Brian J. Robb is the *New York Times* and *Sunday Times* bestselling biographer of Leonardo DiCaprio, Johnny Depp and Brad Pitt. He's also written acclaimed pop culture books on silent cinema, the films of Philip K. Dick, Steampunk, J. R. R. Tolkien, Wes Craven and Laurel and Hardy, and the TV series *Doctor Who* and *Star Trek*. He is co-editor of the popular website Sci-Fi Bulletin and lives in Edinburgh.

Recent titles in the series

A Brief Guide to Star Trek
Brian J. Robb

A Brief Guide to James Bond
Nigel Cawthorne

A Brief Guide to Jane Austen
Charles Jennings

A Brief Guide to Secret Religions
David Barrett

A Brief History of Angels and Demons
Sarah Bartlett

A Brief History of Bad Medicine
Robert Youngston

A Brief History of France
Cecil Jenkins

A Brief History of Slavery
Jeremy Black

A Brief History of Sherlock Holmes
Nigel Cawthorne

A Brief Guide to J. R. R. Tolkien
Nigel Cawthorne

A Brief Guide to C. S. Lewis
Paul Simpson

A Brief History of the Private Life of Elizabeth II
Michael Patterson

A Brief Guide to Jeeves and Wooster
Nigel Cawthorne

A Brief History of Superheroes
Brian J. Robb

A Brief History of the Spy
Paul Simpson

A Brief Guide to Oz
Paul Simpson

A BRIEF GUIDE TO

THE HUNGER GAMES

Brian J. Robb

ROBINSON   RUNNING PRESS
PHILADELPHIA · LONDON

ROBINSON

First published in Great Britain in 2014 by Robinson

A CIP catalogue record for this book
is available from the British Library.

ISBN 978-1-47211-058-9 (paperback)
ISBN: 978-1-47211-071-8 (ebook)

Typeset in Stempel Garamond by TW Typesetting, Plymouth, Devon
Printed and bound in Great Britain by CPI Mackays

Robinson
is an imprint of
Constable & Robinson Ltd
100 Victoria Embankment
London EC4Y 0DY

An Hachette UK Company
www.hachette.co.uk

www.constablerobinson.com

First published in the United States in 2014 by Running Press Book Publishers,
A Member of the Perseus Books Group

Books published by Running Press are available at special discounts for bulk purchases in the United States by corporations, institutions, and other organizations. For more information, please contact the Special Markets Department at the Perseus Books Group, 2300 Chestnut Street, Suite 200, Philadelphia, PA 19103, or call (800) 810-4145, ext. 5000, or e-mail special.markets@perseusbooks.com.

US ISBN: 978-0-7624-5474-7
US Library of Congress Control Number: 2014932739

9 8 7 6 5 4 3 2 1
Digit on the right indicates the number of this printing

Running Press Book Publishers
2300 Chestnut Street
Philadelphia, PA 19103-4371

Visit us on the web!
www.runningpress.com

Printed and bound in the UK

CONTENTS

PART ONE: THE SPARK

PART ONE: THE SPARK

1

LET THE GAMES BEGIN: *THE HUNGER GAMES* PHENOMENON

The Hunger Games has become a huge, worldwide phenomenon. What started with a big-selling young adult novel has turned into a multimillion-dollar blockbuster movie series, and much more besides for the legions of fans of Katniss Everdeen, Peeta Mellark, Gale Hawthorne and Finnick Odair.

The trilogy of young adult books comprising *The Hunger Games*, *Catching Fire* and *Mockingjay* (known collectively as *The Hunger Games* trilogy or saga) by Suzanne Collins follows the ordeals of tough, self-reliant teenager Katniss Everdeen. She becomes a Tribute in the annual Hunger Games, a battle to the death fought by young people from all over Panem (the future United States). More than that, through her actions Katniss also becomes the figurehead of a rebellion against the dreaded Capitol and those who rule Panem in their own interests and not those of the people.

The sales surge of the first book, published in 2008, took publishers Scholastic by surprise. They'd put 50,000 copies of the hardback out, a large number for a new series, but Suzanne Collins was a well-known and successful author thanks to *The Underland Chronicles*, and the advance buzz on the book from editors, stockists and the media had been overwhelmingly positive. Despite this, they'd underestimated the interest, and the book had to go back to print twice, bringing the number of hardback copies up to 200,000. Within two years, *The Hunger Games* had sold to thirty-eight countries in twenty-six different languages and had sold over 800,000 copies in the US and Canada – the first printing of the final book, *Mockingjay*, would reach those numbers immediately.

For over 100 consecutive weeks, *The Hunger Games* featured on the *New York Times* bestseller list. It was followed by *Catching Fire* in September 2009, with an initial print run of 350,000 copies, soon boosted to 750,000 by 2010. The final volume, *Mockingjay*, came out in the summer of 2010, selling 450,000 copies during its first week on release, with a total planned print run of 750,000 increased to an eventual 1.6 million to meet overwhelming demand. Overall, worldwide the three books have twenty-six million copies in print (including the inevitable movie tie-in editions). Suzanne Collins became the first children's or young adult author to sell over one million books for the Kindle ebook reader, only the sixth author of any category to do so. Analysis of the geographical sales of the books in the United States indicated that they were most popular in California, Utah and Florida.

The books have been festooned with awards. *Publishers Weekly* named *The Hunger Games* as one of its Best Books of the Year for 2008, while the *New York Times* acclaimed it as a Notable Children's Book of 2008. *Booklist* editors and *School Library Journal* agreed, similarly praising *The Hunger Games*. As the book spread, so did the fame of its reclusive author. By 2011, Suzanne Collins had been awarded the California Young Reader Medal for *The Hunger Games*, and by 2012 the Scholastic *Parent & Child* magazine listed the book as the thirty-third best book for children of all time, with a special notice for 'best original ending'.

The books struck a chord with teenagers going through high school: the trials and tribulations Katniss faced in the Games arenas were symbolic of those most young people face when growing up. In overcoming their own limitations, facing up to bullies, struggling to escape the influence of their parents, every teen reader of *The Hunger Games* trilogy could see how this exotic dystopian fantasy could nonetheless reflect elements of their own lives. That core identification between the young readers and Katniss, Peeta and Gale is what drove Suzanne Collins's work to be so successful. It also appealed to older, adult readers for many of the same reasons: high school is sometimes seen as the best years of people's lives, but for many others they were the worst years.

The four movie versions of the trio of novels brought *The Hunger Games* saga to a whole new audience. As well as the readers of the novels, the movies – created and promoted as seasonal blockbusters released across a four-year period – were deliberately aimed at everyone. The writers and producers took the books and brought the characters to life in the form of stars Jennifer Lawrence, Josh Hutcherson and Liam Hemsworth, among a host of others. The epic nature of the story and the humanity of the lead characters appealed to the widest possible audience, so much so that the second movie, *Catching Fire*, became the biggest film at the US box office of 2013.

This is the story of *The Hunger Games*: how it began when author Suzanne Collins was flicking through television channels one night, between war footage and reality television gameshows; how she turned that spark of inspiration into a bestselling trilogy of young adult books packed with thoughtful messages; and how the 'girl on fire' came to the screen in a quartet of movie blockbusters led by Jennifer Lawrence as Katniss Everdeen.

Let the Games begin!

Note: As there is detailed discussion of all three novels in *The Hunger Games* saga and the movies made from them, this volume contains many plot-point spoilers so is best read after reading the books and seeing the movies.

2

THE GAMEMAKER: AUTHOR SUZANNE COLLINS

If there is one Gamemaker more important than Seneca Crane or even Plutarch Heavensbee, then it's the author of *The Hunger Games*, Suzanne Collins. Without her original conception of the Games, inspired when she was flicking between television channels covering the Iraq War and a reality show, there would be no Panem, no Katniss Everdeen and certainly no *Hunger Games* phenomenon.

Suzanne Marie Collins was born into an American military family, which meant that from a very early age she had become used to frequently moving around the country. Her life began in Hartford, Connecticut on 10 August 1962 as the youngest of four children, but she was destined to have a disrupted childhood that would feed into her later literary creations.

Her parents, Jane and Michael, already had three children – Kathy, Joanie and Drew. Some of Suzanne's earliest memories are of men in uniform drilling at West Point, where her pilot father (who rose to the rank of Lieutenant Colonel) was teaching military history on loan from the Air Force. 'My father was career military,' Suzanne said. 'He was a veteran [and] a doctor of political science. He taught at West Point and Air Command Staff and lectured at the War College.' Experience of war ran deep in her family. Her grandfather had been gassed in the Great War, and her uncle suffered shrapnel wounds during the Second World War, so the dangers of military life were ever evident. In 1968, when Suzanne was aged six, the Collins family moved to Indiana.

Her understanding of the impact of warfare on family life came a lot closer to home when her father left to serve in Vietnam – an event that helped focus her feelings about war and its effects on the young, both those directly involved and those left behind. 'If your parent is deployed and you are that young,' she remembered, 'you spend the whole time wondering where they are and waiting for them to come home. As time passes and the absence is longer and longer, you become more and more concerned – but you don't really have the words to express your concern. There's only this continued absence.' This would be translated to absent fathers in her fiction, notably Gregor's missing father in *The Underland Chronicles* and Katniss's loss of her father in *The Hunger Games*. The eventual war depicted in *Mockingjay* between the Districts and the Capitol owes something to Suzanne's understanding of the war in Vietnam.

She noticed that her father returned from Vietnam changed. 'I think he felt it was his responsibility to make sure that all his children had an understanding about war, about its cost, its consequences,' she said. He suffered 'nightmares . . . that lasted his whole life,' according to Suzanne. She often awoke in the night to hear him crying out as a result of painful dreams. Suzanne would give similar disturbing dreams to Katniss Everdeen, who suffers Post-Traumatic Stress Disorder following her experiences of the 74th Hunger Games.

Five years after her father's return from the conflict, the family were on the move once again, this time to Europe. The Collins clan moved to Brussels, where young Suzanne studied European history, especially the Second World War, a conflict that had a much more marked effect on the landscape and peoples of Europe than on the US. 'Europe,' she said, was 'one gigantic battlefield.' The family would occasionally take tours of historic battlefields, some of them dating back to ancient times.

A family trip to a castle, expected to be 'fairy-tale magical' by young Suzanne, instead turned into a lesson on fortresses. 'My dad's holding me back from the tour to show me where they poured the boiling oil,' Suzanne remembered, 'where the arrow slits are. And then you're just like, wait a minute! This isn't what I had in mind. I should have known better . . . I felt like I was tutored [by] somebody very experienced in [war], both as a real life and historical.'

These trips were not just to honour the war dead or to provide a distraction for a young family on the weekend. Suzanne's father was a historian, so as well as showing Europe to his daughter and her siblings, he was also filling their heads with detailed histories of each place visited. 'He talked about war with us from very early on,' said Suzanne of her father. 'It was very important to him that we understood things, I think because of both what he did and what he had experienced. If you went to a battlefield with him you didn't just stand there. You would hear what led up to this war and to this particular battle, what transpired there, and what the fallout was. It wasn't like, there's a field. It would be, here's a story.'

The notion of stories and their connections to real places became fixed in Suzanne's mind. She read a lot as a child, but often children's stories were quite separate from the realities of the world in which she lived. She also came to realize that the places in which people lived, especially places that had seen war, were shaped by past events that had taken place there. Those events, and the reasons that things were the way they were in the world, made up the stories of the people who lived there. 'If I took the forty years of my dad talking to me about war and battles and taking me to battlefields and distilled it down into one question,' she said, 'it would probably be the idea of the necessary or unnecessary war. That's very much at the heart of it.'

Stories she'd read also informed Suzanne's experiences of the wider world. For example, a sighting of a field of poppies recalled not the Great War battlefields known as Flanders Fields – the connection her father might make – but the poppies in one of her favourite books and films, *The Wizard of Oz*. 'This moment becomes transformative,' she recalled of her father connecting the poppy field to the war, 'because now I'm looking out on to that field and wondering if it was a graveyard.'

Upon returning to the US, Suzanne attended George Washington Carver High School in Alabama, where she furthered her interest in reading and mythology, having grown more interested in them during her European stay. Suzanne developed a taste for macabre stories in Junior High. 'In fifth and sixth grade [between ten and twelve years old], I went to school in an open classroom. And the English teacher, Miss Vance, was wonderful. On rainy days, she would take whoever was interested over to the side and read us Edgar Allan Poe stories. I remember all of us sitting around just wide-eyed as she read "The Tell-tale Heart" or "The Masque of the Red Death". She didn't think we were too young to hear it. And we were riveted. That made a huge impression on me.'

Suzanne had a variety of favourite books as a child, but

even she found school reading assignments sometimes difficult. *The Mayor of Casterbridge* (1868) by Thomas Hardy was one she found a tough read, so tough in fact that she never finished it. 'It was assigned in tenth grade,' she said, 'and I just couldn't get into it. About seven years later I rediscovered Hardy, and consumed four of his novels in a row. Katniss Everdeen owes her last name to Bathsheba Everdene, the lead character in *Far From the Madding Crowd* (1874). The two are very different, but both struggle with knowing their hearts.'

Books dealing with traditional mythology were a large part of Suzanne's reading growing up. 'I've had a lifelong love of mythology, so I'd have to top the list [of favourites] with *Myths and Enchantment Tales*, by Margaret Evans Price, which belonged to my mom when she was a girl, and *D'Aulaires' Book of Greek Myths*. Fiction standouts include *A Wrinkle in Time*, by Madeleine L'Engle; *The Phantom Tollbooth*, by Norton Juster and Jules Feiffer; and *Boris*, by the Dutch writer Jaap ter Haar, which I still think is one of the best war stories written for kids.'

Suzanne soon developed a list of favourites she'd return to and reread over the years, including family saga *A Tree Grows in Brooklyn* by Betty Smith; George Orwell's dystopian *Nineteen Eighty-Four*, no doubt an influence on the totalitarian regime in *The Hunger Games*; William Golding's *The Lord of the Flies*, which in its tale of children turning on one another is clearly also an influence on *The Hunger Games*; *The Heart is a Lonely Hunter* by Carson McCullers, about a deaf man's experiences in thirties America; and Ray Bradbury's *Dandelion Wine*, inspired by that author's own late-twenties childhood. The book that scared her the most was the real-life account of a virus outbreak, *The Hot Zone* by Richard Preston. The one that got away – the book Suzanne knew she ought to have already read, but has never gotten around to – was Dostoyevsky's *The Idiot*, although she'd come close in reading several theatre adaptations when working for the Classic Stage Company.

Suzanne followed junior school with time at Alabama's School of Fine Arts where she was a Theatre Arts major, graduating in 1980. She later attended Indiana University, leaving there with a double major in Drama and Communications in 1985. Although acting had interested Suzanne in her early teens, she had moved beyond that. Her combined focus on theatre and drama, alongside communications, clearly marked Suzanne out as likely to pursue a career in either theatre or television – not as an actor, but as a writer. During her time at Indiana University she met a young aspiring actor named Charles Pryor, who was widely known as 'Cap' and who would become her husband in 1992.

'When I got out of undergrad,' she remembered, 'I had a degree in theatre and telecommunications. [In] my first job, I was a news reporter for the local stories for NPR [National Public Radio]. Then I was a country-western DJ. I did data entry for a yearbook company. In my mid-twenties, I went back to grad school at NYU [New York University], and I specialized in playwriting.' In 1987, at the age of twenty-five, Suzanne and Cap moved to New York, where she took up a Master of Fine Arts in dramatic writing at New York University. Her big career break was just around the corner. 'I worked in development for a film producer for a year and a half or so, and then I got my first television writing job.'

Suzanne quickly broke into working on children's television in the city. 'The first show I did was in 1991. It was a live-action show called *Hi Honey, I'm Home!*' she remembered. She worked on a variety of shows for younger viewers that aired on Nickelodeon, including *Clarissa Explains It All* (1991–4), *The Mystery Files of Shelby Woo* (1996–8, an episode of which – 1996's 'The Missing Dolphin' – featured Suzanne's husband, Cap Pryor), and *Little Bear*, an Emmy-nominated series for which Suzanne wrote many episodes. She was the co-creator and story editor for the 2000 animated series *Generation O!* Suzanne was nominated for the Writers Guild of America Award for Animation for the 2001 Rankin/Bass seasonal special for Fox, *Santa, Baby* (which she co-wrote with Peter Bakalian). Later she became the lead writer for the show *Clifford's Puppy Days*, based upon a series of books published by Scholastic (who were later to be Suzanne's publisher). Even after being published, Suzanne continued to keep her hand in with children's television, freelancing for the 2008–9 Nick Jr show *Wow! Wow! Wubbzy!* 'It's a fun preschool show that's set in this imaginary town called Wuzzleburg,' she said. 'When I was working on *The Hunger Games* – there's not a lot of levity in it – I'd do a *Wubbzy* script. It was an enormous relief to spend some hours in Wuzzleburg, writing an eleven-minute episode, where I know things are going to work out just fine and all the characters will be alive at the end.'

While working on the Kids' WB show *Generation O!* Suzanne met the show's co-creator, children's writer and illustrator James Proimos (author of the Johnny Mutton series and *Patricia von Pleasantsquirrel*). He encouraged her to think about writing her own children's books. By then she'd had two children of her own, a son Charlie (born 1994) and a daughter Isabelle (born 1999). She set out to put her accumulated knowledge of writing for children via television to work in writing an adventure story aimed at younger readers. The result was *Gregor the Overlander*, published in 2003 when Suzanne was forty-one, her first book and the start of what would come to be known as *The Underland Chronicles*. The series eventually ran to five books published between 2003 and 2007. During 2003 – the year her father died – Collins and Pryor moved with their family from their cramped apartment in

Manhattan to a larger family home in Newtown, Sandy Hook, Connecticut (later infamous as the location of an elementary-school shooting in 2012).

In her work on *The Underland Chronicles*, Suzanne drew influence from another children's story she loved: *Alice's Adventures in Wonderland*. Set in a fantasy land hidden under New York City, *Gregor the Overlander* followed eleven-year-old Gregor and his two-year-old sister Boots on their trip to the underworld after they fall through a vent in the basement of their apartment. In this strange 'Underland' they meet all manner of weird creatures (many of them giant versions of animals and insects familiar to children), before discovering that Gregor is the 'warrior' spoken of in an ancient prophecy and Boots is the 'princess' worshipped by the creatures. The children are caught up in an ongoing war between the strange creatures known as 'gnawers' and the Underland inhabitants. 'We had two [military] superpowers,' she said of her *Chronicles*, 'the humans and the bats, but the humans were dependent on the alliance with the bats, because then they became aerial fighters.'

For the first time, Suzanne tackled the meaning and effects of war in fiction aimed at children. 'I'd like to take topics like war and introduce them at an earlier age,' she said. 'If you look at *Gregor* [*the Overlander*], it has all kinds of topics, but it's in a fantasy. It's played out with a combination of humans and rats and bats. But those topics are there.' The idea to extend the series to five books came from her work on television: 'Having written for television, the idea that you spend all this time creating this world, developing these characters, and then you're only going to use them for one story? [*Gregor*] required a series format. If I had written *Gregor* as one book, it would have been over 1,700 pages . . . For a nine- to twelve-year-old audience, that would have been daunting.'

She had no doubt, however, that children were smart

enough to perceive the messages in the *Underland* books. They'd know there was something important underlying the adventure, and they were clever enough not only to see it, but to handle some quite disturbing adult topics due to the way they were presented in the guise of fantasy fiction. 'Kids will accept any number of things,' she said. '*The Underland Chronicles* – which I wrote for kids the same age as I was when Miss Vance read me Edgar Allan Poe – features death, loss and violence. The third book has biological warfare, the fourth book has genocide, the fifth book has a very graphic war. I wondered if at some point that was going to become a problem. Not for the kids so much, but for parents or schools. It never seemed to. I think somehow if you went on that journey with me from the beginning, you were prepared by what had come before.' It would be a model that would serve her well writing for slightly older readers with *The Hunger Games* series.

While working on *The Underland Chronicles*, Suzanne also wrote a rhyming picture book called *When Charlie McButton Lost Power* (2005), illustrated by Mike Lester. During 2005 Suzanne attended a question-and-answer session with young readers of her *Gregor the Overlander* books at the Reed School in Newtown, a rare personal appearance from an author who continues to avoid publicity despite her rapid rise to fame. Her son attended Reed Intermediate School, while her daughter was at Sandy Hook Elementary School. During this time, Cap Pryor was described in the *Newtown Bee* local newspaper as a 'stay-at-home dad'. In reply to student questions, Suzanne compared her previous collaborative work in writing for television with the essentially solitary role of a fiction author, although she was happy to be in a position to write about the things that intrigued her. She advised students who wanted to become writers to 'write about things you love and feel passionately about'. She told them she generally spent about two months planning and researching her books, followed by a four-month period for the actual writing. She also confirmed that her models for Gregor and Boots had been her own children and their relationship with each other. She then signed each student's book with the motto 'Fly you high'. *The Underland Chronicles* would go on to feature in many local Newtown summer reading programmes over the years. In fact, Suzanne had moved into something of a literary neighbourhood, with Sandy Hook boasting James Thurber as a local author, alongside Pulitzer Prize-winner William Swanberg, poet Louis Untermeyer and *Sesame Street* writer Ray Sipherd.

One evening towards the end of her time working on the final instalment of *The Underland Chronicles*, Suzanne was watching television in a rather tired and distracted frame of mind. 'I was lying in bed, and I was channel-surfing between reality TV programmes and actual war coverage. On one channel, there's a group of young people competing for . . . I don't even know; and on the next, there's a group of young people fighting in an actual war. I was really tired, and the lines between these stories started to blur in a very unsettling way. That's the moment when Katniss's story came to me.'

The idea of a 'reality TV' style competition with life-or-death stakes was mixed in with Suzanne's lifelong love of classical mythology and storytelling. 'It's very much based on the myth of Theseus and the Minotaur,' she said of the world of *The Hunger Games*, 'which I read when I was eight years old. I was a huge fan of Greek and Roman mythology. As punishment for displeasing Crete, Athens periodically had to send seven youths and seven maidens to Crete, where they were thrown into the labyrinth and devoured by the Minotaur, a monster that's half-man and half-bull. Even when I was a little kid, the story took my breath away, because it was so cruel, and Crete was so ruthless.'

The ruthless world of Crete became Panem, a future United States in which a popular rebellion has been put down and the ruling Capitol requires the remaining twelve Districts to put forward two Tributes every year – a young boy and a young girl – to compete in the televised Hunger Games. In the arena, there can be only one survivor as the Games are a battle to the death. 'The message is, mess with us and we'll do something worse than kill you – we'll kill your children,' said Suzanne of her mythological inspiration. 'And the parents sat by apparently powerless to stop it. The cycle doesn't end until Theseus volunteers, and he kills the Minotaur. In her own way, Katniss is a futuristic Theseus. I didn't want to do a labyrinth story, so I decided to write an updated version of the Roman gladiator games. I was also heavily influenced by the historical figure of Spartacus. Katniss follows the same arc from slave to gladiator to rebel to [becoming the] face of a war.'

Suzanne was aware of how television coverage of the Vietnam War was reputed to have had a desensitizing effect on American audiences and she wondered what effect the current twenty-first-century coverage of warfare was having on the new generation. At the same time, many viewers spent their leisure time glued to 'reality' television shows that had spread across almost all channels since the debut of the original *Big Brother* in 2000. 'I worry that we're all getting a little desensitized to the images on our televisions,' she said. 'If you're watching a sitcom, that's fine. But if there's a real-life tragedy unfolding, you should not be thinking of yourself as an audience member. Because those are real people on the screen, and they're not going away when the commercials start to roll.'

Once she started the story, the world of Panem began to develop beyond what she'd originally envisaged. Setting the story in the future allowed for contemporary issues to be brought into her tale, while telling it through the first-person viewpoint of heroine Katniss Everdeen gave her story an immediacy only achievable through direct address to the reader. 'Telling a story in a futuristic world gives you this freedom to explore things that bother you in contemporary times,' said Suzanne. 'So, in the case of *The Hunger Games*, [there are] issues like the vast discrepancy of wealth, the power of television and how it's used to influence our lives, the possibility that the government could use hunger as a weapon, and then first and foremost to me, the issue of war. I don't write about adolescence, I write about war. For adolescents.'

At the core of *The Hunger Games* was a story of violence, with young people forced into an arena where they had to kill each other to ensure their own survival. While not shying away from tackling what that meant in reality, Suzanne had to be careful to remember she was writing for young adults, so she set out not to make the descriptions of what goes on in the arena too graphic. She was content to let readers' imagination do that work. The participants in the Games and those who facilitate them are all depicted equally as victims of a corrupt system – one that Katniss will eventually play a role in overthrowing when she becomes a symbol of defiance across the Districts of Panem.

Although *The Underland Chronicles* had been a series of five books, Suzanne didn't initially set out with *The Hunger Games* to create a new, ongoing series. She had one story to tell, that of Katniss Everdeen's experiences in the Games, and how she survived. However, as she finished the first book, Suzanne became aware there was a larger story. 'Once I'd thought through to the end of the first book, I realized that there was no way that the story was concluded. Katniss does something that would never go unpunished in her world. There would definitely be repercussions. So the question of whether or not to continue with a series was answered for me.'

When she submitted her novel to Scholastic, her

publisher, an editor pointed out some thematic similarities with another young adult novel published in Japan in 1999 called *Battle Royale*, written by Koushun Takami. It told of junior high-school students forced to fight each other to the death when trapped on an island by an authoritarian Japanese government. It became an acclaimed movie in 2000 and a manga (Japanese comic book) between 2003 and 2008. 'I had never heard of that book or that author until my book was turned in,' claimed Suzanne. 'At that point, it was mentioned to me, and I asked my editor if I should read it. He said: "No, I don't want that world in your head. Just continue with what you're doing." '

Scholastic had taken on Suzanne's book in 2006 in a six-figure deal. The publishers saw the author as a sure thing with her previous series *The Underland Chronicles* having sold around one million copies across five books. The fact that the new book was aimed at an older audience was also encouraging, as Scholastic believed it had the potential to be an even bigger hit. 'Usually an editor holds the manuscript to their chest and doesn't share it until everything is absolutely perfect,' said David Levithan, executive editorial director at Scholastic, 'but this one came in such great form, we wanted to get it to as many people as possible early on.' Suzanne worked with long-time editor Kate Egan, as well as Levithan and Scholastic Press editor Jennifer Rees, to shape the manuscript.

The Hunger Games was published in hardcover in September 2008 and made an immediate impact. With an initial print run of 200,000 copies (increased twice from the original 50,000 copies planned due to extraordinary pre-orders), the book was quickly reprinted. A clever advance publicity campaign that involved co-opting online book websites and independent reviewers in the young female target age range paid off. *The Hunger Games* was following hard in the wake of Stephenie Meyer's young supernatural-romance *Twilight* series (the final entry,

Breaking Dawn, was published at the same time), and many lessons had been learned from the success of those books. By November 2008 the book was in the *New York Times* children's bestseller list, where it would remain for over 100 consecutive weeks. The paperback was released in July 2010, giving a further boost to sales.

The Hunger Games received a widely positive critical reception. In the *New York Times*, John Green called it 'brilliantly plotted and perfectly paced . . . the considerable strength of the novel comes in Collins's convincingly detailed world-building and her memorably complex and fascinating heroine. In fact, by not calling attention to itself, the text disappears in the way a good font does: nothing stands between Katniss and the reader, between Panem and America.' *Time* magazine labelled the book 'chilling, bloody and thoroughly horrifying', while Stephen King – who thought he detected some similarities to some of his own work (see Chapter 4) – reviewed the novel in *Entertainment Weekly*, commenting it was 'a violent, jarring speed-rap of a novel that generates nearly constant suspense and may also generate a fair amount of controversy. I couldn't stop reading . . . Collins is an efficient no-nonsense prose stylist with a pleasantly dry sense of humour.' Among the other positive reviews were notices from *Booklist*, *School Library Journal* and *Kirkus Reviews*. Authors writing for readers of similar ages as those *The Hunger Games* was aimed at praised the books, including Rick Riordan, of *Percy Jackson and the Olympians*, and *Twilight*'s Stephenie Meyer, who noted 'I was so obsessed with this book . . . *The Hunger Games* is amazing.'

Sales of the book – in hardback first – were just as amazing. By February 2010 *The Hunger Games* had sold in excess of 800,000 copies. It had been translated into twenty-six languages worldwide, and publishing rights had been sold in thirty-eight different territories. *The Hunger Games* was one of the first books to take advantage of the spread of e-readers, becoming one of the top five bestselling Amazon Kindle ebooks. The author continued to maintain that her success had come from the simplest of places: 'The Hunger Games is full of things that intrigue me; it's dystopia, it's got kids in it, it's gladiators, it's war, there are genetic mutations. The Underland Chronicles has fantasy, animals, sword fighting. If you write about things that you feel passionately about, it is so much easier to write.'

By the time The Hunger Games was well on its way to becoming a phenomenal success, Suzanne was hard at work on the follow-up that she knew the ending of the first book required. Under the working title 'The Quarter Quell', but published as Catching Fire, Suzanne began to consider what happened to Katniss in the months after her victory in the Games and how she had impacted on the viewing millions of Panem, the downtrodden populace. The Catching Fire hardback was scheduled to be published on 8 September 2009, but high retailer demand saw it moved up a week to 1 September, before the Labor Day holiday and the beginning of the new school term. The initial print run exceeded that of The Hunger Games, reaching 350,000 copies. By February 2010 there were 750,000 copies of the hardback in circulation, as several rapid reprintings had been necessary to meet increasing demand.

As with the first book, the critics were overwhelmingly positive, even though this was the middle book in what was now to be a trilogy, so did not complete the story of Katniss Everdeen and her battle with the powers of Panem. Publishers Weekly said the novel 'doesn't disappoint when it segues into the pulse-pounding action readers have come to expect . . . the star remains Katniss, whose bravery, honesty and wry cynicism carry the narrative. Collins has also created an exquisitely tense romantic triangle for her heroine. Forget [Twilight's] Edward and Jacob: by book's end (and it's a cliffhanger), readers will be picking sides – Peeta or Gale?' The *Twilight* comparisons were inevitable, but probably not unwelcome to a publisher who was happy *The Hunger Games* books had become a phenomenon that captured the attention of mainly female teenage readers, but also offered enough action and gripping events to tempt young male readers too.

Booklist said the new story 'matches, if not exceeds, the unfiltered adrenaline rush of the first book', and featured 'perfect pacing and electrifying world building . . . aside from being tremendously action-packed science fiction thrillers, these books are also brimming with potent themes of morality, obedience, sacrifice, redemption, love, law, and, above all, survival'. The *New York Times* continued the praise for *Catching Fire*, describing the book as 'a portrait of how a desperate government tries to hold off a revolutionary tide and as such has something of the epic feeling of Orwell to it. (But for kids.) Collins has done that rare thing. She has written a sequel that improves upon the first book . . . at the heart of this exotic world is a very real girl, the kind lacking even a single supernatural gift. All this is accomplished with the light touch of a writer who truly understands writing for young people: the pacing is brisk and the message tucked below the surface.'

As with any success story, there were dissenters from the generally positive welcome given to the second instalment of *The Hunger Games*. The *Plain Dealer* complained about the pacing of the book, in an otherwise fairly positive review: 'after 150 pages of romantic dithering, I was tapping my foot to move on. Katniss in a pensive mood seems out of step with the kick-butt assassin. Teenage girls may argue that point. Despite its lengthy build-up, when Katniss finally marches into the Games arena, Collins's story skyrockets.' *Entertainment Weekly* – a publication that would become a cheerleader for the movies of Suzanne Collins's books – saw the new novel as a disappointment compared with the first, calling it a 'decidedly weaker sequel' in which the two men in the life of Katniss Everdeen are barely differentiated. 'There's little distinction between the two thinly imagined guys, other than the fact that Peeta has a dopier name. Collins conjures none of the erotic energy that makes *Twilight*, for instance, so creepily alluring.'

Nonetheless, fans lapped up the new novel, with *Time* magazine placing it at number four in the top fiction of 2009, and *People* magazine placing the novel at eighth place on its list of the year's best. *Catching Fire* won *Publishers Weekly*'s Best Book of the Year award for 2009.

With sales of the first two books soaring, boosted by the publication of paperback editions, and audiences worldwide beginning to catch up with *The Hunger Games* saga, Suzanne Collins was ready to wind up her epic tale. The third novel – *Mockingjay* – made its hardback debut in the US and Canada on 24 August 2010. Editions for the UK, New Zealand and Australia were published the following day, showing just how much of an international event the new *Hunger Games* novel had become. The first book was in development as a movie, further increasing the awareness of the story worldwide, with many new readers keen to catch up with the originals before the much anticipated film versions arrived. The third, and according to all involved at the time, final novel in *The Hunger Games* series saw a huge increase in the initial print run from the planned 750,000 copies to an impressive 1.2 million copies worldwide. In the first week alone sales reached 450,000 in hardback and ebook copies. Scholastic immediately ordered an additional 400,000 hardback copies, eventually increasing the overall print run to 1.6 million books. Ellie Berger, president of Scholastic Trade, said sales of *Mockingjay* had 'exceeded all expectations'.

The promotional push for the final novel of *The Hunger*

Games had gone all out, including a video 'trailer' that attracted over 22,000 'likes' to a Facebook page in just ten days. There was an online clock counting down to the release date, and a nationwide competition in which one lucky fan could win a personal visit from Suzanne Collins. Merchandise (before the arrival of the first film) associated with *The Hunger Games* had also taken off, including T-shirts, posters, games and jewellery such as bracelets.

As the author embarked on a publicity and signing tour (dubbed the '13-District Tour'), fans of the books blogged, tweeted and generally sang the series' praises across all forms of social media, helping to identify *The Hunger Games* as a phenomenon any connected teenager should be involved with. Lifting a page from the *Harry Potter* playbook, there were midnight release 'parties' for the novel in selected bookstores across the US, with the 'official' event in New York City at Books of Wonder attended by Suzanne. To keep the crowds entertained while they awaited the midnight unboxing of the books, and to play up the party atmosphere, there were jugglers, magicians, face-painters and even Tarot-card readers laid on. Suzanne read the first chapter of the new novel to the spellbound crowd, but due to a hand injury she had to 'sign' copies using a signature stamp. She also issued an 'open letter' to reviewers and fans who might be quick readers of the final novel to 'avoid sharing any spoilers, so that the conclusion of Katniss's story can unfold for each reader the way it was meant to . . .'

Mockingjay had a lot to live up to given the cliffhanger ending of *Catching Fire* and the outstanding story and character elements needing to be wrapped up satisfactorily. *Entertainment Weekly* gave the new novel a more positive review than the second, calling it a 'riveting final instalment . . . Collins has kicked the brutal violence up a notch in an edge-of-your-seat plot that follows Katniss as she tries to fulfil her role, protect her mother and sister and, in the end, finally choose between her two greatest loves.' *Publishers Weekly* went so far as to dub *Mockingjay* 'the best yet . . . a beautifully orchestrated and intelligent novel that succeeds on every level [with] sharp social commentary and nifty world building'. *Kirkus Reviews* complained that reviewers had been denied the customary advance 'sneak peek' at the new novel, but went on to call *Mockingjay* 'exactly the book its fans have been hoping for. It will grab them and not let go, and if it leaves them with questions, well, then, it's probably exactly the book Collins was hoping for, too.' The *Los Angeles Times* claimed 'fans aren't likely to be disappointed . . . *Mockingjay* finally settles the question of Katniss's true affections, and it takes some truly surprising twists and turns to get there. Unfolding in Collins's engaging, intelligent prose and assembled into chapters that end with didn't-see-that-coming cliffhangers, this finale is every bit the pressure cooker of its forebears.' The subject of the relationship of Suzanne's novels to real life wars that readers were seeing on their television screens during the time the novels were published exercised some reviewers, with the *Baltimore Sun* noting that 'the heartbreaking effects of war and loss aren't sugar-coated. This is one young adult novel that will leave you thinking about the ramifications of war on society, not just the coming-of-age of a young woman.'

There were some caveats delivered by some reviews, such as that in the *New York Times* that claimed that *Mockingjay* was 'not as impeccably plotted as *The Hunger Games*' but still retained 'its fierce, chilly fascination'. The *Sacramento Bee* found the resolution of the epic tale to be lacking: 'The disappointment with *Mockingjay* hits primarily as Collins starts her home stretch. It's almost as if she didn't allocate enough time or chapters to handle all her threads.' Others were reserved in their general praise, with *USA Today* giving the novel just three out of five stars.

* * *

As a result of the runaway success of *The Hunger Games* series, the rather shy and retiring Suzanne Collins found herself something of a celebrity, a situation that would only increase when the film versions of her novels hit the big screen between 2012 and 2015. She'd also made a huge amount of money from the success of the books (and selling the film rights), but hoped that wouldn't change her or her family in any way. 'I'm not a very fancy person,' she said, noting that money from publishing success takes a long time to filter through to the author. 'I've been a writer a long time, and right now *The Hunger Games* is getting a lot of focus. It'll pass. The focus will be on something else. It'll shift. It always does. And that seems just fine.'

By 2010 Suzanne had been named as one of *Time*'s most influential people and that same year Amazon crowned her as the bestselling Kindle author of all time, having written twenty-nine of the Top 100 'most highlighted' passages in ebooks. However, she had already moved on to new projects. Her father – who had so influenced her outlook on the military and the human cost of war – had died shortly before her success with *The Hunger Games*, but everything he'd taught his daughter continued to influence her work. Her next project was another children's book dealing with war, but aimed at a younger age group.

The Year of the Jungle, published in 2013 just as *Catching Fire* set cinema screens alight, was a heavily autobiographical illustrated piece in which a little red-haired girl named Sue awaits the return of her father from war in a foreign jungle: the elements of the author's own story were evident. Even some of the illustrations in the book were based upon personal family photographs. 'I specifically wanted to do this book as a sort of memory piece honouring that year for my family,' said Suzanne, 'and because I know so many children are experiencing it right now – having deployed parents. It's a way I would like to try and communicate my own experience to them.'

Following *The Year of the Jungle*, Suzanne Collins was planning a new young adult series of novels expected to build upon her reputation from *The Hunger Games*. At the same time, many fans were clamouring for further adventures in the world of Panem. Whatever the future would hold, just like her heroine Katniss Everdeen, the odds were ever in Suzanne Collins's favour!

3

THE HUNGER GAMES: DRAMATIS PERSONAE

As the first novel in a series, *The Hunger Games* had a tough job. The book not only had to introduce a cast of characters that would connect with readers, but an entire world of the future that those readers could believe in. The characters and story were designed to grab the readers' attention and drive them through the book, but the world of Panem needed to be fully formed as a real place, complete with the poor Districts and the rich Capitol, as well as the political structure that gave rise to the Hunger Games seventy-five years before. All this the book easily communicated to the reader with simple prose and gripping storytelling.

In the nation of Panem, Katniss Everdeen is a self-sufficient girl of sixteen who lives in the mining area of District 12. A long time ago there was a rebellion and District 13 was obliterated. The remaining Districts were separated and subjugated by the Capitol, who now deploy Peacekeepers to maintain order. As a result of the defeated rebellion, the Capitol instigated the Hunger Games. Each year two young people from each District aged between twelve and eighteen, one male and one female, are selected by random ballot as Tributes and are sent to the Capitol to train for battle in the arena. The rules of the Games mean there can be only one winner, one survivor, so each of the Tributes faces a battle to the death. The events in the arena are screened to audiences in the Districts to help keep them pacified.

When her younger sister Prim is 'reaped' for the Games the first time her name is entered in the lottery, Katniss spontaneously volunteers to take her place – a choice allowed under the rules. It means leaving her sister and her sick mother (who has never been the same since her father died in a mining disaster several years before), but if Katniss can win the Games, they'd be provided for. She is teamed with Peeta Mellark, a young baker who has long admired Katniss from afar, although she has more in common with her hunting buddy Gale Hawthorne.

Katniss and Peeta are taken to the Capitol by their mentor Haymitch Abernathy, a previous winner of the Games over two decades earlier, and Effie Trinket, a superficial representative of the Capitol. Made over as glamorous participants in the Games by stylist Cinna, Katniss and Peeta are trained under the watchful eye of the Gamemakers who design the arena, including its traps and tricks. Haymitch, as their mentor, advises and guides them on strategy, but once they are in the arena Katniss and Peeta are on their own.

In the arena Katniss forms an alliance with twelve-year-old Rue, a girl from District 11 who reminds her of Prim. At the same time she has to deal with Peeta's publicly declared love for her, and the fact that Haymitch suggested she play up to it to please the viewers (while all the time she's thinking of Gale, watching in District 12). When Rue is killed, Katniss defies the Capitol by preparing her body with flowers before the corpse is taken away. A rule change allows there to be two winners, so Katniss and Peeta team up to defeat the other Tributes. When they are the only two left, the Capitol announces a reversion to the old rules: they must battle one another. Katniss and Peeta refuse, with Katniss threatening their suicide through eating night-lock poison berries. Fearing this would ruin the Games, the Capitol powers capitulate and allow both to be Victors. Unknown to Katniss, her defiance sows the seeds of a growing rebellion among the subjugated Districts against the oppressive Capitol.

The Hunger Games takes place in a future America known as Panem, whose seat of power is the Capitol, located in the Rocky Mountains. The remaining nation – survivors of some unspecified apocalyptic event – is divided into twelve Districts with the populations largely kept separate from one another. There was once a thirteenth District, but it was reputedly destroyed during a rebellion against the Capitol. The Games were initiated seventy-four years ago partly as a punishment against the rebellion, but also as a method of social control employed by the dictatorial rulers of Panem.

The Districts all have particular specialisms. District 1 is the favoured and wealthy producer of luxury items, such as jewellery, much admired by those in the Capitol, while District 2, in the Rocky Mountains not far from the Capitol itself, is a centre for the production of weaponry and where the Capitol's Peacekeeper troops are trained. Both Districts 1 and 2 produce what are known as 'career Tributes', who deliberately train for the Games and volunteer to enter the arena, so overcoming the random ballot known as the 'reaping'. District 3 produces electronics and features a population highly skilled in engineering, but is less favoured by the Capitol. District 4 is on the coast, home to Panem's fishing industry whose produce is prized in the Capitol. District 5 is the location of the power plants that keeps the Capitol going, so is especially kept under the thumb of the dictators of Panem with long hours and bad living conditions enforced so the inhabitants cannot strike against the Capitol. District 6 is a transportation hub and seems to be an area rife with drug addiction, while District 7 is a forested area that specializes in lumber and the production of paper. District 8 produces the textiles used to manufacture the Peacekeeper uniforms, and is one of the first to rebel when Katniss is adopted as a symbol of defiance after winning the 74th Games. District 9 produces grain, which helps feed the population of Panem, and District 10 raises livestock, again helping to feed the country's inhabitants. District 11 is a huge area in the south of Panem that focuses on agriculture, while District 12 – where Katniss and Peeta are from – is a mining area that produces coal and where working conditions in the mines are harsh and often dangerous.

The Capitol is the centre of power across Panem, a sophisticated city located in the Rocky Mountains that dominates the country through the exercise of totalitarian control. The twelve Districts surround the Capitol. The citizens of the Capitol live their lives far removed from the deprivation that marks the majority of the Districts. Inhabitants of the Capitol are generally wealthy and enjoy a high standard of living, at the expense of those living in the Districts whose toil allows for their carefree lives. From outside, life in the Capitol appears to be decadent, with an emphasis on outlandish fashion and style, and with continual evidence of conspicuous consumption in total contrast to the hunger and exhaustion of the workers in the oppressed Districts. Capitol people dye their hair and skins, wear fashionable tattoos and employ surgical alteration. Rebels from the

Districts are taken as slaves in the Capitol and are known as Avoxes; their tongues are removed, so depriving them of their voices.

Residents of the Capitol are exempt from participation in the Games, which are part of an annual celebration televised across Panem. Citizens of the Capitol become sponsors of favoured Tributes in the Games, paying for them to be supplied with food or weaponry to aid their survival in the arena. Past Victors of the Games are sometimes attributed celebrity status in the Capitol, and the Capitol's viewers of the Games can often become emotionally involved, something taken advantage of by Katniss and Peeta.

Begun following the Dark Days of almost seventy-five years before, the annual Hunger Games is a form of gladiatorial combat that takes twenty-four Tributes (two from each District) chosen by lottery to participate in a televised battle to the death. There can only be one Victor. At the age of twelve, every inhabitant of each District sees their name entered into the annual 'reaping', the lottery from which the Tributes for the Games are drawn. For each year until they reach eighteen, every young person has their name entered an additional time, and they can purchase extra grain to feed their starving families at the cost of additional entries into the reaping. As a result, some poorer participants have a far higher chance of being selected.

A representative from the Capitol visits each District to preside over the reaping: District 12 is allocated Effie Trinket. Any other citizen can volunteer to take the place of someone selected through the reaping, as Katniss does for Prim. The selected Tributes are taken to the Capitol by their representative and their mentor, a previous winner of the Games from their District (if they have one). The mentor is responsible for their coaching and training in preparation for the Games. In the Capitol, Tributes are given a makeover by a team of stylists and all twenty-four train together for a period before the Games begin. There is also an impressive parade down the Avenue of the Tributes and televised interviews (currently hosted by Capitol celebrity Caesar Flickerman), with additional commentary on the Games once they are in progress.

The Games take place in a specially designed arena and begin with the Tributes entering from underground before rushing to the Cornucopia, a store of supplies and weapons to help them survive. Many Tributes are killed instantly in the fight over the Cornucopia supplies, although some (such as Katniss) opt not to become involved in the opening melee in the hope they can survive longer than those instantly taken out in the scramble. The Gamemakers design the arena with entertainment of the populace at large in mind, so as well as natural supplies such as water and edible plants and berries, there are also traps and predators, such as tracker jackers, Panem's deadly genetically engineered wasps. Throughout the Games, Tributes may form temporary alliances, but in the end they must battle on to win alone.

The Victor embarks upon a post-Games Victory Tour of the Districts, ending with a lavish feast provided by the Capitol for their home District. They then live in the Victors' Village with their families and become local celebrities and mentors to the next generation of Tributes. Victors have dealt with the aftermath of their experience in the Games in various ways, with District 12's Haymitch Abernathy becoming an alcoholic. However, Victors do get to live out the remainder of their lives in some luxury compared to their fellow District inhabitants.

A diverse array of characters populate Suzanne Collins's *The Hunger Games*. Katniss Everdeen is the lead character of the trilogy. She starts out as a mildly anti-establishment, self-sufficient sixteen-year-old who spends her time in the woods beyond the fence that surrounds District 12 hunting to supplement her family's meagre rations, often in the company of Gale Hawthorne, a friend of several years about whom she is developing mixed feelings. Her simple world of taking care of her poorly mother (suffering a form of depression since Katniss's father died in a mine explosion five years earlier) and sister Prim is turned upside down when Prim is 'reaped' for the annual Games. A spur-of-the-moment reaction sees Katniss step forward from the crowd and volunteer to take her sister's place, regardless of the wider consequences.

Her sparky nature is recognized by her Capitol stylist Cinna, who dubs Katniss the 'girl on fire'. Her one advantage in the arena is her hunting proficiency with a bow and arrow, but her innate independence and self-reliance stand her in good stead against the Tributes from other Districts. Most puzzling to her is her fellow Tribute Peeta Mellark, a boy from her District she hardly knows but who declares his love for her during a live television interview. Katniss is confused by the pretend relationship they concoct for the sake of the ever-present cameras. It endears them to the watching Capitol population, who might then be minded to sponsor them with additional supplies or weapons, but it starts to feel rather more real to Katniss as time passes. Her memories of Gale, watching at home in District 12, slowly fade into the background.

Although Katniss cannot avoid having to kill during the Games, she attempts to keep direct confrontations to a minimum, relying on the other Tributes gradually to reduce the overall number of opponents. She takes no pleasure in the killing of her adversaries, and suffers some long-term consequences as a result. Katniss believes she and Peeta have won the Games when the temporary rule change allows for there to be two Victors, but she falls back on her defiant nature in choosing joint suicide with Peeta over having to fight him. She is initially unaware of her status as a Panem-wide symbol of rebellion around which an uprising is slowly forming in the aftermath of the Games.

Gale Hawthorne is two years older than Katniss but the pair have been friends for many years, having met after her father's death when she took up hunting to bring additional food to her family's table. Gale lost his father in the same mining disaster, so he and Katniss have a shared sense of paternal loss, along with a mildly rebellious nature. Gale has two brothers and a sister, and lives with his mother. He's often the object of attention from the girls in District 12, but he reserves his own attention for Katniss. He is emotionally confused by the developing relationship he sees between Katniss and Peeta Mellark through the televised Games.

Peeta Mellark is Katniss's fellow District 12 Tribute for the 74th Hunger Games, a charismatic blond-haired baker's son who is developing his own skills working in the family business. His declaration of love for Katniss before the Games sees him become a star among some of the audience, but it serves to complicate Katniss's feelings for him and for Gale. During the Games, convinced that Katniss will win due to her long-practised hunting skills, Peeta does all he can to protect her and help her to survive. He's called 'Lover Boy' by the career Tributes from other Districts that he pretends to align himself with during part of the Games. Peeta suffers a leg wound inflicted by a Tribute named Cato and contracts blood poisoning. After the Games are over, his leg is amputated and replaced with a prosthetic. The romance between Katniss and Peeta is real enough to cause Capitol sponsors to supply them with vital medicine in the closing stages. When the new rules are reversed to allow for only one Victor, Peeta initially offers to sacrifice himself so that Katniss can win. Her refusal and impetuous idea to stage a joint suicide bid sees them both survive as the Capitol cannot risk ending the Games with two such popular Tributes dead by their own hands. Their actions make them powerful enemies within the Capitol, and Peeta will suffer serious consequences as a result.

Haymitch Abernathy is the middle-aged previous victor of the 50th Games who serves as the mentor to both District 12 Tributes, Katniss and Peeta. He suggests to Katniss she should play up the romance with Peeta for the cameras, no matter how she really feels. Haymitch knows about gaming the system, having used a forcefield at the edge of the arena to his advantage to win his Games, only for President Snow to order the killing of his family as a punishment. As a result of his experiences in the arena and his devastation over the loss of his mother, younger brother and girlfriend, Haymitch became an alcoholic and something of a local joke. He is regarded as a disgrace by those from the Capitol, especially Effie Trinket. District 12 had no further winners of the Games until Katniss and Peeta, perhaps as a result of Haymitch's poor mentoring of successive Tributes. Impressed by Katniss and Peeta, he slowly emerges from his apathetic state to guide them both to success and to begin to look at the wider situation across Panem beyond the fences that surround District 12.

Effie Trinket is the representative from the Capitol who has responsibility for District 12. Every year the preening fashion victim presides over the reaping, and fails to hide her disgust with Haymitch. She chaperones Katniss and Peeta through their preparations for the Games in the Capitol, and is initially delighted by their apparent success and the fame that is reflected on her. Consumed by her life in the Capitol, and happy to dress in the current fashions, Effie is shallow, poorly educated and easily pleased. However, her exposure to Katniss and Peeta slowly opens her eyes slightly to what is going on around her.

There are several characters whom Katniss Everdeen encounters in the Capitol who, while not central to the narrative of *The Hunger Games*, do add great colour to the world of Panem. Prime among them is her stylist, Cinna, who coins the phrase 'girl on fire' to describe his charge, and was inspired to design a stunning flaming dress for her parade prior to the Games. It is his first year as a stylist for the Games and he specifically asked to be assigned to District 12 as he relishes the challenge of dressing the Tributes from the drab coal-mining District. His innovative designs help win the support of the crowd for Katniss and Peeta. Cinna is well aware of the artifice of the Capitol, and tries to do what he can to communicate subversive ideas through the way he dresses and presents Katniss and Peeta to the Games' audiences. He develops a genuine affection for Katniss, caring about her progress in the arena, and he's happy to see her emerge the Victor. Cinna is supported in his makeover efforts by a team of specialized assistants that includes Octavia, Venia and Flavius, all of whom become very attached to Katniss.

Seneca Crane is the Head Gamemaker of the 74th Hunger Games. It is Seneca who institutes the misjudged temporary rule change to allow for two Victors, playing on the popularity of Katniss and Peeta with the audience. His actions disturb President Snow, who apparently overrules the change and forces Seneca to reinstate the old rule. Unfortunately for him, Seneca capitulates to Katniss's suicide threat, declaring both her and Peeta the Victors as he sees no other way out without inflaming the crowds. As a result, he is summarily executed by President Snow and replaced with Plutarch Heavensbee for the 75th Hunger Games.

The popular face of the Games, seen on the television coverage of the event across the Districts, is Caesar Flickerman, the preening host and commentator. It is his task to interview each of the Tributes prior to the Games and to comment on the action in the arena, eventually greeting the overall winner. He is joined in the task by

Claudius Templesmith, who makes announcements heard by the Tributes within the arena.

President Coriolanus Snow is the current mastermind behind the Hunger Games and the dictator of Panem. He is a shadowy figure in the first novel, only seen during the opening ceremonies, and has nothing at all to do with Katniss. However, he is the power that maintains the unequal distribution of resources and wealth between the Capitol and the Districts, and uses the media and the constant threat of the Games to keep the population in line. His presence grows in importance in the later books, and he comes to see Katniss's role as a figurehead of rebellion and symbol of defiance as a potential threat to his autocratic rule.

The various Tributes from other Districts are sketchily outlined in the first novel, but a few of them have a direct impact on Katniss. Prime among them is young Rue, from District 11, who Katniss sets out to protect. Katniss learns a little from Rue about her family and life in District 11, opening her eyes to the way others across Panem live. Rue teaches Katniss a simple four-note tune to be used to signal one another, and she also takes a liking to Katniss's mockingjay pin. Rue is killed by Marvel, a career Tribute from District 1, and Katniss decorates her corpse with flowers in contravention of Games rules. Katniss has a largely silent but understanding relationship with Rue's fellow District 11 Tribute, known as Thresh. She avoids Marvel and Glimmer from District 1 and Cato and Clove from District 2, knowing they are all well-trained career Tributes. Katniss nicknames the wily, feline Tribute from District 5 'Foxface', never knowing her real name. The other Tributes are not named and have little impact on Katniss's journey through the arena to victory.

These characters are affected by the fallout from the victory of Katniss and Peeta in the 74th Hunger Games. Some will rise to the challenge that the growing rebellion across the Districts makes to the Capitol, while others will shirk their responsibilities. Some will be vanquished, often the victims of their own misjudged actions, while others will triumph and bring about change.

4

THE HUNGER GAMES: INFLUENCES AND INSPIRATIONS

The Hunger Games is at its heart a simple tale, simply told, but there lies within it a cornucopia of meaning waiting to be unpacked. In writing the trilogy, Suzanne Collins drew upon a myriad influences and inspirations in shaping the world of Panem. She deliberately, albeit lightly, drew upon a series of social issues from US and world history and from contemporary times, ranging from poverty and starvation to social and economic inequality. Themes like these inform the backdrop to the society depicted in the novels, and sometimes motivate the characters, but they are rarely foregrounded in a heavy-handed manner. Rather, the simple style in which the novels are written allows younger readers to follow and become attached to their favourite characters while the deeper themes lurking in the background come through. Suzanne Collins, while admitting to not necessarily knowing every twist and turn of her story from the beginning, was clear that the three books would follow a thematic development: 'I didn't know every detail, of course, [but] the arc of the story from gladiator game, to revolution, to war, to the eventual outcome remained constant throughout the writing process.'

The story of her initial inspiration from flicking between television channels showing a reality television competition and a news channel showing war reportage is well-known (see Chapter 2). Equally important to the genesis of the first novel was her personal background as the daughter of a military man who had experienced the potential loss and uncertainty of having a loved one involved in conflict. These thoughts were at the centre of her inspiration for *The Hunger Games* novels: how to communicate the real impact of war to the young, while at the same time offering a readable critique of modern media and the society it reflects.

Suzanne grew up in a politically aware household where education was prized and attention to news and current affairs was encouraged. She combined this with her own deep interest in history, both factual and the older myths and legends that form the basis of much storytelling. She drew upon the stories of the Roman era, including their naming conventions, for characters and places for much of the Capitol of Panem. The city's architecture may be brightly coloured, but it is modelled after Roman designs. Characters have names like Coriolanus, Cato, Brutus, Octavia, Venia, Flavius, Plutarch, Seneca, Claudius and Caesar – all Roman in origin. At the same time, there is a layer of older Greek myth behind much of *The Hunger Games*.

The politics of Panem involves the oppression of populations and the effects of dictatorship upon a country where communal resources (the fruits of the Districts) are harvested for private benefit (the living-in-luxury population of the Capitol). It was through the journey of her central character of Katniss Everdeen that Suzanne hoped to gently introduce some of these political topics to her youthful readership. 'The interesting thing about Katniss is when the story begins, she doesn't have much political awareness,' she said. 'There are things she knows about her world to be true and untrue, but no one has ever educated her in that area. It is not in the Capitol's interest that she know anything about politics. There's only one television channel, completely controlled by the Capitol. She is struggling to put things together as she goes, and it's quite difficult, because no one seems to think it's in their interest to educate her, either. Even though hers is an extreme case, I think all of us have to work to figure out what's going on [in the world].'

Some of these political topics are examined in the relationship between the young and the old in society, partially influenced by a failing modern Western economic system where a pensions crisis is growing, with fewer working young people paying taxes that offer support – through their pensions – for an ever-growing population of older people. The inhabitants of the Capitol are almost all older adults: children (although part of that society) are rarely depicted in the first two books. The children readers do encounter most directly are from the Districts and living in poverty and squalor. Then there is the effect of war – as channelled through the Games – on both participants and the wider population watching on television. By the end of the first book and into the second, *Catching Fire*, Katniss is depicted as a sufferer of Post-Traumatic Stress Disorder, while the wider populations of the Districts are also traumatized, frightened and controlled through their viewing of the annual Games on television.

Underlying the central conceit of *The Hunger Games* is a very old story, the Greek tale of Theseus and the Minotaur. The myth relates that in punishment for past deeds, Athens had to regularly supply seven boys and seven girls to Crete, where they were thrown in the Labyrinth and devoured by the Minotaur, a half-man, half-bull creature. Beyond this, the Games are an updating of the gladiatorial arena that entertained the Romans, in which participants were both unwilling slaves or prisoners of war being punished, and well-trained professionals who had careers as famed fighters. 'In keeping with the classical roots, I send my Tributes into an updated version of the Roman gladiator games,' the author said, 'which entails a ruthless government forcing people to fight to the death as popular entertainment. The world of Panem, particularly the Capitol, is loaded with Roman references. Panem itself comes from the expression "*Panem et Circenses*", which translates into Bread and Circuses.'

In the later years of the Roman Republic, and in a move that seemed to define the decline of well-developed Roman civic virtue, handouts of grain (for bread making) to local poor populations were accompanied by huge (and hugely expensive) games, gladiatorial contests and sporting spectaculars. These games could last for days or sometimes even weeks, with many animals slaughtered (the deaths of humans in the games occurred less often than popular fiction and sword-and-sandal movies might suggest). As in *The Hunger Games*, animals would be introduced into the arena to spice things up, and fighters would have to display great cunning or skill to win the approval of the crowds.

The phrase 'bread and circuses' comes from the work of Roman poet and satirist Juvenal: in *Satire X* he identifies the need for bread and circuses as the only remaining responsibility of the new Roman population that has abandoned any practical political involvement that might challenge their rulers or change their living conditions: 'Already long ago, from when we sold our vote to no man, the People have abdicated our duties; for the People who once upon a time handed out military command, high civil office, legions – everything, now restrains itself and anxiously hopes for just two things: bread and circuses.'

That phrase has become a metaphor for a type of superficial appeasement used to keep subjugated populations well-enough fed that they survive but cannot revolt (bread), and entertained enough that they are distracted from the conditions in which they are forced to live (circuses). This is the world of Panem, which Katniss's defiance eventually does so much to disrupt.

The combination of reality-television gameshows with war footage (both featuring mostly young people) may have given Suzanne her initial inspiration, but across the novels she developed a thorough critique of modern media as a backdrop against which the action takes place. The increasingly violent and competitive nature of a certain type of reality gameshow, such as *Survivor*, or certain iterations of the dominant *Big Brother* television series, was playing on her mind. 'They're often set up as games,' she said of these entertainments, 'and, like sporting events, there's an interest in seeing who wins. The contestants are usually unknown, which makes them relatable. Sometimes they have very talented people performing. Then there's the voyeuristic thrill – watching people being humiliated, or brought to tears, or suffering physically – which I find very disturbing. There's also the potential for desensitizing the audience, so that when they see real tragedy playing out on, say, the news, it doesn't have the impact it should. The audiences for both the Roman games and reality TV are almost characters in themselves. They can respond with great enthusiasm or play a role in [participants'] elimination.'

The Games depicted in the novels include many of the elements of current television reality and contest shows, including the dramatic 'makeover' of the participants (by Cinna and his assistants), the need to 'dress to impress' for the pre-Games parade and talent interviews, the real or fake 'showmance' (a romance developed just for show or just for an audience) between Games participants Katniss and Peeta, an all-star reunion of past winners (seen in *Catching Fire*'s Quarter Quell), and the seemingly ageless, artificial gameshow host, personified by Caesar Flickerman.

The complicity of the audience for the Games (in both the novel and for the real-world television diversions) is a factor in their own oppression: the 'bread and circuses' idea is at play here. Give a population enough food and water to cover survival, enough material goods to satisfy, then add an interactive diversion (in the form of reality television, Olympic and other sporting events, or the Hunger Games themselves), and the population will direct their dissatisfaction towards the participants in the games, indulging their apathy, so refraining from any meaningful political action. Any resistance to those who rule or action towards change is diverted into rooting for or against participants in the Games, which also serve to sate the population's bloodlust. 'The Hunger Games is a reality television programme,' said Suzanne. 'An extreme one, but that's what it is. And while I think some of those shows can succeed on different levels, there's also the voyeuristic thrill. I think it's very important not just for young people, but for adults to make sure they're making the distinction. Because the young soldiers dying in the war in Iraq, it's not going to end at the commercial break. It's not something fabricated, it's not a game. It's your life.'

The merging of news and entertainment is in play too. During the Iraq War in particular many media commentators and viewers pointed out the similarities between the video footage shown on the nightly news and the images seen in violent warfare-based video games played mostly by the young and impressionable. The question was sometimes asked, is it possible to tell one from another? The potential confusion also applied to media professionals, as in the case of an ITV news programme that transmitted video-game footage to illustrate a real-world event. ITV's *Exposure: Gaddafi and the IRA* used a sequence of a helicopter being shot down from video game *ArmA 2* with an on-screen caption claiming the imagery was from a 1988 IRA propaganda film, in which terrorists were supposedly using weapons supplied by Gaddafi. The mistake was excused as 'human error', but it was symptomatic of the growing confusion between the real world and simulations of reality, even in documentary.

There is also a criticism of the concept of being fashionable, and being seen to be a part of a particular society, in the novel's depiction of the denizens of the Capitol. This is especially presented through the character of Effie Trinket, who might be considered to be an archetypal 'fashion victim'. It is in her nature (learned through growing up within that world) to stay abreast of the latest shifts of what is fashionable in Panem high society. This season's 'in' colours, wig styles and dress length are all very important to her (and she's far from alone in the superficial world of the Capitol) as these things are signifiers of status, wealth, position and power (even if Effie is apparently at the lower end of the scale). Those with real power, or who aspire to it, can be seen to resist or opt out of these fashions. This is, necessarily as it is a visual medium, much more noticeable in *The Hunger Games* movies. Characters such as Cinna, President Snow and Plutarch Heavensbee dress in fairly reserved, sombre clothing (often traditional suits, perhaps with some fashionable amendments). They are powerful enough (or wish to appear to be) to rise above the need to stay fashionable that drives everyone else: they are figuratively, and often literally, above such trivial things and exempt from this competition.

Some commentators have seen evidence of Suzanne Collins's Catholicism and signs of distinctive Christian religious allegory in the pages of *The Hunger Games* novels. The 'bread' part of 'bread and circuses' is again significant. Peeta, Katniss's partner in the Games, is a baker and through his ability to supply sustenance, a life-giver (usually seen as a feminine attribute). He gave the starving Katniss bread (as used in the Christian sacrament), at great risk to himself. That gift sustains Katniss and her family, giving her a new outlook resulting in her seeing a sign of hope in the first dandelion of spring, something she thought lost in District 12. The image of a 'spark' of life runs throughout the books. Katniss herself says: 'What I need is the dandelion in the spring. The bright yellow that means rebirth instead of destruction. The promise that life can go on, no matter how bad our losses. That it can be good again. And only Peeta can give me that.' Bread recurs throughout, but most clearly in the supplies given to Katniss from District 11 in recognition of the respect she accords their Tribute Rue in death.

Peeta devotes himself to Katniss, even if she only initially returns his love in the form of a performance for the cameras: he carries on regardless, in a selfless manner. He puts her life before his own, offering himself up in a variety of ways as a sacrificial character, from enduring a beating from his mother when he gives away the bread, through to the wounds he sustains in the arena defending her. Unlike Katniss's deafness (and other scars), which can be fixed back in the Capitol, blood poisoning leads Peeta to lose a leg after the Games as it is beyond saving. The biblical resurrection is echoed when Peeta takes a wound intended for Katniss, and is then buried (hiding under leaves by the side of the river), then placed in a cave for several days where he recovers, gains new life and emerges reborn. In many ways, Peeta is the subservient one in their relationship: where Katniss is tough, self-sufficient and willing to kill to survive (normally male attributes), Peeta bakes cakes, decorates his skin (as camouflage) and needs to be repeatedly rescued by Katniss (all perhaps traditionally seen as female attributes in adventure fiction). In *Catching Fire*, he is the one taken prisoner and who needs to be liberated by Katniss.

Of course, Peeta is not the only character who carries the theme of self-sacrifice. Katniss herself is the clearest example – the inciting incident of the story is her substitution of herself for her younger sister Prim during the 'reaping'. A Christian reading of that action would see a character following the example set by Jesus, but for Katniss it is an instinctual act bred from years of looking out for her sister and providing for her family after her father's death (another subtler, longer term form of self-sacrifice).

Hope, although not an exclusively religious virtue, is a centrepiece of the saga. The rebellions in the Districts and the actions of Katniss and her friends are driven by the hope of a better future, a change in the world of Panem. That society, administered by President Snow and created by his forebears, may be read as an example of a world without God or a world where the concept of God has been replaced by the materialism and transient fashions of the Capitol. The morality of not only endorsing but regularly staging a public spectacle in which children kill each other for the entertainment of the masses is the result of such thinking. The theory behind many religions is that a moral framework can only come from a set of rules created by a deity and enforced by his representatives on Earth. This outlook suggests that the rules of society are only followed because a moral code enforces punishment, and a religious view sees religion as central to any moral code. Humanists and others would disagree, refusing to see a lack of religion as equivalent to a lack of morals. While the world of Panem is a satire or an exaggeration of the real world, many of the characters the reader is asked to sympathize with show clear positive moral qualities (not least in their battles against the Capitol) without any obvious endorsement of an all-pervasive religion or god figure.

Whether these biblical echoes are deliberate on the author's part, emerged naturally from her outlook on life, or are just examples of an author using some of the classic tropes of good storytelling and character design is not clear, but what is clear is that some readers of *The Hunger Games* come to the work through a religious filter and find within stories, parables and examples that reinforce their faith.

In the end, the stand taken by Katniss is an expression of her innate individualism. Her survival and hunting skills that put food on her family's table and that serve her so well in the Games arena are a necessary product of her sense of responsibility for others (her family, Gale, the wider community – such as the black-market trading centre of The Hob – of District 12) and a product of the conditions in which the Capitol has trapped the populace. These aspects of her character came from Suzanne's own past and her family experience. 'Some things I knew from listening to my dad talking about his childhood,' she said. 'He grew up during the Depression. For his family, hunting was not a sport but a way to put meat on the table. He also knew a certain amount about edible plants. He'd go into the woods and gather all these wild mushrooms and bring them home and sauté them. My mom wouldn't let any of us go near them, but he'd eat them up and they never harmed him, so I guess he knew which ones were safe, because wild mushrooms can be very deadly. I also read a big stack of wilderness survival guidebooks. And here's what I learned: you've got to be really good to survive out there for more than a few days.'

Katniss is a version of the many female warriors of myth, legend, literature and popular culture. From ancient times there are stories of real-world female fighters, from the Far East through to nineteenth-century Russia, taking in such figures as Sui Dynasty Princess Pingyang, Spartan princess

Arachidamia, British queen Boudicca, Roman gladiatrix arena fighters and French martyr Joan of Arc – Katniss Everdeen contains some aspects of the spirit of them all. Folklore adds other examples, such as the Amazons, a tribe of all-female warriors, through to American Civil War heroine Annie Oakley, to such fictional creations as Buffy Summers (of television series *Buffy the Vampire Slayer*), Wonder Woman, and *Alien*'s Ellen Ripley.

The most appropriate tale for Katniss Everdeen might be that of Spartacus, the slave and gladiator who led a slave revolt against the Roman Republic in around 73 BC. The specific details are lost to history, but the story is generally interpreted as a model of an oppressed people rising up and fighting for their freedom against an oligarchy, just as the Districts eventually do in relation to the Capitol. The story has been retold in a myriad of forms and has been an inspiration to many significant political thinkers. She doesn't know it in the context of the fiction, but Katniss is certainly following in the footsteps of Spartacus.

In naming some of her favourite reading while growing up, Suzanne Collins also exposed some of the chief literary influences on her creation. Two of the books – William Golding's *Lord of the Flies* and George Orwell's *Nineteen Eighty-Four* – provide the keystones to Panem. From Golding's 1954 novel comes the idea of children killing each other and questions of survival. *Lord of the Flies* follows the misadventures of a group of pre-adolescent children stranded on a remote island, the result of a plane crash which itself follows the evacuation of mass populations due to a nuclear war. Their attempts to build a functioning society quickly break down and the children turn violently on one another. The conch shell used by the children to communicate echoes the horn-shaped Cornucopia. Orwell's 1949 dystopia is set in 'Airstrip One', a future version of the British Isles, a totalitarian state engaged in an endless war. The population is oppressed and the dictatorship is personified in the figure of 'Big Brother', a symbol of the all-seeing surveillance state. He is assumed to be always watching the populace, just as the Gamemakers are always watching the Tributes. The language known as Newspeak is a twisted version of English, so meanings are reversed or obscured, as with *The Hunger Games*'s military enforcers being called Peacekeepers. The influence of the novel on culture and society is exemplified by the continual use of 'Orwellian' to describe any aspect of the state that is seen as oppressive.

Although Stephenie Meyer's *Twilight* books had given teen fiction a new lease of life, Suzanne avoided the supernatural soap-opera romance of Meyer's approach, instead embracing the science fiction of dystopia for her fantasy world. There's nothing supernatural in *The Hunger Games*, with the world of Panem a strictly scientific one, in which the tracker jackers are genetically engineered and 'muttations' – more genetically engineered creatures – are used as weapons by the Capitol. The constant surveillance society of *Nineteen Eighty-Four* is reflected in the Jabberjays, artificially created organisms that can mem-orize and repeat entire conversations, so reporting back to the authorities any outspoken dissent within the Districts. The mockingjay that is so symbolic throughout the trilogy is an accidental offshoot due to interbreeding between Jabberjays and mockingbirds. Their ability to repeat song notes and the mockingjay as a symbol of rebellion (derived from the pin worn by Katniss) are central to *The Hunger Games*.

The romance in *The Hunger Games* is minimal, largely confined to thoughts in Katniss's head as she plays along with Haymitch's plan to promote her and Peeta as a couple (an idea that Peeta is living out in reality). Gale, left back in District 12, is only recalled through her guilty thoughts of him. This is not the full-blown romantic triangle that provided such angst for the characters (and the readers) of Meyer's books, but it is present enough for those readers who enjoy that aspect to make more of it than is actually present if they wish.

That Suzanne's favourite reading should inform her work is no real surprise. However, there are several other key texts can be seen to have echoes in *The Hunger Games*. Shirley Jackson's 'The Lottery' is a short story from 1948 (the same year that Orwell was writing his *Nineteen Eighty-Four*) that describes an annual ritual known as 'the lottery' in which an unfortunate selectee from within a community is stoned to death. It is suggested that this is part of an ancient ritual of an offering to the gods to ensure a good harvest the following year. It provides a model for the basic idea of the reaping process in *The Hunger Games*, although Suzanne has extrapolated from it and created her own version with multiple entries made in return for additional food rations. The catchphrase 'may the odds be ever in your favour' was originally intended as a good luck wish bestowed upon someone, but has become a general greeting. However, given that each community has an easily defined number of twelve- to eighteen-year-olds, and it could be determined from record keeping how many times each person's name had been entered for each annual reaping, it would be a fairly simple statistical exercise for every individual's exact odds of being chosen to be worked out.

The Japanese novel *Battle Royale* by Koushun Takami, published in 1999, is often cited by fans and critics of *The Hunger Games* as being the obvious precursor. Better known through the movie released in 2000, the story is set in an alternate-reality, authoritarian Japan in which the rulers enact 'the programme'. This annual event, originally a military research programme but now used to reduce the likelihood of organized resistance or insurgency, sees one class of schoolchildren selected for participation. The class are isolated on an island, given survival packs and a randomly selected weapon, and forced to battle each other to the death. They are each fitted with electronically armed collars that contain tracking and listening devices, so if anyone attempts escape or no one has been killed in the first twenty-four hours, the collars will be detonated and no winner will be declared.

The version of social control through the sacrifice of young people in *Battle Royale* did not feature any televised coverage of the event so central to *The Hunger Games*, and therefore lacks the media satire Suzanne embedded in her work. However, it is a powerful story that made an equally powerful film – although Suzanne claimed never to have heard of either before she submitted *The Hunger Games* to her publisher. Susan Dominus, writing in the *New York Times*, noted that 'the parallels are striking enough that Collins's work has been savaged on the blogosphere as a bald-faced rip-off,' but added the proviso that 'there are enough possible sources for the plot line that the two authors might well have hit on the same basic set-up independently'.

Of course, the idea of people hunting others is a very old one, dating back at least as far as the Richard Connell 1924 short story 'The Most Dangerous Game' (also known as 'The Hounds of Zaroff'), which became a movie in 1932. Based on big-game hunting safaris in Africa, the story had aristocratic hunter General Zaroff hunt down and kill people washed up upon his isolated island. Zaroff calls the hunting of people 'the most dangerous game of all'. The movie starred Fay Wray and was made by Ernest B. Schoedsack and Merian C. Cooper – the team who also made 1933's *King Kong*. The idea behind the story has been adapted and retold in various permutations ever since, of which *The Hunger Games* is merely the latest and one of the most successful.

The survival-in-the-wild skills displayed by Katniss were seen in the 1958 young adult novel *My Side of the*

Mountain by Jean Craighead George, which is about a twelve-year-old boy named Sam Gribley who hates living in the urban jungle of New York with his eight brothers and sisters, and who runs away to his grandfather's abandoned farm in the Catskill Mountains wilderness. There he builds his independence and self-sufficiency while surviving on the fruits of the surrounding forests. The book was one of three awarded the Newbery Medal in 1960 and it formed the basis for a 1969 movie and several sequel novels.

In Geoffrey Household's 1939 thriller *Rogue Male*, an unnamed British sportsman sets out to use his accumulated skills to hunt and kill a European dictator (obviously based on the then current figures of either Hitler or Mussolini) whose totalitarian regime was responsible for the death of his girlfriend. Household's work was an acknowledged influence on David Morrell's 1972 novel *First Blood*, in turn the basis for the Rambo series of movies.

Science-fiction author Robert Sheckley's 1953 story 'Seventh Victim' (published in *Galaxy* magazine) is set in a future in which murder is legal and televised, with both victims and 'hunters' able to secure corporate sponsorship and assistance to aid their survival or their killing – some successful participants go on to become professional, corporately branded celebrity killers. It was loosely adapted as the Italian movie *The 10th Victim* (1965), starring Marcello Mastroianni and Ursula Andress. Similarly, Sheckley's 1958 short story 'The Prize of Peril' followed a man who entered a television gameshow competition in which he had to evade assassins out to kill him for a period of one week in order to win a large cash prize. Some critics see 'The Prize of Peril' as one of the first published works to allude to the phenomenon later known as 'reality television', and it considerably pre-dates Stephen King's conceptually similar *The Running Man*.

Several works by King have been cited (not least by the author himself) as possible precursors of the world of

The Hunger Games. Both *The Long Walk* (1979) and *The Running Man* (1982), each published by King under his Richard Bachman pseudonym, do have marked similarities to Suzanne's later work. During the release of the *Catching Fire* movie King remarked: 'It's not unlike *The Running Man*, which is about a game where people are actually killed and people are watching: a satire on reality TV.'

Both *The Long Walk* and *The Running Man* (which became a movie in 1987 starring Arnold Schwarzenegger) feature satires of a totalitarian America that uses some form of Olympic-style games to control the population. In *The Long Walk*, the event is an endurance hike in which 100 boys take part and keep walking – at a regular speed of four miles an hour – until only one survives. The walk is watched by people lining the routes, with certain participants picked out as favourites to watch and potential 'winners'. The event is organized by a 'gamemaker' in the form of 'The Major' and is policed by soldiers who can shoot on sight any participants who deviate from the route, as well as supplying water and food to the walkers each day. The victor is granted 'The Prize': anything he wants for the rest of his life, although few winners go on to live long and fulfilling lives after the event (shades of Haymitch Abernathy's plight). At one point, two young walkers stage an act of defiance in which they march away from the route into oncoming machine-gun-fire, their middle fingers raised in defiance to the troops and the watching crowds.

The Running Man is set in 2025, a time when the worldwide economy is in ruins, international violence is increasing and the US has become a totalitarian dystopia. Ben Richards takes part in a television gameshow called 'The Running Man' in which participants are allowed to travel anywhere in the world with a twelve-hour headstart in their efforts to outrun assassins, called 'Hunters', set on their tracks. This is only one of the many violent game-shows transmitted on the government-owned channel The

Games Network. Every hour a contestant stays alive and escapes capture he earns $100, with an additional $100 for every Hunter he kills. If the contestant survives for thirty days he wins one billion 'new dollars'. Television viewers can also earn cash rewards if they spot the contestant in their neighbourhood and inform the Network of their whereabouts. The record survival time is eight days and five hours, and no contestant has lasted long enough to claim the big prize. In his favourable 2008 review of *The Hunger Games* novel in *Entertainment Weekly*, King wryly commented: 'readers of *Battle Royale* (by Koushun Takami), *The Running Man*, or *The Long Walk* (those latter two by some guy named Bachman) will quickly realize they have visited these TV badlands before'. And that's the point – at a time when according to some critics every story has already been told, novelty comes from how an author remixes the old ingredients and as a result creates something new.

The climax of *The Hunger Games* deliberately echoes a much older classic text. When Katniss and Peeta decide they will kill themselves by taking the poisonous nightlock berries they are replaying one of the great romantic suicide pacts of fiction, that of the madly-in-love ('starcrossed lovers' perhaps, as Katniss and Peeta are called by Caesar Flickerman) title-character teenagers in William Shakespeare's romantic tragedy *Romeo and Juliet*. Katniss realizes that 'without a Victor, the whole thing would blow up in the Gamemakers' faces. They'd have failed the Capitol. Might possibly even be executed, slowly and painfully while the cameras broadcast it to every screen in the country.' Their victory presents Seneca Crane with little choice – he cannot leave the millions watching on television across Panem without a winner, and a live double suicide would be very damaging to the Capitol and the Games. This results in his hasty decision to declare them both Victors, a decision that leads to his execution being ordered by President Snow (alluded to in the books, depicted in the movie). This is a moment of new maturity for Katniss: throughout the Games she has used her hunting craft to prolong her survival by avoiding conflicts and making the best of what the forest provides. At the end she crosses into the political arena, making a choice (and co-opting Peeta in her choice) to publicly defy the Capitol and the Gamemakers (and, by implication, the ultimate symbol of the Capitol's power, President Coriolanus Snow). Her act of defiance will be the spark that ignites a revolution.

With *The Hunger Games* conquering cinema box offices every year as well as the book sales charts, it is appropriate that both the books and the movies should have been inspired by a handful of key films of the past. Several were movies made from novels already covered, such as *The Most Dangerous Game* (1932, and its 1945 remake, *A Game of Death*) and *The Running Man* (1987), and over many decades had spread widely the concept of deadly games or competitions.

Most often, as with the latter two examples, these games were an offshoot of a totalitarian society and used as one of several methods of controlling and pacifying (or distracting and punishing) what might otherwise have the potential to be a rebellious population. The prime example of an exaggerated life-or-death sport being co-opted by the state to provide the circuses component of 'bread and circuses' to the oppressed population is the 1975 Norman Jewison film *Rollerball* (remade, poorly, in 2002). William Harrison's screenplay is based on his own short story 'Roller Ball Murder' (1973). The movie is set in 2018, with a global corporate state in control. The game of Rollerball pits two armoured teams who traverse an enclosed arena on skates or motorcycles in pursuit of a steel ball which they must get into the opposing team's goal. Anything goes, with the violence played up by the game organizers to please rabid television audiences (in the short story the aim of the players is to kill their opponents, with the game doubling as a form of population control). The teams are sponsored by the corporations and skilled players can become stars. While the game is intended as pacifying entertainment, one of the corporate directors notes that it also serves to show those watching the futility of any individual effort. Problems arise when one star player, Jonathan E (James Caan), refuses to retire when instructed, becoming ever more popular and a figurehead, giving the population hope (a dangerous thing, according to Panem's President Snow). The rules are altered to make the game ever more dangerous (like the Quarter Quell), the aim being to terminally eliminate Jonathan E. (a precursor of Katniss E.) as he is now counter to the stated purpose of the game. A staged championship becomes uncontrollably violent, more of a Roman gladiatorial contest than a sport, with only two players remaining. Jonathan E. refuses to kill his final opponent, instead scoring the only point of the game and taking a victory lap of the arena to the acclamation of the crowd. By his actions, he has defeated the controlling state and inspired the millions watching, becoming a symbol of rebellion and resistance. The film was hugely influential.

There were other game-based films, such as *Death Race 2000* (1975), in which the Transcontinental Road Race has become a form of deadly entertainment. Racers score points by killing each other and mowing down pedestrians during the coast-to-coast three-day race. This America is a single-party state dictatorship that uses the televised race to keep its citizens in line. Drivers become stars, recognizable due to their trademark outfits, personae and vehicles. Live commentary is delivered by an egotistical over-the-top sportscaster, just like Caesar Flickerman. A resistance group sabotage the twentieth Annual Race in an attempt to overthrow the regime by kidnapping Frankenstein (David Carradine), one of the leading racers. The film was produced by Roger Corman, who wanted to take advantage of the publicity for the then-in-production *Rollerball*, getting his movie into theatres two months earlier. These themes were played out (often to diminishing returns) in other similar movies, such as the television movies *Deadly Game* (1991, 'People are dying to play') and *Futuresport* (1998), as well as other *Most Dangerous Game*-derived 'people hunting' movies like *Surviving the Game* (1994).

In a similar vein are theme-parks-gone-wrong movies such as *Westworld* (1973) and *Jurassic Park* (1993, both from Michael Crichton novels). In both, recreated people, places and creatures are presented as entertainments, but they soon get out of control and turn deadly, echoed in Panem's Games arenas. Both spawned sequels, with *Futureworld* (1976, and the short-lived television series *Beyond Westworld*, 1980), and the ongoing *Jurassic Park* series. Fake reality movie *The Truman Show* (1998) was also echoed in *The Hunger Games* (more in the movie depiction of the Games control room).

Reality television was one of Suzanne Collins's main inspirations for *The Hunger Games*, and several movies have played with the idea of exaggerating television shows such as *Survivor* to include contestants killing one another (seen by some cynics as the ultimate form of such shows that inflict ritual humiliation on those taking part). Often overlooked, Nigel Kneale's 1968 British television play *The Year of the Sex Olympics* got there first. The elite are in control of the media, feeding the masses a stupefying diet of common-denominator entertainment and pornography. A new programme – 'The Live Life Show' – follows a group stranded on a remote Scottish island, but low audience figures sees the show's controllers introduce a psychopathic killer to the island to spice things up. The resulting murderous rampage results in soaring ratings, making the show a success.

The growth of real-life equivalents, such as *Big Brother*

(1999–present), *Castaway 2000* (BBC, 2000–2001) and *Survivor* (an international format that began in 1997, but started in the US in 2000 and the UK in 2001), at the turn of the century was parodied in movies where reality television turns deadly. *Series 7: The Contenders* (2001, 'Real people in real danger') purported to follow the six contestants participating in the seventh series of *The Contenders*, where players selected annually by national lottery are armed with pistols and set out to hunt and kill one another for the entertainment of the viewing audience. The main character of Dawn is a previous champion, returning once more to the game (as Katniss does in *Catching Fire*). Others ploughed the same furrow, such as *Live!* (2007), in which contestants play Russian roulette with real bullets live on television (a gimmick employed on British television by illusionist Derren Brown in 2003), and television series *Siberia* (2013), which drew on the *Castaway/Survivor* model with contestants stranded in a Siberian forest encampment, but followed shows like *Lost* (2004–2010) in adding a seemingly supernatural element explained by the camp's proximity to the location of the 1908 Tunguska 'event'. The 2006 Thai horror/comedy *13: Game of Death* featured a reality gameshow in which a contestant is directed by mysterious phone calls to attempt thirteen tasks that become increasingly immoral or deadly as it progresses, climaxing in a one-on-one murder.

There are other elements of the world of *The Hunger Games* that devoted fans can spot in all manner of preceding television shows and movies. For example, the reaping is echoed in the age-related 'capping' ceremony in the British television serial *The Tripods* (1984–5, based on the John Christopher young adult novel series), while in the movie *Logan's Run* (1976, derived from the 1967 novel by William F. Nolan and George Clayton Johnson) those who reach the age of thirty (twenty-one in the novel) are taken to the Carrousel [*sic*], where they are euthanized with a promised random chance of 'renewal'. Similarly, Panem's white-clad, helmet-wearing Peacekeepers might owe something of a debt to the black-clad android enforcers seen in *THX 1138* (1971), the debut movie from *Star Wars*'s George Lucas.

How much of this material had a direct influence upon the creation of *The Hunger Games* can only be known to Suzanne Collins. At the very least, it is evidence of how ideas and inspirations float around in a culture, available to be picked up, reworked, repackaged and re-examined to suit the current age. For many younger readers and viewers, *The Hunger Games* saga serves as a gateway to a host of other (some more adult) dystopias in fiction, film and television.

5

JENNIFER LAWRENCE: THE GIRL ON FIRE!

The producers of *The Hunger Games* movie struck it lucky in choosing rising star Jennifer Lawrence to play Katniss Everdeen. Early in a career marked out by a series of indie character roles, Jennifer scored an Oscar nomination for Best Actress, an award that she'd go on to win while making the first movie of an eventual four. The production had caught a young star on the rise, and the subsequent blockbuster success of the following films was in no small part down to her charms and talents.

Jennifer Shrader Lawrence was born on 15 August 1990 in the suburban Indian Hills neighbourhood of Louisville, Kentucky. Her father, Gary, owned a construction firm called Lawrence and Associates Concrete Design that offered building and repair services – he's since sold the business. Her mother, Karen Koch, still runs a children's camp and activity centre called Camp Hi Ho in Shelby

County. Jennifer may have been a latecomer, but she completed the Lawrence family, joining two older brothers, Ben and Blaine.

As the youngest, Jennifer's tastes were formed by whatever her older siblings were into. 'I got all of their hand-me-downs, so I was watching *MacGyver* and listening to Vanilla Ice,' she once said. By the age of five she was regularly quoting from 1995 Adam Sandler comedy *Billy Madison*, and re-enacting Cheri Oteri routines from *Saturday Night Live*. Her favourite movies were also those that cracked her brothers up, including the Jim Carrey movies *Ace Ventura: Pet Detective* and *Dumb and Dumber* (explaining her eagerness to appear in a cameo in 2014's twenty-years-later sequel, *Dumb and Dumber To*). 'We nicknamed her "Nitro" because she was so hyper,' said brother Ben, who is ten years older than Jennifer and works in web design and video production.

Jennifer went to Kammerer Middle School and then on to Ballard High School, and at each stage she never missed an opportunity to deliver a performance, whether it was appropriate or not. She was taught history at Kammerer by Christopher Noah, who recalled a seventh-grader with a different approach to the Greek myths. 'If we were doing something about Cupid and Psyche,' Noah said, 'Jen would take the role of Psyche and change her voice and mannerisms.'

Jennifer did the usual school and church plays as a child, but it was clear that she was far more serious about it than her contemporaries. Her first time on stage was at her local Christ Methodist Church in a play about the Book of Jonah, playing a prostitute. This role didn't seem to faze young Jennifer or even her mother. 'She played the best prostitute,' said Karen. 'This little extra just took over . . .' Jennifer then went on to take the dramatic role of a playing card in *Alice in Wonderland* at Music Theatre Louisville.

By the age of fourteen, Jennifer had already been

unmistakably bitten by the acting bug. 'I've always had this obsession with stories,' she said. 'If I wasn't watching TV or a movie, I was reading or you had to be reading to me. I never did theatre or took classes, which I think has helped me. I just had instincts and they were right.' She played Desdemona in Shakespeare's *Othello* at Walden Theatre, a local Louisville community theatre that had been running since 1976. Charlie Sexton, the theatre's artistic director, knew Jennifer was special almost immediately. '[She] stood apart from the standpoint of seeing herself in a career. Most eighth-graders weren't thinking that far ahead, but she was ready to get to LA.'

For school spring break, Jennifer persuaded her parents to take her not to Los Angeles but to New York, and 'as soon as my feet hit the sidewalks' she felt she'd found her spiritual home. She was interviewed by a couple of modelling agencies, one specializing in acting. 'We went to get this out of her system,' Karen Lawrence told *Louisville Magazine*. If that was the plan, it certainly didn't work.

Watching street dancers in Union Square one afternoon, Jennifer found herself the centre of attention. A scout for an H & M clothing commercial spotted her, and approached for permission to take her picture and put her under consideration for the ad. 'This guy was watching me, and he asked if he could take my picture,' remembered Jennifer. 'We didn't know that was creepy, at the time. So we're like, "Sure." So he took my mom's phone number, and all of a sudden all these [modelling] agencies are calling. And that's when it all started.'

While she viewed doing the odd commercial as a way into film and television acting – her true goal – Jennifer knew early on that she didn't want to simply become a model. 'I decided I wanted to be an actress, and I would only sign with an agency if they would let me audition for commercials and act as well,' she said. 'One of them gave me a script, to audition the next day, and I read the script . . . It was the first time I had that feeling like I understand this. I was fourteen, my brothers were star athletes, one of them was a straight-A student. I always felt I sucked at everything, that I could never find the thing that I liked. I auditioned and I probably sucked, but I had decided 100 per cent that this is what I wanted to do.'

Jennifer tried out with a variety of acting agencies and seemed to be a natural at auditions. 'They said it was the best cold read [having never seen the script before] they'd ever heard from a fourteen-year-old,' she said of one agency. 'My mom told me they were lying. My parents were the exact opposite of stage parents. They did everything in their power to keep it from happening. But it was going to happen no matter what. I was like, "Thanks for raising me, but I'm going to take it from here." '

Realizing their daughter was not going to be dissuaded, Jennifer's parents decided to cut a deal. They'd support her acting ambitions, but she'd have to graduate from school first. Jennifer knew this was sensible – just in case she wanted other options. She didn't doubt that she'd succeed in acting, but agreed to the deal. Like many things in her young life, she applied herself to achieving her goal. The result was her graduation from school two years early, with a 3.9 grade average. 'I never considered that I wouldn't be successful. I never thought, "If acting doesn't work out I can be a doctor." The phrase "If it doesn't work out" never popped into my mind. And that dumb determination of being a naive fourteen-year-old has never left me.'

The next few months were spent travelling to auditions in New York, with the reluctant support of both parents. 'I just started getting an overwhelming feeling of being exactly where I needed to be, exactly when I had to be there,' she said of her early experiences trying to start an acting career. 'Every time I would leave an agency and stop reading a script, I just wanted to keep going and going.' By the end of that summer she'd changed geographical direction, heading westwards to Los Angeles for a series of movie screen tests.

It seemed Jennifer was serious about acting, so Karen and Gary contacted local acting coach Flo Greenberg – who'd worked with such stars as *Friends*'s Matt LeBlanc and *Spider-Man*'s Kirsten Dunst – to have their daughter's true potential assessed. If they hoped to have back-up for their view that she should drop her acting ambitions, they were in for a big surprise. 'I was eager for her to pursue her acting career immediately,' said Greenberg. 'I don't say that about many people. Sometimes, you need to know when to keep your hands off and let somebody's natural technique blossom.'

Ben and Blaine, Jennifer's older brothers, were heavily involved in sports, as was their father, while their mother had run her kids' activity camp for many years. Her parents tried to interest Jennifer in softball, tennis and field hockey, as distractions from acting, but the nearest the young would-be actress got to athletics was in perfecting cartwheels. Even the older boys were begging their parents to let their younger sister follow her star, so apparent was it to them that she would not be driven off course. 'In our family, everything was about sports. If she could've thrown a baseball, we would have been able to tell that she could pitch,' said Karen Lawrence. 'We just didn't recognize her talent.'

Before she knew what was happening, Jennifer Lawrence was a professional. She started small, with a couple of modelling photoshoots for clothing retailer Abercrombie & Fitch, before stepping up to a handful of commercials, including one for fast-food chain Burger King. Jennifer also appeared in a dialogue-less role in two television promos for the MTV series *My Super Sweet 16*. Spoofing the kind of spoilt rich kids featured in the series, she appears in the first promo as Lisa, about to blow out the candles on a giant cake when a disco glitterball falls from the ceiling, hitting the cake and splattering her in icing. In the second promo she's being carried on a chaise-longue-style sedan chair, which she promptly falls off. They were short clips, but as would be her way, Jennifer made an unforgettable impression. As always with such a driven young actress, there was a good reason for taking on these slight roles: they were enough to earn her a Screen Actors Guild union card, the first step towards a professional screen-acting career.

In 2006 Jennifer landed a part in a television drama pilot episode for a show called *Company Town*. Created and written by Elwood Reid (a writer on *Cold Case*, *Hawaii Five-O* and *The Bridge*, among other shows), it starred *ER*'s Sherry Stringfield as Angie Amberson and concerned the lives of government agents who live near one another in the same Washington neighbourhood. Jennifer played Caitlin, but the pilot made for Paramount was not sold as a series and remains unaired. The following year another unsold pilot followed, with Jennifer playing the small role of an unnamed 'frantic girl' in *Not Another High School Show*, a parody of teen dramas like *Beverly Hills 90210*, *Laguna Beach* and *Dawson's Creek*.

At the same time, Jennifer began landing small roles in episodic series. She played the role of a basketball 'mascot' in a 2006 episode of *Monk* titled 'Mr Monk and the Big Game', starring Tony Shalhoub, a part that saw her on screen for only a few seconds, and most of that hidden under an animal-mascot costume. She did get one line, though. An episode of crime series *Cold Case* followed in 2007. In 'A Dollar, A Dream' Jennifer played Abby Bradford (sharing the role with Darcy Rose Byrnes, who played a younger version in flashbacks). Abby is the daughter of a missing woman whose body is found in a car dredged up from a lake, a mystery that attracts the cold case team.

Jennifer then featured in two episodes of mystery series *Medium*, which starred Patricia Arquette as real-life psychic investigator Allison DuBois. In the first, 'Mother's Little Helper' from the show's third season in 2007, Jennifer was Claire Chase, a girl who helps solve a murder by appearing to Allison's daughter Ariel in her dreams. The show's casting director had noted young Jennifer's resemblance to star Patricia Arquette and kept her in mind for when an episode required a younger version of the character to appear. As a result, her second episode, 'But for the Grace of God' in the following season, saw Jennifer return as the younger version of Allison DuBois herself, also in dream/psychic vision sequences involving Ariel.

While living in New York and LA in search of acting opportunities, Jennifer was continuing her studies, working for her General Educational Development tests that completed her high-school education. The small roles she was scoring in television episodes were great experience, but Jennifer was looking for something more long-term that would allow her to really get to grips with working on the development of a character. She finally got her chance on *The Bill Engvall Show*, a situation comedy for TBS. Co-created by and starring Bill Engvall, the show was a comedy about a family therapist who discovers his own family may be in need of some therapy themselves. Jennifer won the role of Lauren Pearson, the daughter of Engvall's Bill Pearson and Nancy Travis's Susan Pearson. As in Jennifer's real life, her character had two brothers, although they were both younger. The show was even set in suburban Louisville (albeit the one in Colorado), so Jennifer could draw on her own life growing up to play Lauren. Her role was to be the leader of the three children whenever they cooked up wild schemes or hatched plans against their parents. 'At fifteen, I signed a seven-year contract,' Jennifer said of *The Bill Engvall Show*. 'Then I realized that I had an absolute passion for deep, dark indie movies, which is the exact opposite [of the show]. I love the show, and I love the people on it . . . but if I had to turn down a movie for the show, I would die. That was always my biggest fear.'

Thankfully, Jennifer didn't have to make such an agonized choice. While popular, the show was cancelled in 2009 after three seasons and a total of thirty half-hour episodes, freeing Jennifer from her seven-year commitment (a standard clause in most television contracts). The role, however, allowed the actress to develop keen comic timing as well as the skills needed to handle the comedy's occasional dramatic developments.

The biggest movie audition Jennifer Lawrence had faced up to that point had come in 2007. She was up for the leading role in a young adult fantasy franchise based upon a trilogy of bestselling novels. However, then-seventeen-year-old Jennifer lost out on the part of Bella Swan in the first *Twilight* movie to Kristen Stewart, who won the role and the media and fan attention that came with it. Within a few years, Jennifer would be in command of her own young adult fantasy franchise based on another bestselling trilogy, and she'd be much better able to cope with the attention then. 'I'd had no idea *Twilight* would be such a big deal,' she said of what she later came to see as a narrow escape. 'I remember when the first movie came out, seeing Kristen Stewart on the red carpet and getting "papped" [having her photo taken by the paparazzi] wherever she went. For me, and assuming for her, it was just another audition. Then it turned into this whole other thing.'

The first of Jennifer's 'deep, dark indie movies' was the little seen *Garden Party*, a coming-of-age drama written and directed by Jason Freeland based on his own short stories. She only scored a few minutes of screen time as Tiff, one of a group of teenagers in Los Angeles exploring their emerging sexuality. Her character was pretty far removed from Lauren, the good-as-gold teenager from *The Bill Engvall Show*, but Jennifer was able to hold her own in this ensemble movie. From the film's cast of relative unknowns, she is the only one to emerge in career terms. Certainly none of the others have become household names – or Oscar winners! *Garden Party* clearly wanted to be *Short Cuts* (1993) for modern teens, but the *Village Voice* dubbed the film 'trivial'. Released in the summer of 2008, it took only $20,000 at the US box office. The film remains little more than a footnote in the Jennifer Lawrence story.

Her next part was another small one, playing the young version of Rosamund Pike's character Zoe in the thriller *The Devil You Know*, but the movie would quickly become legendary as the 'lost' Jennifer Lawrence film. Although made in 2007, when Jennifer was seventeen, the movie wasn't released until 2013 (and then only on video-on-demand) to capitalize on her new-found Oscar-driven fame. The movie starred Lena Olin as reclusive movie star Kathryn Vale who is hiding a secret while grooming her daughter, Zoe, to follow in her footsteps. Although another minor entry on her CV, the rather shapeless would-be enigmatic thriller got some attention simply because Jennifer was in it. It's not a performance anyone would have missed if it had remained unreleased.

For *The Poker House*, released in 2008, Jennifer finally had the lead role and a bigger name director in actress Lori Petty. Petty was making her debut as a director with a movie loosely based on her own childhood experiences. She'd appeared in plenty of movies and no doubt was able to give her young leading actress good advice on developing her craft and dealing with fame. Petty – best known for *Point Break* (1991), *A League of Their Own* (1992) and *Tank Girl* (1995) – was the daughter of a Pentecostal minister, raised in rural Chattanooga, Tennessee. In the movie, Jennifer plays the oldest of three sisters who all live with their mother Sarah (Selma Blair) in the 1970s in a home that doubles as a gambling den and a brothel. Sarah is on the run from the girls' father, a violent minister, but has found herself in a worse situation with pimp Duval (Bokeem Woodbine). Depicting the events of just one day, the part of Agnes set quite a challenge for the now eighteen-year-old Jennifer. As well as dealing with the family situation, Agnes suffers rape and threatened prostitution, but eventually escapes to New York to take up a life as an artist. Her younger sister, Cammie, was played by Chloë Grace Moretz, later star of the *Kick Ass* movies and the remake of Stephen King supernatural thriller *Carrie*, as well as a potential movie Katniss Everdeen. The *Los Angeles Times* called *The Poker House* 'harrowing . . . its indomitable fourteen-year-old heroine, Agnes, is so acutely well-drawn and so beautifully played by Jennifer Lawrence', and noted that the film succeeded because of 'Lawrence's shining portrayal'. Urban Cinefile called Jennifer's performance 'sensational', while Movie Metropolis perceptively noted, 'Lawrence is so persuasive we must mark her as a rising star'. It was the first time the actress had received any notable critical coverage.

'Rising star' was right, but Jennifer knew she still had a lot to learn, even if working with an actress of Petty's experience had helped her hone her craft. 'From fifteen to sixteen I sucked, because I had no idea what I was doing,' Jennifer admitted. 'Then I slowly stopped sucking. I never think I'm above reality or exempt from disaster. But I'm a hard worker, and when I set my mind to something, it usually happens.' One director who clearly remembered seeing and being impressed by young Jennifer Lawrence in *The Poker House* was Gary Ross, later her director on *The Hunger Games*.

Looking back on her first leading role, Jennifer now realizes what a breakthrough the performance in this dark drama was. 'Well, I was young. Now that I'm older, I can see what an amazing, brilliant script it is and how it grabs you and it has teeth. It's real and it's ugly. All [these] things that aren't usually appealing really appeal to me. When I was young, I thought it'd be fun. Now I can really look back on it and appreciate it. I learned a lot.'

Working with Lori Petty was Jennifer's first time with a female director, and one who'd also been an actress (she'd later work with Debra Granik and Jodie Foster as directors). 'She would give me direction, weird directions that wouldn't really make sense at the time and then I'd realize how much it helped me,' she said of Petty. 'She just knows how to communicate with you. I guess that's because she was an actress and so she knows how to really get to me. I've learned a lot from her.'

That on-the-job education would be put to good use in her next role, in writer–director Guillermo Arriaga's *The Burning Plain* (2008). Arriaga had been the screenwriter on the multi-story, multi-cast dramas *Amores Perros* (2000) and *Babel* (2006), both directed by Alejandro González Iñárritu. *The Burning Plain* reflected those films in its multi-tiered storyline following a mother and a daughter as they attempt a reconciliation after the daughter's difficult childhood.

For this one, an ensemble movie led by Charlize Theron, Jennifer was again much further down the cast list playing Mariana (the younger version of Theron's character), one of a pair of teenagers searching a New Mexico border town for information about their parents' broken lives. Mariana was another troubled young character for Jennifer to sink her teeth into. At this early stage in her career, though, the young actress wasn't consciously picking darker roles. 'I think it chose me more than anything,' she said of *The Burning Plain*, Arriaga's uneven directorial debut. 'When you first start acting, you can't pick and choose. Those were the roles I was booking. It was me, the girl from Kentucky with the wonderful family. Everyone was seeing this ability to go to this dark place that I didn't know I had. I auditioned for every comedy, everything under the sun. I'm not going to pretend that I've been so smart to pick these things. I've auditioned for all of those, but the comedies and the lovey-dovey movies didn't pick me. The dark, dark dramas, the dirty indies picked me, and I couldn't be happier.'

Director Arriaga was quickly convinced that Jennifer was the actress he wanted to play the young Theron. He called the older actress to give her the news: 'The first day of casting, he called me and he said "I found her,"' said Theron. 'I said "All right, calm down. Very happy for you, but you have three weeks of casting." And, he was like "No, no, no! I've found her." He sent me a tape and I've never been that blown away by an audition. I mean, never in my life have I ever given an audition like that.'

For her part, Jennifer was unfazed by the process of working on a bigger movie than she'd ever been part of before. 'I had no idea what I was doing. I memorized my lines and I showed up and was like "Hey, I'm here to shoot a movie." I feel like I can't really prepare for it. Now, I know that I can read the script and I know what I'm doing, but until you get there and you get the wardrobe and you're on the set . . . Then you start talking to the director and everything, that's when it really starts developing. I don't want to be closed-minded enough to already have it set in stone before I even show up. I have my thoughts on what I want to do, but it's also important to be mouldable, to be able to [say] "Well, why don't you try it this way?" Before I start filming, I don't have all of the answers, ever. It's just developing, adapting and reacting. It's a lot of different things that happen during the filming.'

It was another small role that made a big impression on everyone who saw the movie, and it put Jennifer next to two Oscar winners in Theron and Kim Basinger. 'Kim is in it the entire time,' said Jennifer. 'She comes to set completely in her character and does not leave. And Charlize is like me, joking around, and once the director yells "action", she gets right to it. It's just so funny to watch the opposites. I've learned so much from them.'

In *The Burning Plain* her troubled teenager's actions lead to unexpected and tragic events, so her role was pivotal to the overall plot, even if her screen time wasn't that extensive. Far more attention was paid to *The Burning Plain* than to *Garden Party* or *The Poker House*, although the film didn't perform as well as hoped at the box office and was met with mixed reviews based on high expectations from Arriaga's previous work. It was, however, the second performance for which Jennifer won an award. She won the Marcello Mastroianni Award at the 2008 Venice Film Festival that September, a prize that honours the best young actor or actress to emerge from a movie screened at the event. This followed the Outstanding Performance Award from the Los Angeles Film Festival for *The Poker House* given in June that year. However, she had yet to score her breakthrough role.

By 2009, Jennifer Lawrence was a well-enough known face to star in a pop video. Parachute signed her to appear in the video for their single 'The Mess I Made' that saw her appear bathed in an ethereal light as the apparent romantic partner of lead singer Will Anderson. 'She was amazing,' remembered Anderson. 'We could tell when we met her that she was going places. Here was this amazingly talented actress, and just an incredible person who also happened to be gorgeous. How could we not ask her to be in the video? Seeing her get nominated for the Oscar was amazing. No one deserves it more than her and it's awesome to see her getting cast in such rad roles!'

Both *The Poker House* and *The Burning Plain* came out around the same time, creating an image of Jennifer Lawrence as an intense young actress who was interested in roles that depicted pain and suffering. That couldn't be further from the truth. 'Jodie Foster once told me that twenty years from now I would look back at my career and see a pattern, and understand what it had to do with my life. Now, I'm just like, "I don't know." I'm just as puzzled as everyone else. It's always been about the script and the director for me. There are directors that I want to work with and that I admire. You can love a script, but if it doesn't have a good director, it won't be that [one I take].'

However short her screen time, however minor the role, or whether it was the lead character or just one part among many players, Jennifer Lawrence used her time on television and her first few movie roles to her best advantage. Every appearance was a learning opportunity, every film a chance to discover more about what went on behind the scenes. Curiosity had always been a driving impulse in Jennifer, and while much of her talent seemed to come naturally, she was determined to use these early experiences to figure out how the movie business worked. 'I've always wanted to direct,' Jennifer admitted. 'Ever since the first movie. Lori Petty was directing, and I was imagining being a director. I love filmmaking. I love acting, but I don't feel married to being just in front of the camera.'

Jennifer was also learning how to handle the media appearances that were a necessary part of promoting her work. Giving interviews and attending press junkets was all new for the girl from Kentucky, but she quickly figured out how to handle it. Her shoot-from-the-hip style would win her many admirers in a few years' time, but none of her seemingly crazy pronouncements are simply the work of a ditzy actress. 'I don't think I'm always right,' she admitted. 'I'm a good listener, and I'm open to being told I'm wrong. But by the time I say something, it's already gone through the nine levels in my head, and probably it is right. So I might as well say it.'

She also found that so-called 'Method' acting, where actors draw on real-life emotions for their characters, was not for her. She could not draw on her own experience to inform her roles, as at age sixteen or seventeen she'd had precious little. 'All I'm really doing is memorizing my lines,' she said. 'I understand each word coming out of my mouth. It's never my real emotions that are invested in it. If I'm thinking about me and my life to put fear across my face or make me cry, then I'm reacting as Jennifer. And, also, I'm not a mental case, so I'm not going to be able to believe everything that's going on in a scene. If I'm in a movie and my dog just died, well, I know that my actual dog didn't just die.'

Her childhood and teenage years didn't resemble those of Agnes or Mariana or the roles she'd played on *Medium*. The nearest was perhaps the family-friendly comedy of *The Bill Engvall Show*. For the other roles, she had to draw on reserves other than experience. 'I've never been through anything that my characters have been through. And I can't go around looking for roles that are exactly like my life. So I just use my imagination,' she said. 'If it ever came down to the point where, to make a part better, I had to lose a little bit of my sanity, I wouldn't do it. To you [the viewer] it looks emotionally straining, but I don't get emotionally drained, because I don't invest any of my real emotions. So many people, after they've seen my movies, expect me to be intense and dark, and I'm not at all.' Her policy to withhold her real emotions when acting in movies would be sorely tested by her next film. This one would prove to be a huge breakthrough for the young actress: *Winter's Bone*.

Everything before *Winter's Bone* for Jennifer Lawrence had simply been prelude. She brought everything she'd picked up in her roles to date to the character of Ree Dolly, an Ozark teenager forced to draw upon her own inner resources to survive a harsh life while unravelling a dark family secret. It was the screenplay by director Debra Granik and Anne Rosellini, adapted from Daniel Woodrell's 2006 novel, that attracted Jennifer to the challenging part. 'I admired her,' Jennifer said of the book's central character. 'She has a strength that I could never possess, and she doesn't take no for an answer. You just find yourself fascinated with the life that she has and the attitude that she has toward it.' *Winter's Bone* would be good training for playing Katniss Everdeen.

Mostly set in the Missouri Ozarks, Woodrell has dubbed his fiction 'country noir' for the dark drama his works depict. *Winter's Bone* was no exception as it follows the trials of sixteen-year-old (seventeen in the movie) Ree Dolly as she tries to protect her two younger siblings, brother Sonny and sister Ashlee, while attempting to track down her missing father, who has jumped bail following a charge of cooking crystal meth. There's an urgency to her quest, as she faces losing the family home to the bail bondsman, so she and her siblings will become homeless unless she can find her father. Other family members are little help on Ree's quest, especially her shifty uncle known as Teardrop (John Hawkes). This insular and close-knit community seems determined to thwart Ree's mission, making her all the more determined to discover their secrets.

It was Ree's single-minded 'kind of blind pursuit of what she was finding,' that sold Jennifer on the role. She saw the character as having a 'kind of tunnel vision, that none of us have, of seeing what you need and what you want and what needs to happen, and not seeing anything else other than that'. Jennifer had not read the book before reading the screenplay, but she had heard about it from Karen Lawrence, her always supportive mother. 'My mother actually read [the book] five years before and told me that if they ever made it into a movie, I'd be perfect. I didn't listen to her, because she's my mother, but five years later I got the script and the audition.'

Some 200 actresses of the right age range read for the main part, some in New York, some in Los Angeles and many more at a Missouri open casting call. Where Jennifer had come from made her appealing to director Debra Granik, whose previous work included the short film

Snake Feed that went on to be expanded to become her first feature film, *Down to the Bone* (2004). As with *Winter's Bone*, that film was also about drugs, following the efforts of a woman (played by Vera Farmiga) to kick her crippling cocaine habit. Although based in New York by that point, Jennifer moved back to Kentucky for a while in order to re-familiarize herself with the culture of rural south-central America where she'd grown up. Her immersion in country life meant picking up a few skills she'd need for the film, including chopping wood, handling firearms and cleaning out stables. In order to be adaptable in other roles, Jennifer had put some effort into losing the Bluegrass State inflections in her speech, but now she had to quickly reacquire them to play Ree Dolly. Jennifer's transformation into Ree meant wearing a minimal amount of make-up, painting her teeth with a yellow polish to make them look worse than usual and pulling a knit cap over her blonde hair. All that effort and her earlier preparation paid off in her performance. 'It would have been a lot harder if I was from New Jersey,' she said. 'The lifestyle is different [from Louisville], but some of the sayings were the same. I was comfortable in the dialect.'

For six weeks, shortly after Jennifer had turned eighteen, cast and crew relocated to the remote Ozarks. The movie was shot in Missouri's Taney and Christian Counties during February and March 2009 for some twenty-five very chilly days. The intensity of filming on location in such a short period was something of a blur for Jennifer. 'I just remember feeling so overwhelmingly grateful and happy that I didn't have time to really think about things,' she said, 'because when you're filming the movie you're in that zone, that filming zone. It's all in bits and pieces. I don't think I felt pressure, I just felt intensely happy and grateful [for the role]. I went up there to the location the week before, and I spent some time with the family on whose property we were shooting. Little Ashlee in the movie, the girl who's my sister, she lives there. She was part of that family, and we actually became close. We were basically shooting a movie about a girl who happens to live there. In the movie, these characters aren't really made into heroes or villains. It's just true.'

Winter's Bone was met with an overwhelmingly positive critical reception upon release. The *Illinois Times* noted that 'Lawrence delivers a dynamic performance', while the *New Yorker* called the movie 'extraordinary' and the *San Francisco Chronicle* praised Jennifer for delivering 'a performance of ferocious, fully mature, self-possession that recalls a young Jodie Foster. In scene after scene, she holds her own against a cast of older standouts.' The low-budget independent film took $6.5 million at the US box office.

Beyond the box office, the film was festooned with awards, including the Grand Jury Prize: Dramatic Film and Best Screenplay Award at the 2010 Sundance Film Festival, two awards at the 2010 Berlin Film Festival and three at the 2010 Stockholm International Film Festival, including Best Film and Best Actress for Jennifer Lawrence. The Chicago Film Critics Association awarded her the Most Promising Performer Award, while the Detroit Film Critics Society gave her the Best Actress and Breakthrough Performance awards for the film. Several other critics' groups and film festivals nominated or accorded awards on Jennifer for *Winter's Bone*, but the big surprise was her Oscar nomination for Best Actress in a Leading Role, alongside co-star John Hawkes as Best Supporting Actor. Neither was to win on this occasion, but the nomination was enough at this stage for the now twenty-year-old Jennifer. She said: 'I am honestly speechless and wish I had an eloquent way to say how excited and grateful and surprised I am to be nominated in the company of four amazing actresses. When I was younger, I watched the awards and dreamed that one day I might be able to go, but at the time it seemed so far away . . .' That February 2011 night the winner was

Natalie Portman for *Black Swan*, but Jennifer only had to bide her time; she'd be up on the Oscar winner's podium soon enough.

Jennifer Lawrence had achieved her breakthrough performance with *Winter's Bone*, becoming better known (especially after the Oscar nomination) and making a splash within the industry as a rising star many writers, directors and other actors wanted to work with. She'd done it all while growing up on screen. 'I'm not smarter than other nineteen-year-olds, or more mature than other nineteen-year-olds,' she once said. 'I just haven't gone through the gradual maturing that happens when you go into grades. You move with your classes, and I didn't have a class. I was with adults all day, mimicking them. So I just matured on my own, and I think Ree and I have that in common.'

Having now 'made it' in the movies and arrived at the much sought-after 'big time', down-to-earth Jennifer didn't see the process or her prospects differently than before. She was as determined as ever to go wherever the roles took her. 'There's something that's so beautiful and character-building, really, when you make an indie [movie], and you're starving and cold and exhausted and not one of you is there for the money. You're only there for the film, and then when you see it – when I watched *Winter's Bone* – I just got chills, because I know how hard we all worked. Then you do a studio movie and you work just as hard to make sure that it's good. There's more leniency to have a little bit more fun – I can enjoy living life in London [on *X-Men*], as well as going to work every day. It's just different. The filmmaking is still the same. You still take it as seriously.'

She also now had a new level of fame. 'Fame hits people differently when it happens suddenly,' Jennifer said. 'I never have given value to myself or viewed myself differently through my work, through my job. It doesn't give me a big head or anything, it just means I worked hard, and it paid off. I'm grateful that people love the movie. But there were hundreds of people that went into making [it]. I'm just a tiny part of it.'

In the immediate wake of making *Winter's Bone* – before it was released and before the film and Jennifer Lawrence became the 'next big thing' – the actress continued to work in smaller roles in smaller films. Released in 2011, *Like Crazy* and *The Beaver* were two very different movies, but both had unique experiences to offer Jennifer as she mapped out her career. *Like Crazy*, co-written and directed by Drake Doremus, followed a transatlantic love affair as a British student, Anna (Felicity Jones) falls in love with an American, Jacob (Anton Yelchin). The pair struggle to keep the relationship going when they are separated on different continents, but Jacob starts a new relationship with Samantha, played by Jennifer, while they're apart. 'I saw *Winter's Bone*,' said Doremus of casting Jennifer. 'We shot in June, and pretty much right after we shot the movie, [her Oscar buzz] started to ramp up in the fall. We got in when she was still under the radar. That was a good bet we made, for sure.'

By coincidence, Anton Yelchin was in Jennifer's next movie, too. *The Beaver* starred Mel Gibson and was directed by Jodie Foster, a one-time child actor who'd grown up in Hollywood and taken up a role behind the camera, as well as in front of it – a model Jennifer hoped one day to follow. As with *Like Crazy*, this was a smaller role for Jennifer, but one that saw her directed by Foster, the third female director the young actress had worked with. In *Interview* magazine, Foster asked her young star about her career plans in Hollywood. 'I'd like to think that I have a plan, but you can't really pick what scripts you're going to get or what movie is going to come along, so I'll have the idea of, "Maybe I should do something lighter now",' Jennifer said. 'After *Winter's Bone*, I was like, I need to do something with a bigger budget and more resources now. And then I got *The Beaver*, with you, which was lighter and bigger, but never anything I could have anticipated. So maybe it is more about whatever script speaks to you and whatever part is available to you in a given moment, because you really don't have the kind of control where you can plan. I suppose you can have a general idea of where you want to go. [My films are] all dark. I think there's something of artistic value about them. When I did *The Burning Plain*, I was going through that turning-into-a-woman phase and discovering what it was like to be a woman, and going through hell – and that was what was happening to my character in the movie. Then, when I read *Winter's Bone*, I was getting to a place where I would've done anything for that movie – and I did. So I think there is some kind of a pattern, but I don't know. I know certain roles are important to me. I know that I really want to play them. I know I can do a good job. But I can never put into words why – and you have to have an answer because you get asked that question.'

Her experience with Foster saw both actresses confess that they saw a lot of themselves in the other. 'We both walked away thinking the same thing: "I've never met anybody who reminds me of me more." As far as methods go, neither of us have one. Like me, she doesn't take any of it to heart. We both think of this as a job, and don't understand why you suddenly have to become an a-hole when you become successful at it. We're both perfectly fine with technical directions: "Hunch your shoulders more, lift your head up higher." And we both hate b.s. directing, like, "Imagine your puppy just died." If you want me to cry, just say "cry".'

Her work with Foster served to reinforce Jennifer's opinion that while there was a lot of star-driven razzmatazz to working in Hollywood, it was best to treat it like any other job. 'I think that growing up in a completely normal house, in a normal city, has made me crave normal. This is just a job for me. I watched my parents work hard on something they were passionate about, and that's what I do now. I think growing up in Louisville has helped me have an eye for seeing the normal side of things. It's a weird job I have, but it's still a job.'

Jennifer's next role couldn't have been more different, as it entailed spending much of the movie virtually naked and painted blue. In 2011's *X-Men: First Class* Jennifer was playing the younger version of shape-shifter mutant Mystique, a role previously portrayed by Rebecca Romijn. The eight-hour multilayered body-paint application needed the attention of up to seven make-up artists. It was a tiresome process, but Jennifer got through it by re-watching some of her favourite movies, such as *Dumb and Dumber*. 'It was like a really bizarre sleepover where I was just standing up naked being painted and scaled and glued,' she said. 'There were so many points where I'd think, "There is nobody else in the whole world who is doing this right now. Literally!"'

However testing the make-up application, it made for a striking image in the movie, even if it required Jennifer to go places on screen she'd never gone before. She also had to endure a twice-a-day training regimen and a high-protein diet that allowed her to sculpt, yet maintain, her curves. 'I knew that if I was going to be naked in front of the world, I wanted to look like a woman and not a prepubescent thirteen-year-old boy. I'm so sick of people thinking that's what we're supposed to look like.'

The next role that Jennifer Lawrence would secure would unexpectedly change her life. Director Gary Ross and studio Lionsgate ran a comprehensive search for the right actress to fill the role of Katniss Everdeen in the movie version of the hit young adult novel *The Hunger Games*. Up to thirty actresses were formally auditioned, some older and some younger than the target age of sixteen or seventeen required for the character. As in the Games, there could only be one Victor.

Director Gary Ross explained why he put the future of a hugely budgeted movie franchise on the shoulders of up-and-coming actress Jennifer Lawrence. 'I was just a fan,' he said, simply. 'When you do what I do, any time you see an actor like this emerge – I think everybody's head sort of snapped, you know? Both from *Winter's Bone* and other work that she's done, I was just always very aware of her. Then I had a meeting with her, and I was just as impressed, and then she came in and read for us and she blew me away. I think that an actor like this comes along once a generation.'

As far as her spectacular career rise in Hollywood went, Jennifer Lawrence was definitely the 'girl on fire'.

6

CASTING *THE HUNGER GAMES*

The casting search for an actress to play Katniss Everdeen in *The Hunger Games* movie was exhaustive and exhausting. A trawl of all the likely actresses in the right age range had produced a shortlist of around ten finalists, cut down from a longer list of up to thirty likely candidates. Although she was in the final list, Jennifer Lawrence didn't think she'd be first choice.

'I pictured [Katniss] as another face, with a braid,' she said, when asked who she thought might win the role. Thinking of herself in the part 'would be slightly narcissistic'. The call confirming her casting was very welcome when it came, even if filming on *X-Men: First Class* meant an early wake-up call when the news was delivered. 'It was the middle of the night in England, and I was in bed when I got the call,' remembered Jennifer. 'I was so in love with the books and the script, and suddenly it was right in my face – and the size of the decision was terrifying.' It took the actress a whole three days to finally say 'Yes', securing a payday of $500,000 for the first movie (equivalent to what Kristin Stewart had received for the first *Twilight* movie, but a modest amount for the leading role in a would-be blockbuster). Her income from *The Hunger Games* series would soar over the subsequent movies as built-in contractual 'escalators' related to the film's box-office success kicked in.

Readers are often vocal on the internet if they disagree with the choice of actors for the main roles in movies of favourite books, and reaction to *The Hunger Games* casting news was no different. The complaints were mainly because those chosen didn't match an individual reader's specific mental images of Katniss, Peeta and Gale, or because they had set their hopes on one of the other candidates up for each role. It all kicked off in March 2011, when it was announced that Jennifer Lawrence had won the role of Katniss.

The first bone of contention was Jennifer's age: at twenty she was seen by some as too old to portray the (in the book) sixteen-year-old Katniss Everdeen. The problem director Gary Ross and author Suzanne Collins faced was finding an actress with the dramatic range to carry the role, and it was unlikely – though not impossible – that someone younger would be up to the task. Many media commentators had expressed a preference for Hailee Steinfeld, who was just fourteen when she starred in *True Grit* (2010) as Mattie Ross. She had been in the running alongside actresses including Chloë Grace Moritz (*Kick Ass*), Kaya Scodelario (*Clash of the Titans*), Malese Jow (*The Social Network*), Abigail Breslin (*Little Miss Sunshine*), Emma Roberts (*Valentine's Day*), Saoirse Ronan (*Atonement*) and Shailene Woodley (*The Descendants*).

According to Ross, Jennifer displayed 'an incredible amount of self-assuredness, you got the sense that this girl knew exactly who she was. She came in and read for me and just knocked me out; I'd never seen an audition like that before in my life. It was one of those things where you just glimpse your whole movie in front of you. I just thought she was phenomenally talented, riveting and amazing, and had so much power. I found her to be just a completely compelling, intelligent person.'

Ross was clear that age was not his primary consideration, Jennifer's cinematic potential was. 'Suzanne [Collins] saw every single audition. And not only did Suzanne not have an issue with Jen's age, she felt you needed someone of a certain maturity and power to be Katniss. This is a girl who needs to incite a revolution. We can't have an insubstantial person play her, and we can't have someone who's too young to play this. Suzanne was very concerned that we would cast someone who was too young. In Suzanne's mind, and in mine, Katniss is not a young girl. It's important for her to be a young woman. She's a maternal figure in her family. She's had to take care of Prim, and in many ways her mother, since her father's death. She's had to grow up pretty quickly.'

Many readers had taken Collins's descriptions of Katniss as grey-eyed, olive-skinned and dark-haired to imply she might be mixed race (at the very least it was a description that left her ethnicity an open question), so the green-eyed, white, blonde-haired Jennifer Lawrence may have been something of a shock. It was something Ross and Collins had considered in making their selection. 'Suzanne and I talked about that as well,' said Ross. 'There are certain things that are very clear in the book. Rue is African-American. Thresh is African-American. Suzanne had no issues with Jen playing the role. She thought there was a tremendous amount of flexibility. It wasn't doctrine to her.'

Ross clearly knew that simply by making these decisions he would be trampling all over some readers' sincerely held images of the main characters. 'I think one of the wonderful things about *The Hunger Games* is that everyone has such a personal relationship to the material that they feel they have a very specific idea about the character and who the character is,' he said. 'I think a lot of the debate that has gone on about who Katniss is, is fantastic. People feel very passionately that their take on the character is unique and correct. But the one that I've honestly listened to the most has been Suzanne, who conjured this girl out of her own imagination.'

In an open letter to readers of *The Hunger Games*, Suzanne addressed the issue directly: 'As the author, I went into the casting process with a certain degree of trepidation. Believing your heroine can make the leap from the relative safety of the page to the flesh and bones reality of the screen is something of a creative act of faith. But after watching dozens of auditions by a group of very fine young actresses, I felt there was only one who truly captured the character I wrote in the book. In her remarkable audition piece, I watched Jennifer embody every essential quality necessary to play Katniss. I saw a girl who has the potential rage to send an arrow into the Gamemakers and the protectiveness to make Rue her ally. Who has conquered both Peeta and Gale's hearts, even though she's done her best to wall herself off emotionally from anything that would lead to romance. Most of all, I believed that this was a girl who could hold out that handful of berries and incite the beaten down Districts of Panem to rebel. I think that was the essential question for me. Could she believably inspire a rebellion? Did she project the strength, defiance and intellect you would need to follow her into certain war? For me, she did. Jennifer's just an incredible actress. So powerful, vulnerable, beautiful, unforgiving and brave. I never thought we'd find somebody this amazing for the role. And I can't wait for everyone to see her play it.'

If the search for Katniss Everdeen had been challenging, the hunt for actors to play the rest of the major roles in

The Hunger Games was no less difficult, if a little less pressured. Finding the two significant men in the life of Katniss Everdeen led the crew of *The Hunger Games* to Josh Hutcherson for Peeta and Liam Hemsworth for Gale.

Born Joshua Ryan Hutcherson in October 1992, Josh grew up in Union, Kentucky with his mother, Michelle, who was an employee of Delta Airlines, and his father, Chris, who worked as an analyst for the Environmental Protection Agency. He knew he wanted to act from about the age of five, but it'd be four more years before the precocious Josh made his formal movie debut. A local screen test took him to Hollywood in 2002 and a role in a television pilot, *House Blend*, and an appearance in an episode of hospital drama *ER*. He quickly secured other roles, including a small role in *American Splendor* (2003) and a part in *The Polar Express* (2004) that required a motion-capture performance. He quickly made his mark in a series of children's films, including voicing a character in *Howl's Moving Castle* (2004) and appearing in *Zathura* (2005), a film about a game that becomes all too real, fantasy adventure *Bridge to Terabithia* (2007) and *Firehouse Dog* (2007). In between he played the son of Robin Williams's lead character in comedy *RV* (2006).

All these parts brought Josh to the attention of young movie fans, and he soon began to get coverage in teen magazines such as *Bop* and *Pop Star*. Two family fantasy movies added to his credentials as a teen heart-throb in *Journey to the Centre of the Earth* (2008) and *Cirque du Freak* (2009), both based on fantasy novels. 'I love doing movies that are different from each other. That's why I like to be an actor because I get to play different characters and pretend I'm different people going through different situations,' he said. More 'grown-up' parts followed in the acclaimed drama *The Kids Are All Right* (2010), where he played Laser, and the ill-fated remake of *Red Dawn*, shelved until 2012.

In April 2011 it was announced that Josh would be

playing Peeta Mellark, rival District 12 Tribute to Katniss Everdeen in *The Hunger Games*. 'I was fortunate enough to be in the room with Gary Ross when Josh came in to audition,' said Suzanne Collins. 'Three lines into the read I knew he'd be fantastic. Josh totally captured Peeta's temperament, his sense of humour and his facility for language. I'm thrilled to have him aboard.' For his part, Josh saw the role as a major opportunity. 'I love Peeta,' he said. 'The character is so much who I am – self-deprecating, a people person.' In winning the role, Josh beat out other contenders such as Hunter Parrish (*Weeds, RV*), Alex Pettyfer (*I Am Number Four*), Evan Peters (*American Horror Story*) and Alexander Ludwig (who later won the role of Cato, a Tribute from District 2). 'Mentally, [auditioning] was rough,' declared Josh, 'because I've never connected with a character more than I have with Peeta. It drove me crazy. They were the toughest few weeks of my life because I wanted it so badly.'

Director Gary Ross was relieved that finding Peeta had not proved as tricky as he thought it might. 'When I read the book,' he said, 'I thought Peeta would be the hardest role to cast, and I feel so lucky that we found someone who embodies every aspect of such a complex character.'

Announced on the same day in April 2011 in the part of Gale Hawthorne was Liam Hemsworth. Liam was two years older than Hutcherson, so had slightly more movie experience. Born in Melbourne, Australia, in 1990, where his mother, Leonie, was an English teacher and his father, Craig, was a social services counsellor, Liam got his first break in the soap opera *Neighbours*, which had also featured the oldest of the three Hemsworth brothers, Luke. Middle brother Chris (who started in soap *Home and Away*) was initially the most successful with major roles in *Star Trek* (2009) and playing the Marvel superhero in *Thor* (2011), but Liam was rapidly catching up.

A potential role opposite Sylvester Stallone in *The*

Expendables (2010) brought Liam to Hollywood (however, he wouldn't appear until the 2012 sequel), where he auditioned for the part of Thor before losing the role to Chris. Instead he starred opposite Miley Cyrus (his on-off girlfriend) in teen romance *The Last Song* (2010), which ideally placed him for the part of Gale Hawthorne. 'Gale is a young man who uses words very sparingly, so the onus was on the actor we cast to capture him by showing, not telling,' said producer Nina Jacobson of Liam. 'This was accomplished so beautifully in Suzanne's writing, and Liam was able to translate it so naturally to the screen. At the same time, Gale's journey across the three books transforms him, and Liam's performance left no doubt that he would take us there.'

Six-foot-three, blue-eyed Liam was half asleep when director Gary Ross called to offer him the role. 'Gale is someone who wants to stand up to this thing but can't,' Liam said. 'He's pretty powerless. It's one of the hardest things to think about: one of your best friends, or someone in your family, basically going off to war. And that's what happens to Gale in the first book. As much as he's against the government and wants to stand up to them, he really is helpless. I just thought it was such a gut-wrenching kind of thought.'

Producer Jon Kilik was carefully monitoring the casting of the movie. 'Casting *The Hunger Games* was like fitting pieces of an epic puzzle together,' he said of the exacting process. 'Liam as Gale was one of those perfectly matching pieces. He's got such a strong physical presence, and a kind of natural heroic quality, that really embodies who Gale is in the book.'

With the first three main members of the cast announced, *The Hunger Games* hit more casting controversy. There was yet another fan fuss over the choices of Josh Hutcherson and Liam Hemsworth as Peeta and Gale, following the

April 2011 announcements. In the case of Peeta, *Weeds*'s Hunter Parrish was the firm fan favourite, so many readers had to make rapid adjustments when dark-haired Josh secured the blond-haired role. Liam's selection as Gale was similarly controversial and led to many Twitter and blog disagreements before the film had even entered production.

The casting of Amandla Stenberg as Rue was criticized by some fans who took Collins's comparisons of Rue to Katniss's sister Prim far too literally. From that comparison some saw her as blonde-haired and blue-eyed just like Prim, rather than having the brown skin and eyes clearly described in the text. Twitter was awash with 'fans' of the books complaining about the casting of a black actress (in what was clearly a black role, as recognized by Gary Ross). It was just more confirmation that visualizing characters in a much-loved novel can be fraught with difficulties and can (literally) colour a viewer's response to the resulting movie.

Willow Shields – one of twins – won the small but pivotal role of Katniss's sister, Primrose Everdeen. Born in 2000 in Albuquerque, New Mexico, her first acting job was a voiceover narrating the short film *Las Vegas New Mexico 1875*. It told the story of a dying gunfighter making his way home to see his wife and daughter one last time, and was made by a volunteer cast and crew. She appeared in an episode of *In Plain Sight* in 2009, a television series about the Federal Witness Protection Programme. Hallmark Hall of Fame television movie *Beyond the Blackboard* followed in 2011, before Willow secured her part in *The Hunger Games*. 'I'm excited to grow up with Prim's character, because I have three more movies . . . I'm going to be fifteen or sixteen by the end, but I started off when I was ten,' she said. 'So it's going to be really interesting to go start to finish, just to see what a difference [there is in] my acting.'

Willow managed to fit in a couple of extra projects

between the first two *Hunger Games* movies, including an episode of R.L. Stine's *The Haunting Hour* and the movie *A Fall from Grace* (2014), directed by Jennifer Chambers Lynch, daughter of David Lynch. 'It's so exciting to find an amazing young actress like [her],' director Gary Ross said. 'Prim is an emotionally demanding role and in many ways she is the cornerstone of the story. Willow Shields will make an amazing Prim and we're very lucky to have her.'

Another small role was that of Katniss's mother, who is not named in either the books or the films. The role fell to experienced actress Paula Malcomson, perhaps best known for her television roles in *Deadwood* (2004–6), *Sons of Anarchy* (2008–), and *Ray Donovan* (2013–). Born in Belfast, Northern Ireland in 1970, Paula made her movie debut in 1992 in *Another Girl, Another Planet*. Major movie roles include parts in *The Green Mile* (1999), based on a Stephen King novel, and *AI: Artificial Intelligence* (2001), directed by Steven Spielberg.

According to producer Nina Jacobson, the role required 'an actress with some gravitas, someone who could really transport herself, and audiences, to a place as tough as District 12'.

Although *The Hunger Games* director Gary Ross had gone for little known or virtually unknown actors for some of the major roles (with the exception of Jennifer Lawrence, whose profile was building following her Oscar nomination for *Winter's Bone*), he knew there were roles in the movie that he could fill with some rather better known Hollywood names in support of the younger cast members.

The first was the role of Effie Trinket, the escort for the District 12 Tributes Katniss and Peeta, who drew their names at the reaping and then accompanied them on their trip to the Capitol to prepare for the Games. To carry this small but distinctive part, Ross turned to actress Elizabeth Banks, who'd previously worked with the director on

Seabiscuit (2003), the story of an award-winning racehorse popular during the Depression.

'I just love Effie,' said Elizabeth. 'She's a lovable villain and it's very hard to find those and be fun and have as much fun as I did. I was a huge fan of the books and of Suzanne Collins, the creator of this entire pandemonium. I read the book when it was published and immediately fell in love ... then I heard [it was] to be a movie. I called everyone I knew the minute I knew that they were making a movie. Gary [Ross] and I worked together on *Seabiscuit*, so when he got the directing job, I sent him a little email like, "Just so you know, I'll totally play Effie, ha ha ha!" Then Gary went through his process and a long time later, after we had a couple more conversations, here we are.'

Elizabeth's previous roles leaned towards comedy in productions like *The 40-Year-Old Virgin* (2005) and *Zack and Miri Make a Porno* (2008), as well as serious drama in *W* (2008), in which she played First Lady Laura Bush and thriller *Man on a Ledge* (2012). She saw Effie as offering her the best of both worlds: 'Frankly, Effie is very much my personality,' Elizabeth said. 'She's the comic relief in a lot of ways. She's a very flamboyant person, but she's also very scared. She's very in-tune with the pressure around her and she's someone who travels to the District, so she sees first-hand exactly what's going on, whereas I think most of the Capitol citizens live in bliss. I think she's very knowledgeable that at any moment, as much as the lives of these kids are at stake, her lifestyle is at stake as well.'

Another figure with comedic potential, but with an underlying sense of drama and even tragedy, was Haymitch Abernathy, the only living Games Victor from District 12, who is supposed to function as a mentor to Katniss and Peeta for the 74th Games. However, he's a broken man. After winning the 50th Games, his family were killed on the order of President Snow due to his tactics. Abernathy became a drunk, drinking more heavily because the

Tributes he trained over the next twenty-three years were all killed, until Katniss Everdeen and Peeta Mellark were triumphant.

Ross knew the role required an actor who could balance the comedy of the character with the deeper pathos that informed his backstory. His first choice was Woody Harrelson, still best known perhaps for his time on the much loved television sitcom *Cheers* (1982–93), but he almost turned the role down. 'My initial interest was [director] Gary [Ross],' said Harrelson, whose career has included such movies as *White Men Can't Jump* (1992), *Natural Born Killers* (1994), *The People vs. Larry Flynt* (1996), *The Messenger* (2009) and *Rampart* (2011). 'I really think he's a tremendous filmmaker. Then I started to become aware that this was a little more of a phenomenon than I realized. I knew people liked the book, but . . . Ironically, I turned it down at first because I just didn't feel like there was that much to do. It wasn't an *uninteresting* part, I just didn't see the whole picture. I'd already started reading the book and got swept up in it. Gary called me and he says, "You gotta do this. I don't have a second choice." I said, "Okay. Well, let's do it then." I was really happy to do it because what a great experience it was to be, hanging out with this cool group of people in North Carolina.'

An equally experienced actor was required for the role of Caesar Flickerman, the host for the Games who anchors the television coverage. The flamboyant Flickerman interviews each of the Tributes before the Games begin, intending to bring out the best in them and so make the event more entertaining for viewers in the Districts. Twenty-five-year veteran of Hollywood Stanley Tucci (he first appeared in *Prizzi's Honour* in 1985) proved himself ideal for the role after playing the part of fashion fan Nigel in *The Devil Wears Prada* (2006). He was another actor who'd previously worked with Ross, providing a voice for the animated film *The Tale of Despereaux* (2008).

For Stanley, a big part of the appeal of his character was the opportunity to transform himself. 'We knew what we wanted the fellow [Flickerman] to look like,' he said of his involvement with the character's visual development. 'Then we experimented with stuff. I said, "I'd like to try teeth. I'd like to try some noses. I want him to have a tan. We have to really make it look like he has plastic surgery." The noses ultimately didn't work, but all the other stuff ended up working. When I got to North Carolina, we played around and we started shooting the next day. I was only there for about a week, but it was fantastic.'

Producer Nina Jacobson knew that Stanley was the right choice for Flickerman. 'When I saw Stanley in his blue wig being so funny and extreme in a kind of *Cabaret* way, it was all so wrong and yet so right for the character.'

Playing Flickerman's co-host Claudius Templesmith was character actor Toby Jones (son of Freddie Jones, best known for appearing in several David Lynch movies). He was born in London in 1966. Following an early career largely in British film and television, Toby became better known to international audiences after voicing Dobby the house elf in the *Harry Potter* movies (from 2002). He was one of two actors (the other was *Catching Fire*'s Philip Seymour Hoffman) to play writer and personality Truman Capote within two years, appearing in *Infamous* (2006). He has appeared in such diverse films as *The Mist* (2007, drawn from a Stephen King story), fantasy *City of Ember* (2008) and *Frost/Nixon* (2008). He took the role of Claudius Templesmith, the announcer for the 74th Hunger Games and the only voice from the Capitol the Tributes are able to hear during the event. 'When I talked to Gary [Ross], he was talking about how he wanted to make it,' said Toby, 'and I think everybody was surprised by the different styles he used within the film. It's not a standard blockbuster. When he said, "Do you want to come improvise with Stanley Tucci," I said, "Yeah, I do want to do that." Also, my children love those books.'

* * *

Head Gamemaker Seneca Crane was behind the unusual rule change for the 74th Hunger Games that allowed two Tributes to win instead of just one. Although the decision didn't work out too well for Crane, it did mean that both Katniss and Peeta could emerge victorious. Playing the vital role of the Head Gamemaker was actor Wes Bentley, best known for *American Beauty* (1999) and as the villain in *Ghost Rider* (2007). For Wes, he knew his role would be a one-film opportunity. In the event, he'd almost be upstaged by his own facial hair. It took a lot of effort to get his look right.

'The first one was a bit more dramatic,' said Wes of his weird beard, 'and a bit more sinister. The hooks were just a little bigger and sharper. Gary [Ross] loved it, but he wanted to tone it down a little bit because in the end, Seneca's not the devil. He's not metaphysical – he's a human being and he's trying to do a job. He's evil and he's ignorant to the fact that he's creating consequences, that people are actually paying for this, but he's not the actual bad guy.'

It took make-up artist Ve Neill up to three hours every day to get Crane's beard just right. 'I usually come to set with a beard and my hair as long as I can get it so there are options. I saw Ve before we started shooting and she was excited I had a beard, because she had something special in mind. It was all her. She went at it for like three hours trying to find the right shape; it was cool. The beard did half the work [for me].'

While taking a break from filming, Bentley would sometimes run to the local store in North Carolina, complete with satanic beard, something that always brought him more than a few questioning stares. 'I got some crazy looks. I don't know what they assumed,' said Wes. The actor took the opportunity of his role in *The Hunger Games* to discuss his past drug addiction and how it was a consequence of early fame. Clean since 2009, Wes saw Seneca Crane as a chance for a Hollywood comeback, even if it meant wearing a beard like no other.

Gary Ross had definite ideas about the character: 'I thought Wes could create something so interesting with this character,' he said. 'Seneca is someone who is drunk on his own youth, ambition and success, and Wes reveals how that becomes self-propelling.' It was an angle that Wes could run with. 'In talking to Gary, I realized he's not quite the cynical bad guy,' said Wes. 'He's more a product of the Capitol's corrupted culture. He's not conniving to be a terrible human being. He's really a tech wizard and a showman who's trying to make his mark, yet he's not really paying attention to the consequences of his work.'

Perhaps one of the odder choices when it came to casting *The Hunger Games* was that of musician Lenny Kravitz as Tribute fashion designer and stylist Cinna. Born in New York in 1964, Lenny won the Grammy Award for Best Male Rock Vocal Performance four years running between 1999 and 2002. Although his mother was an actress (Roxie Roker played Helen Willis in the 1970s television sitcom *The Jeffersons*) and his father was a news producer, Lenny had carved a career in music rather than in acting or in television. Prior to *The Hunger Games* his roles had consisted of a voiceover for *The Rugrats Movie* (1998) and cameos as himself (or rock star characters very like himself) in movies such as fashion satire *Zoolander* (2001) and *The Diving Bell and the Butterfly* (2007), or appearing in documentaries such as *Being Mick* (2001, about the Rolling Stones's Mick Jagger) and in Mexican soap opera *Rebelde* (2004).

Lenny made his biggest splash playing Nurse John in 2009's *Precious*, which brought him to the attention of Gary Ross. 'I was just knocked out,' Ross said. 'It was quiet and strong and understated and open-hearted: all qualities which define this character [Cinna].' His role in *Precious* won Lenny a host of award nominations and set him on the path to *The Hunger Games*. The musician and actor already had a connection to Katniss actress Jennifer Lawrence; she had acted alongside Lenny's daughter Zoe during the making of *X-Men: First Class* in London and the pair had become great friends.

Lenny was working in his home studio in the Bahamas finishing off his album *Black and White America* (2011) when Gary Ross called to offer him the role of Cinna. 'Gary Ross called me because he'd seen *Precious* and he liked how I underplayed the character,' said Lenny. 'It's not a similar role, but in a sense it's got a similar quality. I didn't have to audition, so I'm lucky. I like clothes, and I like playing with clothes. I enjoy fashion as an art.'

Lenny was quick to catch up with *The Hunger Games* phenomenon and work out an approach to the character of Cinna, knowing that his interaction with the main character of Katniss would be pivotal to the sequel. 'I already had a decent sense of who Cinna was. He's this guy who works for the Capitol but you know, he ain't really buying it, but he's got to do what he's got to do within the system. And he meets this girl who he sees something in. She's the underdog, she's supposed to be the last person who's able to win and he admires her bravery for taking the place of her sister. From the day she walks in, he's got a heart for her. And there's only so far that he can go, but he's busting his ass and creating the best pieces for her, to try to help her forge this impression. Because a lot of winning the game is about being likeable.'

Producer Nina Jacobson noted of Lenny's participation: 'We needed somebody for Cinna who could be strong, sexy and have great appeal without a lot of adornment. This is a character who is handsome on his own terms and a rock star in his own right. So we got a guy who's a rock star in real life.'

One of the most sinister, if not the biggest, roles in *The Hunger Games* is that of President Coriolanus Snow, the ruthless President of Panem. He is the man behind the oppression, and Snow is the first to recognize the potential danger in someone like Katniss becoming an underdog survivor and so a symbol of possible rebellion to the masses. Director Gary Ross knew immediately that he'd need a veteran actor, someone charismatic yet with an inner power of steel. 'You have to have a real gravitas,' he said of the actor who landed the plum role. 'Donald Sutherland is someone who was able to bring a tremendous amount to President Snow in just a few key scenes.' For his part, it was the director's script that sold Sutherland on taking part. 'He's a brilliant writer,' said the actor. 'The script was really compelling and I thought it could be significant in reaching young people.'

Canadian-born Donald Sutherland was in his mid-seventies when cast in *The Hunger Games*, probably the oldest actor on the production. Although his career had begun with sixties horror movies like *Die! Die! My Darling!* (1965) and *Dr Terror's House of Horrors* (1965) in London, he became well known for his role in the film *M*A*S*H* (1970). He starred in a variety of films in the seventies, including *Klute* (1971, opposite Jane Fonda), *Don't Look Now* (1973) and the first remake of *Invasion of the Body Snatchers* (1978). His later films included *Ordinary People* (1980), *JFK* (1991) and *Pride and Prejudice* (2005). He is the father of *24* television star Kiefer Sutherland.

Donald was happy to discover his role was being expanded even while production was under way. 'Just before shooting began, Gary added three scenes set in the Presidential Rose Garden that make lucid the concept of an oligarchy, of the privileged, of the hegemony of the Capitol over the rest of the states [Districts]. When I read it, I thought it had the possibility to be [a] most influential American film. What we're dealing with is the destroyed fabric of a once-upon-a-time empire. And the empire is obviously here [America].'

Donald was another latecomer to *The Hunger Games*

phenomenon, but was happy to be involved in fleshing out Suzanne Collins's original ideas. 'I knew nothing about the books or the fascination with them. We were in North Carolina, talking about the nature of these oligarchies of the privileged, and how to administer them. Gary [Ross] said, "I think what we have to talk about is hope and fear." Those [extra] scenes are not in the book. He wrote them, and Suzanne Collins loves them. It so perfectly defined what an administrator or bureaucrat, like Coriolanus Snow, has to do. How do you keep that underclass under control? You offer them a little hope.'

A political activist in real life, Donald was very happy to bring his own view of the world to bear on his portrayal of Snow. 'He expects someone to come and challenge his position. He's very confident. You see that he looks different from the people in the community. He's much older and he comes from a different generation. I think he sees challenge, and I think he sees something in Katniss Everdeen that's been let loose. He sees the challenge that he's been waiting for. This particular girl is someone who you can't just kill. You have to find some other way of controlling and containing her.'

One of the many casting challenges for the movie was in filling the roles of the Tributes (twenty-four in all) who take part in the 74th Hunger Games. With the two main roles already cast, the team behind the movie still had to find twenty-two young actors to play these roles, only a handful of which were important enough for their characters to even have names in the novel.

Alongside Amandla Stenberg as Rue was Dayo Okeniyi as fellow District 11 Tribute Thresh. He was born in Lagos, Nigeria, and was playing his first major role. Jack Quaid, son of actors Meg Ryan and Dennis Quaid, made his acting debut as Marvel, the tough Tribute from District 1, while Leven Rambin – who had appeared on TV in

Grey's Anatomy and *All My Children* – played his female counterpart, Glimmer. Both were relatively unknown, fresh-faced actors who proved to be an antidote to some of the casting controversy that had surrounded the main roles in 2011. Career Tributes Clove and Cato from District 2 were played by Isabelle Fuhrman and Alexander Ludwig. Jacqueline Emerson, another unknown whose only previous role had been to voice a character in 2004's *Father of the Pride* television series, won the role of the sly Foxface, who doesn't speak in the book or movie. Chris Mark, an actor and stuntman, scored the unnamed part of Foxface's fellow District 5 Tribute.

During the pre-production and casting process on *The Hunger Games* movie, Suzanne Collins found her role developing beyond that of just producing the first draft version of the screenplay (which director Gary Ross then reworked with her). Unexpectedly, having developed a closer working relationship with Ross, Collins found herself also consulted on the all-important casting decisions. 'Any time you read a book and get attached to the characters, to me it's always a shock when it goes from page to screen and it's not exactly what was in my head or what I was imagining it should be,' said Suzanne. 'So there's always that period of adjustment. But I think we feel so solid about our casting choices, and so thrilled that we've gotten these three young people in those [main] roles, that nothing can really eclipse it.'

Ross was happy to have the original author on board offering her opinion of how closely his choices fitted with the roles as she imagined them. 'It's wonderful that people have such a vivid image of Katniss and Peeta and Gale and they hold it so dearly,' said Ross. 'Suzanne and I have the advantage of having seen these guys audition for these roles, and I would never judge any role or any actor until I've seen them perform it.'

Suzanne noted of the search for *The Hunger Games* main players: 'People should know that of course we're taking the gravest care in casting these characters. It's not arbitrary. It's of the utmost importance to us that we get the actors who can best bring these characters alive on the screen. Every one of those kids earned those roles by virtue of the auditions they gave. Those three kids? They were all our first choice.'

7

MAKING *THE HUNGER GAMES*

Released on 23 March 2012, *The Hunger Games* movie grossed $691 million at the worldwide box office against a production budget of just $78 million, and was listed by Box Office Mojo as the no. 1 all-time moneymaker in the categories of action movies with a female lead and young adult book adaptations (beating *Twilight*), as well as the most profitable film in the post-apocalyptic genre. The book had been a hit, but how had Suzanne Collins's future world of Panem on the page become Hollywood's next big thing on the screen?

Experienced movie producer Nina Jacobson had been quick to recognize the film potential of *The Hunger Games* novel, snapping up the movie rights in 2009 just as the book was beginning to attract a following. She'd worked in film development since the late eighties, and had been involved in such films as *Dazed and Confused* (1993), *Twelve Monkeys* (1995), *Antz* (1998) and *What Lies*

Beneath (2000), rising to the role of President of Buena Vista Motion Pictures Group, part of the Disney empire. There she'd helped shepherd *The Sixth Sense* (1999), *Pearl Harbor* (2001), *The Princess Diaries* (2001) and *The Chronicles of Narnia: The Lion, The Witch and the Wardrobe* (2005) to the screen. Jacobson left that position in 2006, and set up her own production company – Color Force – which had a 'first look' deal with Dreamworks. Their first project was *Diary of a Wimpy Kid* (2010).

It was actually Bryan Unkeless, a reader within her company, who brought *The Hunger Games* to Jacobson's attention (he'd later be a producer on the movie). It was part of his job to evaluate newly published books as potential films. When she caught up with the adventures of Katniss Everdeen, Jacobson was very keen to make sure she was the one to bring Suzanne Collins's work to the screen. 'I read it and couldn't put it down,' Jacobson said. 'I really became obsessed with the thought of producing it, and was completely bothered by the idea that anybody but me could produce it. I felt that there were so many things that could go wrong, in adapting it, and I had this fierce desire to protect this book . . .' She got access to the second novel, *Catching Fire*, while it was still in manuscript form. Then began the job of persuading Suzanne Collins that Jacobson was the right choice to make the movie. 'Of all the producers we met,' said Suzanne, 'I felt Nina had the greatest connection to the work. I believed her when she said she would do everything she could to protect its integrity.'

After shopping the property around the major studios, all of whom saw the potential but were not willing to take the risk, Jacobson took the project to Lionsgate. The small studio, whose biggest hit to that time was the gory *Saw* horror series, quickly agreed to fund the film. For Suzanne, the choice of studio was crucial: she didn't want to be involved in something too huge. 'Everyone we needed to get the movie going was right there on the phone,' the author recalled. 'The studio was small enough for that to be possible and I felt it would be our best chance of seeing the story become a film.' Jacobson herself noted that 'Lionsgate was a hungry company that was very aggressive and very committed from the beginning. It's harder to get a bigger studio to look at a project with that kind of commitment at an early stage.'

Jacobson's biggest role in deciding the shape and tone of the movie would be in the choice of director. 'It was very important to me to choose a director whose instincts come from character, who's a storyteller, and who puts characters first,' she said. 'I was certain that there was a great movie to be made – but one that had to be treated with care.' She was intrigued by fifty-three-year-old Gary Ross, as his work seemed to lack a signature style: he adapted himself from movie to movie as appropriate, always putting the material first and never repeating himself. Although four-times Oscar nominated, he hadn't made a movie in seven years and initially didn't seem a likely candidate to helm a $78 million female-led teen-focused blockbuster.

Nonetheless, Ross was invited to discuss the project. Ross remembered: 'I'd heard people raving about *The Hunger Games*, and when I asked my kids about it, they kind of exploded . . . I had to stop them from telling me the whole story. Their enthusiasm was so infectious, I went upstairs, started reading, and by 1.30 a.m., I said "I have to make this movie." It was that impulsive.' He arrived for the meeting at Lionsgate armed with a set of storyboards outlining the movie as he saw it and a seven-minute video of a group of *Hunger Games* fans – including his own children – discussing what they loved about the books.

Ross was nervous pitching his take on the movie, presenting work by German expressionist artist Max Beckmann (among others) to give an idea of the style. He knew other directors, with more recent track records of success, were circling *The Hunger Games*, including Sam Mendes (*American Beauty*) and David Slade (*Twilight: Eclipse*). Lionsgate's President of Production Alli Shearmur said: 'After this show of tremendous understanding and sensitivity, we all agreed that [Gary] Ross was the man for the job. He's known both for the fantastical vision of *Pleasantville* and the visceral emotions of *Seabiscuit*, and it was that balance that was so essential.' Jacobson focused on Ross as a director of strong characters as much as a movie-maker who could deliver strong visuals. 'Getting the book right was such a big responsibility, and Gary's understanding of how Katniss's point of view had to be the heart and soul of the story was spot on,' she said.

It was clear to Ross that while the novel told a story of survival, it had within it a series of set-pieces and scenes, as well as a range of diverse environments and characters, which were easy to visualize – if done right. The producers and Suzanne Collins felt he was as keen as they were to balance characterization with spectacle, both being vital to a successful movie franchise, which all concerned hoped *The Hunger Games* could become. The first task was to create a script that would provide a blueprint for the entire production.

It helped Gary Ross win the directing gig on *The Hunger Games* that he had a history of working on movies with strong connections to displaced teenagers. The Tom Hanks-starring *Big* (1988) – for which Ross wrote the screenplay – saw a teenager awaken in the body of a grown man, while *Pleasantville* (1998) – his directorial debut – saw two contemporary teens transported to the kind of nostalgic fifties setting seen in many television sitcoms. His take on *The Hunger Games* was equally clear – it was all about Katniss Everdeen. 'The essential thing is that you are in Katniss's shoes,' he said of the book, which is narrated exclusively from the first person point of view. 'In [racehorse movie]

Seabiscuit (2003), I wanted to viscerally put the audience on the racetrack. In *The Hunger Games*, the audience has to be in Katniss's head. You know what she knows. You don't know more. You're in this experience 100 per cent with her. To that end, the film required a very subjective style. It had to be urgent, immediate and tightly in with Katniss the whole time.' It wasn't a style the resulting film could stick with exclusively, however.

For Nina Jacobson, developing the script meant returning to the source. 'Suzanne was very involved in the development of the script,' she said. 'She wrote the first draft.' At the time, Suzanne was deep in drafting the third novel, *Mockingjay*, and was determined to keep its plot developments secret. So that the script of the first movie would help set up the events of the end of the story, the author felt she should have first crack at writing a screenplay. 'I attached myself as the first screenwriter,' Suzanne said. 'When I look at the development of the script, there was the draft I did condensing down the book – what could be cut out, and then filling out the backstage stories. The one thing I had never been able clearly to see was not "What's the dramatic question?" because the dramatic question is fairly forthright: Is she going to live? But it's the emotional arc that exists between Katniss and Peeta.'

Suzanne was happy to have assistance with her first ever movie screenplay. Veteran screenwriter Billy Ray was brought in to the project to further develop the script. He had written and directed films like *Shattered Glass* (2003) and *Breach* (2007). Suzanne said of Ray, 'He was a complete pleasure to work with. Amazingly talented, collaborative, and always respectful of the book. His adaptation further explored the world of Panem and its inhabitants.'

Director Gary Ross – an experienced screenwriter in his own right – also reworked the in-progress screenplay, putting his stamp on it. 'Both Suzanne and Billy Ray had done wonderful work, but I told Billy when I began – and he's a director as well and a very good one – that I would have to put this into my own voice. I wanted to get back as close as I could to the essence of the book and the emotional arc. To get inside Katniss's skin and understand how she grows, largely through her relationship with Peeta.'

The author of the novel was glad to discover that Ross was such a collaborative writer. 'Gary seemed like a really nice guy and he made these great movies, but we didn't know each other. I saw in Gary's draft that it was the first time it had been successfully done as an overall arc. Without it you have a film, a story, but you risk losing the kind of emotional impact the film might have.'

Working on what would be the final draft screenplay saw Ross and Suzanne bond over the core of the story, both recognizing that film was a very different medium than a novel. 'The essence of this [story], I thought, was her relationship with Peeta,' said Ross. 'Suzanne felt the same way. Obviously, all the major elements that were in the book are in the movie, and we are faithful to that. There's a craft in adaptation where you have to find the essence of something and distil it down for reasonable narrative. We did the last draft of the screenplay together. And Suzanne understands that some things work in a book, some things work in a screenplay. Plus, she has a ton of fun making up new stuff for the movie. The idea that we can sit in a room and pitch and come up with new things, that's a ball for her.'

As the backer of the movie, Lionsgate was taking a huge gamble on *The Hunger Games*. The studio needed a hit after a series of recent flops, including the Taylor Lautner-starring thriller *Abduction* (2011) and the re-boot of *Conan the Barbarian* (2011). The studio's stock price had tumbled on Wall Street, attracting the interest of investor Carl Icahn, who was plotting a hostile takeover. Lionsgate executives faced a similar battle for survival to that awaiting Katniss in the arena. The studio could not afford for *The Hunger Games* to fail.

Ross had agreed to a deal that would pay him less than $4 million (a lowball figure for directing, given he could make more in a year through script doctoring) and would involve spending a great deal of time away from his family during the almost two years the film was in production. He had good reason, though. 'I hadn't seen a piece of material that touched the culture and moved me the same way in a very long time,' he said. 'If you fully commit, you fully commit.' He knew he had a challenge ahead of him, as Lionsgate were working to a very tight budget of just $78 million, required months of location shooting and would also need an estimated 1,200 CGI (computer-generated imagery) shots to bring the world of Panem to the screen.

From District 12, home of Katniss, Peeta and Gale, through to the dazzling Capitol and into the arena in which the Games take place, the film would have to visually conjure up a variety of distinctive locations that had only previously existed in the minds of Suzanne Collins and her millions of dedicated readers. 'The backstory of Panem that has to be alluded to is that a variety of forces – global warming, scarcity of resources, lengthy wars, all these things – ripped away at what used to be American culture and culminated in a very oppressive state. When the Districts rebelled, the Capitol instituted the Hunger Games as a means of control, to keep the people in line,' noted Ross.

This was a vision of a future America that would draw much from world history, principally Roman society at its height, a culture that was built around arenas and gladiatorial combat. 'The Games are like a Roman spectacle but they're also a lot like the reality TV we see right now,' said Ross. 'People are riveted by the Games because we all have this need to root for someone to make it. When President Snow says "The only thing stronger than fear is hope", it's because he knows hope is what gets people so involved in the contest. It's one of the brilliant things that Suzanne does in the book – she shows the best way to control people is not to subjugate them, but to get them to participate.'

While District 12 would depict the poor, careworn environment in which Katniss grew up – a land of coal mines, forests, mountains and rural hard graft not unlike that seen in *Winter's Bone* – the Capitol, the centre of decadence in Panem, would be a place of large open squares, tall majestic buildings that speak of their builders' power and self-image, and people who use outrageous fashion, style and make-up to flaunt their wealth. Crucial to turning the filming locations in North Carolina into the world of Panem was the movie's production designer Phil Messina.

Producer Nina Jacobson felt that the hiring of Messina 'was a big decision. He's so gifted, and his ideas were always so smart and rooted in American history and architecture. Nothing feels like it's not us, or couldn't be us, and I think that's very important. In the evolution of the movie, Gary and I talked a lot about "tonal bandwidth" and making sure that the look and feel and style and choices of the movie stayed within a certain consistent bandwidth. In the book, it's great when she [Katniss] can push a button and food comes up. We didn't do that because we felt that it would be too fanciful and too "Oz" [a reference to the 1939 film fantasy *The Wizard of Oz*], and that the Capitol had to be ominous. It had to be a mind-blower, but it had to be ominous.'

Messina wanted to create a plausible future, a 'lived-in' environment that looked as though it had grown out of what had come before, a look he dubbed 'retro-futuristic'. Messina explained: 'It's as if you took early mid-century, Depression-era America and suddenly brought it into the distant future, with twists of high technology. The book created an alternative universe where on the one hand, you have people scratching in the dirt to survive; and on the other, you have flying hovercraft.'

Everyone on the project was determined to stick to the details of the book as much as possible, so rather than drop something that seemed too difficult or find a way of working around it, the team set about finding ways of accomplishing it, or producing something equivalent. 'We were determined to design ourselves out of difficult situations in order to be as faithful as possible to the novel,' said Messina. Throughout the pre-production design phase, Suzanne Collins was regularly shown sketches and drawings of the various environments of Panem as envisaged by the movie's design team. 'She would sometimes say "That's exactly how I pictured it,"' Messina said. 'Could there be a better comment from the author who came up with this world?'

The first audiences see of the world in which Katniss lives is 'the Seam', the poorest area of District 12, whose economy is focused on coal mining. An abandoned mill town in North Carolina was used for the film, and Messina found a group of 1920s homes that he felt were a good stand-in for the area described in the novel. 'We couldn't have imagined it falling in our lap any better than that,' said Messina. He set out to create an environment of squalor and decay, where individuality has been stamped out and all the houses look the same. Gary Ross described them as 'cookie cutter . . . [They] feel like they're made by a company and not people. Phil [Messina] found the perfect location to bring out the regimented sameness surrounding Katniss.'

An old cotton gin – a factory where machines separated cotton seed from short staple cotton fibre – in Shelby, North Carolina, provided the location for the town square where Reaping Day takes place, a scene that required 400 extras to form the crowds of District 12's downtrodden inhabitants. Tracks were laid for the rail system that transports the coal through the town and out to the Capitol. In all, 300 feet of railroad track was laid and the cargo trains had to be lifted on to it by crane. Crowds were also required for the scenes set in The Hob, the souk-like marketplace of District 12, where all kinds of materials are bought, sold and exchanged – a black-market trade that the Peacekeepers employed by the Capitol generally turn a blind eye to. The detailed set-dressing and the costumes used for the hundreds of people in the marketplace all helped to bring to life how deprived the residents of the area are, in stark contrast to the later scenes in the Capitol.

The studio sets for the Capitol and many of the interiors seen in the film were built in an old Philip Morris tobacco factory in North Carolina. Messina could really let his imagination loose on these extravagant sets, while still placing his designs within a recognizable reality. 'You see the Capitol through Katniss's eyes in the book and we wanted to reflect the opulence and vastness of scale she sees,' he said. 'I was thinking of these buildings from the 1936 World Fair in New York that were temples of industry, we really riffed off that. The Capitol had to be imposing, but also outrageous because to the people who live there it's like Marie Antoinette's decadent court.'

Katniss and the other Tributes parade through the Capitol on horse-drawn chariots and these were some of the first things that Messina turned his attention to. 'I tackled the chariots early on,' he said, 'and we looked at zeppelin-style designs that would echo the Capitol's high-tech Maglev trains. We painted the chariots with automotive paint in black and chrome and even though they are mean looking, they also have the beautiful lines of sculpture. I think they hearken back just the right amount to Rome.'

The chariots and the imposing architecture of the Capitol all recalled ancient Rome, and Messina continued this influence through many of the interior sets, including the all-important training centre. As well as a gym for the Tributes to practise their skills and learn new ones, the training centre had to be an intimidating environment in its own right. In the minds of the film's designers the training centre had to be the scariest high-school gym imaginable, thereby tapping directly into the everyday fears of much of the teen audience who'd be seeing the movie. The place was to be scary and dark, but also echo some of the Roman influences on the exteriors. Then Messina faced tackling one aspect of the book he knew would be a huge challenge: the Cornucopia. 'I was a bit scared of how the Cornucopia was going to look,' he said. 'In the end it is one of my favourite pieces in the whole movie – a huge, nasty sculptural horn in the middle of a field. We looked at Frank Gehry designs and a lot of modern architecture with folded planes and fractal surfaces and riffed on that. It looks like it fell from the sky on to this field.'

The forests in North Carolina were ideal for the hardwood trees the film needed: a coniferous forest was simply not intimidating enough. Even so, finding just the right trees where Katniss could hide or bed down for the night, or were just right to hold the tracker-jacker nest, was not easy. It was important that the trees match what was needed, that they have enough branches, be tall enough and look capable of holding the on-the-run Tributes who hide in their foliage. It would be in and around these branches that one of the film's most important character scenes would take place, when Katniss meets Rue and the pair form a short-lived alliance.

The Hunger Games was a huge project for Messina, but it was one he felt he'd got to grips with. 'I've done bigger movies, but nothing as creative and fun as this design-wise,' he noted. The most important person who had to feel these environments reflected the book after the author was Katniss herself. Jennifer Lawrence said: 'The sets were so helpful to creating Katniss. I'd never seen anything like them and I felt like I was in some kind of wonderland for most of the shoot. From my house in District 12 to the woods, everything was even better than I'd imagined it.'

Something sure to be prominently featured in the film was the flamboyant make-up and clothes of the decadent inhabitants of the Capitol. Key to bringing these aspects of Panem to life were costume designer Judianna Makovsky and lead make-up designer Ve Neill, a three-time Oscar winner. Many of the looks were clearly described in the novel, such as Caesar Flickerman's hair and suit both in delightful shades of blue, the gold eyeliner worn by stylist Cinna and President Snow's defiantly scruffy beard. However, much of it was challenging for the designers, who had to satisfy not only a watchful author, the director and the cast, but also legions of waiting fans who'd endlessly studied the novels for clues about the world of *The Hunger Games*.

'This isn't the type of design we usually do,' said Makovsky of the unusual demands of this film. 'It gets into realms of fantasy fashion in the Capitol, but we also wanted the look to be recognizable and relatable, taking today's haute couture a step further. For me it was a wonderful challenge. How often do you get the chance to do such outrageous clothing, hair and make-up?'

There was an obvious place for Makovsky and her colleagues to begin their consideration of the clothing to be worn by various characters: the dramatic contrasts between District 12 and the Capitol. Clearly, the clothes in District 12 would be worn out, often hand-me-downs, plain, simple workwear or peasant-style clothing. Even here, though, the residents make an effort when they dress up for Reaping Day – although more formal attire might be necessary for the white-clad Peacekeepers. 'The Peacekeepers needed to stand out enough to be scary, but I didn't want them to look like they came from another planet,' said Makovsky.

'The uniforms follow the basic shape in motorcycle cops and SWAT teams, but we take it a step further. And since they don't really have hand-to-hand combat but use electronic wands, they can look very elegant.'

For her Reaping Day outfit, Makovsky had Katniss wearing the blue dress as described in the book, using a simple, vintage fabric. The colour palette used on the clothing of those living in District 12 was limited to greys and blue-greys, earthy colours that fitted with the bleak environment of the coal-mining area that was once the Appalachians. The idea was this would make a dramatic contrast to the Capitol, where many pastel shades would feature among brighter colours, like fuchsia and turquoise. Bridging the gap between the two environments would be Katniss herself, as her dress style changes as she transitions through the Capitol on her way to the arena. 'When she gets to the Capitol, her chariot costume is a leotard and tights with tall boots and it all has a very shiny, dramatic aspect,' said Makovsky.

The makeover of Katniss upon her arrival in the Capitol is down to Cinna, the stylist assigned to her. Given his profession and role in the story, the look developed for Lenny Kravitz was of utmost importance if this cinematic world was to remain convincing. 'Cinna's a very elegant man,' noted Makovsky when thinking about the 'girl on fire' dress for Katniss. 'We thought he would design an elegant dress, and only when it twirls would the flame within the bottom of the dress suddenly become visible. We wanted the dress to feel more high fashion than *Dancing with the Stars*. We added Swarovski crystals so it sparkles when she moves, but when she's standing still, it's just a beautiful dress with flame-like pleats.'

Elizabeth Banks was involved in developing the distinctive look for Effie Trinket. Although she appears wildly over-dressed when in District 12, when Effie returns to the Capitol it becomes clear she'd been 'dressing down' for her visit. 'We agreed that Effie is both a little prim-and-proper and outrageous,' Makovsky said of her consultations with Banks. 'There's a bit of "schoolmarm" about her, but she's also a bit sexy. When she's in District 12, she contrasts starkly with the people there. But when she gets to the Capitol, her look gets wilder and crazier. Her sleeves get larger, the colours get brighter and she changes wigs with every costume, from pink to green to lavender . . .'

There was a temptation with someone like Haymitch to go too far in depicting him as a debauched drunk. Actor Woody Harrelson preferred something dishevelled but not disreputable, a kind of 'bon vivant' in appearance. 'With Haymitch's look,' said Makovsky, 'there's a sense that he's created an outward persona that isn't who he really is – he's putting on a bit of an act. There's this sort of Edwardian dandy style to him.'

As described in the book, each of the Tributes wears identical outfits when they are plunged into the arena to battle each other to the death. The filmmakers, however, felt this might be a little monotonous, so decided to colour-code the participants, making it easier for viewers to distinguish between them. It was director Gary Ross who suggested giving each District a jacket in a signature colour for each pair of Tributes to wear, so marking them apart from one another. Apart from their jackets, their outfits would remain uniform. Another consideration in the design of the jackets was making sure they allowed for the covert attachment of harnesses or ropes for scenes requiring stunt work.

Ve Neill regarded *The Hunger Games* as 'a make-up designer's dream, with everything from high-fashion and avant-garde beauty to prosthetics and injuries, a vast scope and challenge for any artist'. Her inspiration came not only from the books, but also from the costume-design work already under way. It was important that the make-up, however subtle or distinctive it was meant to be, fitted well with the looks already apportioned to each character. Those remaining in District 12 were made up in shades of beige, while the denizens of the Capitol were painted in a riot of colours. For Katniss and Peeta, their looks would evolve subtly from the plainness of their home through their journey into the Capitol. Once in the arena, though, the make-up used on each of the Tributes would be stripped right back, with priority given to dirtying each of them down depending upon their individual experiences. There was also a requirement for some realistic-looking wounds and bruises, especially on Katniss and Peeta as they struggle to survive amid the career Tributes. 'The idea was for the Capitol to be visually stunning in a way very close to the book, but without looking silly,' said Neill, whose work brought her Oscars for *Mrs Doubtfire* (1993), and Tim Burton's *Beetlejuice* (1989) and *Ed Wood* (1995). 'The men of the Capitol are extremely groomed with coloured hair and the women all have bleached eyebrows, giving them a very austere look. [The arena] became about dirt and cuts and tracker-jacker wasp bites . . .'

Hair design is often overlooked in movies, but for *The Hunger Games* hair could help define character. Lead hair designer Linda Flowers could go as wild as she liked for the hairstyles of those living in the Capitol, but she also had to create a realistic, downtrodden look for the inhabitants of District 12. It was, however, the less obvious elements than lime-green hair that brought her the most satisfaction, such as maintaining the signature hair braid that is a part of Katniss's look. It took twenty minutes to prepare for each day of shooting. The other Tributes had slightly more elaborate styles, from ponytail balls on Clove to fishbone braiding for Glimmer and a simple, innocent look for Rue.

For Jacobson, the most important thing was that the future that Suzanne Collins envisaged in her novel should be represented visually on screen in a way that viewers, whether consciously or not, could relate to American history and tradition. 'Judianna Makovsky and Ve Neill created a look that doesn't feel outlandish, but one rooted in the history of American customs,' she said. 'One of Gary's strengths on this film was maintaining a consistent tone throughout, from the Capitol's eccentricity to the intense physicality of the Games, and the design team brought all the right instincts to do that. It all feels like one story.'

For the main cast members there was an intensive eight-week period of physical training prior to shooting beginning on *The Hunger Games*. It was important that the central actors were in good enough shape in order to convince as the hungry Tributes battling for survival in the arena. Jennifer Lawrence studied archery for about six weeks, as well as rock climbing, tree climbing, combat, running and vaulting. There was more to the training than just physical fitness, as the cast had to eat a particular diet to bulk up and increase muscle, as well as be faced with a variety of psychological situations that would prepare them for their time in the arena. 'We had to take a cast, most of whom had no previous action experience, and turn them into stunt people capable of firing bows, throwing spears and climbing trees,' explained Ross. 'There was a massive training component to making it all real.'

Running the sessions were the movie's stunt coordinators Chad Stahelski and Allan Poppleton, who started out by teaching combat choreography to the key actors. Although all the actions would be rehearsed and would be safe, the director was insistent that they should not appear so. 'We tried to create a more spontaneous feeling of wild, emotional struggle,' said Stahelski. 'We looked at each character and talked about their skills, their energy levels, the way they move and, working with all of those elements, ran with the action sequences from there.'

Stunt trainer Logan Hood established a unit gym where

he could focus on the physical fitness of the cast. Weight-lifting, push-ups, pull-ups, rope climbs and box jumps all featured, ensuring each actor was at the peak of their fitness levels for the start of shooting. Each had a custom programme designed to their strengths and to make up for their weaknesses. They even had a period learning 'free running', the acrobatic urban gymnastics that had been heavily in vogue in the run-up to the filming of *The Hunger Games* (and seen in movies from the Bourne trilogy to the James Bond series). 'The training had to transfer directly to their characters' personalities and backgrounds,' noted Hood. 'We weren't interested so much in creating "gym bodies" as in creating seamless, believable performances for each of the Tributes.'

Although normally quite athletic in her off-screen life, Jennifer found even she had to up her game in order to be prepared for what was to come. 'Since half the movie for me is running, I worked extensively with a running coach. All day long I was running down mountains, through sticks and brush, and doing it over and over again. I also worked a lot on climbing, both at rock gyms and on real trees, as well as on vault stunts and even more on archery.'

Key among the skills Jennifer had to master was archery, as Katniss was a dab hand with a bow and arrow. She began by learning traditional bow-and-arrow skills, with an emphasis on how they would be used in hunting animals, before switching to take on the heavily designed 'recurve' futuristic bows used in Olympic-level competition and adapted for use in the movie. 'Archery is a real mind game, all about total focus,' she said of the experience, 'and if you do one thing wrong, you get whipped with a string going like a hundred miles an hour and it's painful! I developed a real love-hate relationship with it.'

The production hired Olympic bronze medallist archer Khatuna Lorig to teach Jennifer how to handle her bow. 'When they called me, they told me, "We want to make

her look like a professional, to shoot like a professional,"'
Lorig said. 'From the beginning, I told [Jennifer], "Listen.
If this is going to work, we're going to do it in a professional way." It's a physical sport – even though I had her
with a very light, barely twenty-pound or eighteen-pound
Olympic style wooden bow. She was getting sore. I think
she was working out in the morning, then coming shooting
with me, then going to work out again. I told her I would
be very proud when I see her onscreen.'

Beside Jennifer during the training session were the
actors playing the other main Tributes, primarily Josh
Hutcherson as Peeta. 'I had to eat a lot of food and work
out hard five days a week with a lot of heavy weightlift-
ing,' said Josh. 'The training was rigorous, but it worked. I
loved doing all the running, jumping and evading people.'
During the course of the pre-filming training, Josh would
add fifteen pounds of muscle to his already fit frame. 'We
had to learn to go from hanging out with your fellow actors
to finding all kinds of fear and aggression against them. It
was a very drastic transition every day, but we had amazing actors who brought that out physically.'

Alexander Ludwig (Cato), Dayo Okeniyi (Thresh) and
Jacqueline Emerson (Foxface) were all involved in getting
into as good shape as they could. As career Tribute Cato,
it was all right for Ludwig to look muscle-bound and more
than capable of holding his own, but the others were supposed to be 'ordinary' people selected from their Districts
at random to take part in the Games. Nonetheless, Okeniyi
gained twenty pounds to play Thresh, as well as undertak-
ing sword-fighting lessons, bodybuilding work, boxing and
hand-to-hand combat training. Emerson was more focused
on building strength and stamina to play the wily Foxface,
who is always running into and away from situations in
the arena, outfoxing her fellow Tributes. Her training
consisted of acrobatics, practising somersaults, running
obstacle courses and learning balance and jumping skills.

*   *   *

Prior to the first day of shooting on *The Hunger Games*, director Gary Ross had worked up a detailed shot list, something he felt was vital to the production especially if he was to pull off his planned 'guerrilla' filmmaking approach to shooting the arena-based section of the Games. His plan was to film that portion of the movie in a hand-held style, both to give the Games an edge-of-the-seat immediacy, but also so they contrasted dramatically with both the subdued District 12 scenes and the much more flamboyant and colourful Capitol sections.

Something he hadn't reckoned with was his leading actress being rushed to hospital mere days before the first day of filming. On the final day of her training in North Carolina, Jennifer Lawrence threw herself into her tasks with a little too much enthusiasm. 'I had to do ten "wall runs",' she said, 'where you run at the wall as hard as you can to get traction. I ran at it and my foot didn't go up, so I caught the wall with my stomach. My trainer thought I had burst my spleen.' Her treatment upon arrival at hospital sounded like something straight out of the future of *The Hunger Games* itself. 'I had to get a CAT scan and go into a tube where they put this fiery liquid in your body.'

Thankfully, Jennifer was in great shape even before beginning her training for this movie, as she'd bulked up for her role in *X-Men: First Class*: 'A lot of the training was getting muscle back, heightening the muscles without building them.' Having been checked out by the hospital, Jennifer and the entire movie production crew were relieved to learn that she'd only suffered some bruising and nothing had been broken in her encounter with the wall, so filming could go ahead as scheduled.

Ross and the producers were determined to film *The Hunger Games* in specific American locations, ignoring pressure from Lionsgate to go somewhere where the subsidies available were larger, such as Eastern Europe, or even elsewhere in America, such as Louisiana or Georgia. Ever since scouting the locations, though, Ross had been sure that North Carolina held everything he needed. It wasn't a location without problems, such as the estimated 300 wild bears supposedly living in the woods in which they planned to film, as well as the 100°F degree temperatures in the summer months when they'd be filming, and the daily rain downpours that would hit the unit at almost precisely four o'clock every day. There was a strong possibility that between these factors and other unforeseen interruptions, the unit would only manage to actually film for around four to five hours each day. The location part of the shooting took place first, before the crew could relocate to the ex-cigarette factory that was being converted into studio sound stages.

Filming officially began on 23 May 2011 in Asheville, North Carolina, and would continue for another eighty-four days. Much of the cast and crew had begun work on location a few weeks earlier, under the codename 'Artemis', appropriately the Greek goddess of the hunt. Local casting had taken place at the end of April, mainly to fill out crowd scenes, especially the reaping scene, and for background artists in scenes in The Hob and throughout the District 12 sequences. Extras were also shipped in from Georgia, Michigan, New York, Virginia and Tennessee. Local outfitters supplied boots and waders for cast members. The area around Henry River Mill village was a hub of activity, where various buildings were remade using movie signage and other temporary adjustments, such as the addition of stairs, to become locations in District 12, including Peeta Mellark's family bakery. All the activity was having a positive effect on the local economy. 'All the hotels are full,' said Jackie Sibley, director of Tour Cleveland County. 'They've hired off-duty police officers. They're renting space, eating at local restaurants. They're spending a lot of dollars.'

The streets of Shelby were closed for the first time between 25 May and 3 June as filming got under way. Around thirty trucks and personnel vehicles were used to ferry cast, crew, props and set elements into the town. Over 750 people were involved in the first few days of filming, 150 being crew members, with 600 extras on the first two days and 400 on the other two. Among the first scenes shot were the reaping scene near the beginning of the movie, offering onlookers (many of whom were fans charting the film's progress for social media) their first glance of Jennifer Lawrence in action, wearing her blue dress as Katniss volunteers to take her sister's place as Tribute.

The area had a long history of movie-making, especially when independent filmmaker Earl Owensby established a 200-acre movie studio there used during the seventies and eighties. Dozens of low-budget B-movies aimed at the area's drive-in cinemas were produced, including Owensby's own *Death Driver* (1977) and *Wolfman* (1979). The filmmaking entrepreneur was instrumental in bringing James Cameron to the area to make *The Abyss* (1989) at a former nuclear power plant. Prior to *The Hunger Games* the last movie to film in North Carolina had been 2008's *Blood Done Sign My Name*.

Production in Shelby continued at the P&M Warehouse complex, where exteriors for stores in District 12, The Hob, the train station and the Halls of Justice were all filmed. Set designers raided local antique shops and thrift stores in surrounding towns to pick up items to decorate The Hob marketplace. Filming in early June included scenes from the end of the movie when Katniss and Peeta return triumphant to District 12. The second week of June saw the production decamp to the DuPont State Forest and Pisgah National Forest where scenes in the Games arena were shot. Willow Shields wrapped her scenes as Katniss's sister Prim by June 18. By June 20, the production unit had relocated to the North Fork Reservoir in Black Mountain, where further scenes in the arena were shot. One of the most dramatic scenes – and one of the most dangerous to shoot – saw Jennifer as Katniss confronted by a wall of fire that she must outrun. On screen the fire had to appear deadly, as though it was in danger of catching up with Katniss at any moment, while in real life safety had to be uppermost. This required a good deal of coordination between the stunt supervisors, the special effects experts and the visual effects people who would work on the footage. The starting point was the construction of several false trees built around steel cores strong enough to withstand fire. The on-location blaze would later be built up by visual effects supervisor Sheena Duggal. Location special effects man Brandon McLaughlin said, 'Gary's idea was to keep everything real as possible. So instead of a ten-foot fireball that defies reality, he wanted a six-foot fireball moving at Katniss in a way that you really feel it.'

To shoot the tracker-jacker sequence, a special crane had to be constructed on a platform built high up in the branches of the trees in order to achieve the dramatic angles to capture the scene in which Katniss drops the nest down on the career Tributes. 'This was like shooting in Vietnam,' director Gary Ross joked. 'I felt like I was making *Apocalypse Now!* The thing was so rigorous. We spent something like six weeks outside in the jungle every day, hiking up and down mountains with cameras, in the mud and in driving rain storms. We all felt it, but nobody felt it as much as Jen[nifer] did. It's been an intense physical experience for her.'

All the scenes taking place in the Capitol were shot in the Charlotte and Concord areas, taking up most of August. 'I think that we've done a tremendous job bringing the Capitol to life, and I think that's going to be really exciting for people to see,' said Ross during shooting. Ross had some welcome filmmaking company during this period when his friend and fellow director Steven Soderbergh turned up on location to help out with some second-unit filming. Soderbergh explained that Ross would rather have someone he knew handle the scenes than hiring in someone unknown. 'What's fun about it, for me,' said Soderbergh, 'is my job is to come in and duplicate exactly what Gary and [cinematographer] Tom Stern are doing. To mimic as closely as I can their aesthetic. If I've done my job properly, by design, you won't be able to tell what I did. It's supposed to cut seamlessly into what they're doing, that's the whole point. That's why he asked me to come down, because he knew that I would be rigorous about matching what they were doing.'

On 15 September 2011, Lionsgate announced an official 'wrap' (the end of filming) for *The Hunger Games*. Five lucky winners of The Ultimate Hunger Games Fan Sweepstakes had visited the production during its later stages in August, visiting the sets and meeting the cast and crew. In all, the film had used 3,000 extras, all of whom required some element of styling for their hair or make-up in order to appear as inhabitants of District 12 or the Capitol.

'I don't know how I ever could have done this movie without Jennifer,' said Ross of his star. 'I'm not sure I would have done it without her. She's that important. More important than any other piece – including me. She's Katniss Everdeen.'

Between the wrap on the filming of *The Hunger Games* in September 2011 and the film's release in March 2012 there was still much to do. Post-production on the movie took several months, from editing the footage to tell a coherent story to adding sound, music and visual effects. The use of CGI was essential to fully bring the world of Panem to life. Nearly every scene of the movie would be enhanced with the use of CGI, whether it was immediately obvious or not. Some of the more obvious uses were in the creation of the mutated 'mutts' who attack the final three Tributes, the deadly, genetically modified tracker-jacker wasps and in some of the cityscapes and environments of the Capitol. Colour grading of the film made the District 12 scenes darker and more 'earthy', while the scenes in the Capitol were brightened considerably to make it seem a superficially happy place, but still retain the sense of oppression that runs through Panem.

Lon Bender, supervising sound editor, knew the often overlooked importance of sound to creating a convincing movie world. He quickly read the books then began to develop his sound mix. 'In designing the sound there was a lot of thought on my part and my team's part about how we would stay true to the book in terms of sonic signatures as well as expanding upon it. It was all about an intimate understanding of the experience of Katniss Everdeen. From a sonic perspective, we always strived to play things from her perspective.' The sound crew wanted to keep that subjective experience intact for the film audience, sometimes mixing the sound down to a single mono production track. Interior 'room tones' and even exterior sounds, such as those of birdsong, were altered to reflect the mood or feelings of Katniss. The same applied to scenes in the arena. Real-world sound was recorded or created (a process known as 'foley') and then altered to fit scenes in the movie, such as a flaming torch waved in front of a microphone to create the sound of fireballs. Every sound heard in the film had to be specially created and recorded.

The first look that the general audience got of *The Hunger Games* was the reveal of sneak-peek scenes at the MTV Music Awards on 28 August, in front of an audience of 12.4 million viewers. For the cast and crew, the hardest, most physical part of bringing *The Hunger Games* to screen was finally over.

'It was brutal at times,' said actor Jack Quaid (Tribute Marvel) of filming in the summer of 2011. 'We had torrential downpours, flooding, scorching heat and then a bear would wander on to the set. But it was an amazing bonding experience. For most of us, this is either our first or second movie, and here we were flung into this crazy world. We definitely all had a great story to tell about what we did on our summer vacation.'

8

RELEASING *THE HUNGER GAMES*

With the movie finished, the special effects completed and the sound mix concluded, *The Hunger Games* movie was ready to be revealed to impatient audiences awaiting its release worldwide in March 2012.

Aiming to reach the book's core audience of twelve-to-eighteen year-olds, Lionsgate was determined the film should have a PG-13 rating in the US. Producer Nina Jacobson was clear on the fine line the movie would have to walk in bringing Suzanne's story to the screen faithfully. 'The situations are so intense and frightening; it's just going to be a matter of creating suspense,' she said. 'The power of movies can be just as much about what you don't see as what you do. What Suzanne managed in the book is to explore violence and exploitation without it feeling exploitive or guilty of its own themes. It's critical . . . Suzanne was rightly concerned that it had the potential to be turned into something she hated, glorifying the violence the book is meant to critique.'

Director Gary Ross was in agreement with Jacobson on the movie's rating, even if some older fans felt that a higher rating could allow the film to tackle the book's suggested violence full on. 'It's not going to be an R-rated movie because I want the twelve- and thirteen- and fourteen-year-old fans to be able to go see it. This book means too much to too many teenagers for it not to be PG-13. It's their story and they deserve to be able to access it completely. I wouldn't rate the book "R". I think Suzanne has a lot of restraint. It isn't that she has written an overly graphic book. Even in things like the tracker-jacker sequence, while horrific, it's the ideas that Suzanne has created that are so terrifying.'

As soon as the movie was announced, fans of *The Hunger Games* became part of the promotional effort. While speculation was rife about who would be cast in the main roles and fans pledged their allegiance to various actors, they were also busy creating fan-made movie trailers – before a single frame of footage had even been shot. One of the first combined real-world news footage with movie clips to create a convincing minute-and-a-half glimpse of what *The Hunger Games* could look like on screen. By August 2010, when *Mockingjay* concluded the trilogy of novels, 470,000 people had viewed this fan-made trailer. By the time of the release of the movie of *Catching Fire* in 2013, the figure was over four-and-a-half million views. Another two-and-a-half-minute trailer was shot by a group of fans, starring themselves in the main roles. Posted in December 2009, it had received 25,000 views by the time of the release of *Catching Fire*. Others used *The Sims* gaming format to retell parts of the story in online 'webisodes'. This fan devotion and creative effort was harnessed by Suzanne Collins, the filmmakers and the studio to help promote the first movie.

Fans took tours of the remaining sets in March 2012, long after filming had concluded, photographing what they could of signs that the filmmakers had been there and posting the result on widely seen fan websites. Their attention was grabbed by games released on social media platforms in the run-up to the movie's debut. The biggest thrill was the release of the genuine first trailer for *The Hunger Games* on 14 November 2011. Online the trailer scored over eight million views in just twenty-four hours. Lionsgate president Joe Drake noted: 'We were the number one Twitter trend on the planet. Since then, the book sales have jumped 7.5 million copies. That kind of data gives us enormous confidence.' In the run-up to the release of *The Hunger Games*, the film made many 'must see' lists and was rated by MTV as 2012's 'most anticipated' movie, ahead of other teen favourites like *Twilight: Breaking Dawn, Part 2*, and comic book movies *The Avengers*, *The Dark Knight Rises* and *The Amazing Spider-Man*.

The reviews for *The Hunger Games* surprised many by being largely positive, given that the source material was a young adult novel and the film was the first in a franchise aimed at a devoted teen audience. The *San Francisco Chronicle* dubbed Gary Ross's movie 'solid if unexceptional', before declaring it 'better than any of the *Twilights*'. The *Los Angeles Times* described the film as 'popular entertainment with strong narrative drive'. *Rolling Stone* announced, 'Hollywood didn't screw up the film version . . . It has epic spectacle, yearning romance, suspense that won't quit and a shining star in Jennifer Lawrence', and called it 'a zeitgeist movie'. Roger Ebert, in the *Chicago Sun-Times*, called it 'an effective entertainment', while *Entertainment Weekly* called the film 'a muscular, honourable, unflinching translation of Collins's vision'. Hollywood trade publication *Variety* dubbed the film 'proficient, involving, ever faithful to its source and

centred around Jennifer Lawrence's impressive star turn
... This much-anticipated event picture should satiate fans,
entertain the uninitiated and take an early lead among the
year's top-grossing films', while the *Hollywood Reporter*'s
Todd McCarthy wrote that *The Hunger Games* 'has such a
strong narrative structure, built-in forward movement and
compelling central character that it can't go far wrong'.

Jennifer Lawrence was widely praised for her performance, with the *Washington Post* noting that 'Lawrence is
never less than grounded and believable as a young woman
forced by circumstance to assume wisdom far beyond her
years'. Roger Ebert called the actress 'strong and convincing in the central role', while *Entertainment Weekly*
praised 'her gravity, her intensity, and her own unman-
nered beauty, about as impressive a Hollywood incarnation
of Katniss as one could ever imagine'. The *Hollywood
Reporter* noted Jennifer's 'impressive gravity and presence'
in the lead role.

Some reviews were not as positive, with *Time* magazine
dubbing the movie 'pedestrian', claiming that 'the film
rarely combusts'. The *New Yorker* described the movie as
'pretty much a disaster – disjointed, muffled, and even, at
times, boring', while David Thomson, writing in the *New
Republic*, thought the hype was all about box-office grosses:
'The phenomenon of *The Hunger Games* is depressing just
because you can't feel its $90 million [*sic*] on the screen,
yet we're overwhelmed by the gold rush of its revenue'. He
then added: 'I grieve for Jennifer Lawrence to think that
vital years will be given over to the drivel of this franchise'.
It was unlikely that the newly bankable Jennifer Lawrence
felt remotely the same.

According to Lionsgate sources, *The Hunger Games*
needed an opening weekend in excess of $100 million at
the American box office if they were to proceed with the
sequel, *Catching Fire*. Although it was a March release,

well in advance of the usual summer blockbuster season, the predictions tracking advance ticket sales suggested that reaching that target was eminently possible: the question many pundits were asking was how much over the $100 million mark would the opening weekend be – $120 million? $130 million?

According to ticketing website Fandango, *The Hunger Games* was selling ten tickets per second through their site in the days just prior to the movie's release. The film was accounting for 96 per cent of all advance ticket sales, with over 3,000 screenings nationwide completely sold out. Fandango would ultimately handle 22 per cent of all tickets sold for *The Hunger Games* on opening weekend. In the days before release, the film was just behind *The Twilight Saga: New Moon* and *Harry Potter and the Deathly Hallows, Part 2* in advance ticket sales records. Those two movies were good indicators of where *The Hunger Games* might land in terms of opening box-office takings, with *New Moon* taking just under $143 million and *Deathly Hallows* $169 million. Big box-office openings are usually sequels or a new instalment in an ongoing series, so *The Hunger Games* had much to prove in terms of meeting the expectations of rabid fans and box-office pundits alike.

Whether or not ticket sales would be enough to justify Lionsgate committing to a sequel, Jennifer Lawrence was definitely on board. '[It's] exciting, which is weird because I remember signing on to it and thinking, "Well I'll probably have fun on the first one and be miserable for the others,"' she said just before the movie opened. 'I'm excited to get back into training, I'm excited to get everybody back together, that was such a fun movie to shoot. Where an actor gets to do a character and a story that they really love and feel so strongly about, that happens maybe once in a lifetime, maybe once every ten years. It doesn't happen a lot and I get to do it once a year.'

While Jennifer was confident she'd play Katniss a second

time, it was down to actual box-office numbers whether that would happen. Thursday night previews, including midnight and 3 a.m. screenings, started off very promisingly, bringing in just under $20 million (making the film the seventh highest midnight opening ever). Among those in attendance at a midnight screening were *The Hunger Games* superfan (and *Veronica Mars* star) Kristen Bell. Diehard fans of the books were the main audience for the early screenings, but many were expected to return (after some sleep!) for repeat viewings over coming days and weeks. The competition wasn't strong that March weekend, with several films opening in limited engagements, among them *The Raid*, *4:44 – Last Day on Earth* and *The Deep Blue Sea*, all appealing to different audiences than those lining up for *The Hunger Games*.

After the midnight screenings, Hollywood took notice, with many predicting that the movie could exceed its $100 million target within three days (making it only the twentieth film ever to do so). Positive reviews, good word of mouth, huge media coverage and fan enthusiasm all combined to create a perfect movie storm. The official opening-day box-office take was $68.25 million, a record March opening for a non-sequel and the fifth highest Friday opening of all time. While Jennifer Lawrence was visiting Whole Foods, her movie was pulling in a huge audience. As Twitter was flooded with fan approval, and critics gave the movie the thumbs up, more people were drawn to cinemas to see what the fuss was about.

Before the final weekend numbers were in, Lionsgate announced the sequel was underway – a script had been in development for several months just in case, but now they added the release date of 22 November 2013. Gary Ross was expected to return to direct once more. Lionsgate's confidence was well placed, as when the opening weekend's final box-office numbers came in they were a very healthy $152.5 million, exceeding most expectations and making *The Hunger Games* the third biggest opening of all time (to that date). It was just behind the final *Harry Potter* movie at $169.2 million and the second film in the new Batman trilogy, *The Dark Knight*, at $158.4 million (a target some thought *The Hunger Games* might surpass). The takings made *The Hunger Games* the number one non-sequel film of all time, exceeding the previous record holder, Tim Burton's *Alice in Wonderland*, which took $116 million. Included in the box-office figures was the $1.3 million gross of the midnight IMAX screenings, the fourth highest grossing midnight IMAX release to that date, behind record holder *Harry Potter and the Deathly Hallows, Part 2*, which had taken over $2 million upon its IMAX release.

The film had also opened at number one at the UK box office, taking just under £5 million ($7.8 million) opening weekend gross in a country where the book was nowhere near as successful (before the film) as it had been in the US and where concerns had been raised about the movie's 12A certificate leading to some minor censor cuts. The British Board of Film Classification removed seven seconds of footage, including what they referred to as 'an emphasis on blood and injury'. The Board reported: 'These cuts, which were implemented by digitally removing sight of blood splashes and sight of blood on wounds and weapons, were made in accordance with BBFC Guidelines and policy. An uncut 15 classification was available.' When released on DVD in the UK, the Blu-ray would feature the uncut 15 certificate version of *The Hunger Games*, while the DVD carried the edited 12A certificate UK theatrical release.

Positive reviews and a release during UK school holidays helped boost the film's takings there, resulting in the movie topping the £2.5 million taken in the opening weekend by the first *Twilight* movie in 2008. Lionsgate's UK head, Zygi Kamasa, noted: '*The Hunger Games* was always destined to be this phenomenon in the US. Book sales have been strong in the UK, but it's not on the same scale. We hoped to be better than *Twilight*'s UK opening, and in fact we are very nearly double that.' *The Hunger Games* phenomenon didn't have quite as high a profile overseas, with Australia contributing $8.5 million, France adding $3.8 million, Russia bringing an additional $6.6 million, and Germany adding $4.3 million to the movie's overseas total of $59.25 million (including $3.6 million from Mexico and $3.1 million in Brazil), contributing to a worldwide first weekend total take of $211.8 million.

With US box office on the Monday after release adding a further $10 million to *The Hunger Games*'s takings, the movie seemed on course to dominate the US box office for a second week. Competing movies opening that second weekend included fantasy sequel *Wrath of the Titans* and Snow White-inspired drama *Mirror, Mirror*. Six days on release saw *The Hunger Games* reach $181.6 million, the sixth best showing for a six-day run. BoxOffice.com analyst Phil Contrino noted that the movie 'is holding up very well. It's quite clear by now that it's not going to suffer from a sharp decline the way that *Twilight* did. The reason for that is the fact that adults are into it and they don't always rush out opening weekend.' Contrino's website predicted an additional $72 million for *The Hunger Games* on its second weekend, noting: '*The Hunger Games* definitely has a shot at hitting $400 million domestically. It's a great accomplishment for the first film of a franchise to hit that mark.' If it hit the $350 to $400 million level, then *The Hunger Games* would prove itself more successful than either the first *Twilight* or *Harry Potter* movies.

Wrath of the Titans had a strong start taking $1 million at late night previews, while poor reviews scuppered *Mirror, Mirror* in advance. *The Hunger Games* went on to retain the number one spot, heading towards a possible total of $250 million over the weekend by taking an additional $18.65 million on the Friday (a 72 per cent drop on the previous week, but that was better than *Twilight: New Moon*'s 76 per cent drop and *Twilight: Breaking Dawn, Part 1*'s 77 per cent drop). By the close of the second weekend, *The Hunger Games* had added $58.5 million to a cumulative total of $248.4 million, falling just short of the hoped-for target of $250 million in under ten days (it took one more day for the film to pass that milestone). Over that weekend, the number two film *Wrath of the Titans* took $32.2 million (half of the previous film *Clash of the Titans*' opening $61 million), while *Mirror, Mirror* trailed at a poor number three with just $19 million. Internationally, *The Hunger Games* added a further $34.8 million in the second week, putting the non-US cumulative two-week total at $113.9 million. Having taken $365 million globally in two weeks, pundits began suggesting *The Hunger Games* was on target to reach a worldwide total take of $600 million.

In its third week on release, *The Hunger Games* faced new competition from the re-release of James Cameron's *Titanic* in 3D and *American Reunion*, an *American Pie* comedy sequel. *The Hunger Games* continued to take less at the box office over ensuing weeks, with another $33.1 million on week three, $21 million on week four and $14 million on week five. In its sixth week on release, the movie took an additional $10.8 million (each week on release thereafter the film took under $10 million). By September 2012 the film had been open for twenty-four weeks and had taken a cumulative total of $408 million at the US box office. The non-US gross totalled $283.1 million, making for a worldwide cumulative total take of $691.2 million, in excess of the $600 million optimistically predicted during week two.

Lionsgate's gamble with *The Hunger Games* had paid off. With the film costing just $78 million to make and a low $45 million to market (the books and media interest had already paved the way), the studio were overjoyed with the opening grosses. They needed a hit, after low-grossing

instalments of the *Saw* franchise, with their previous
biggest successes being *The Expendables* and the documentary *Fahrenheit 9/11*: now *The Hunger Games* franchise
put them in place to rival some of the bigger studios who
depended on such 'tentpole' film series for their sure-fire
summer successes.

Pent-up demand stoked by the novels and fan attention meant that the first film in the series performed at the
box office as though it were a sequel, with a huge pre-sold
audience eager to see the movie multiple times. It certainly
seems like the odds were ever in the movie's favour.

Inevitably, in making a movie from a much-loved novel
there were going to be changes in adapting the work to the
screen that not every fan of the book was going to understand or agree with. Some thought the film failed to convey
the inner thoughts of Katniss as expressed through the
novel's first-person point of view and that a voiceover was
required to make some of the key points that the movie
otherwise did not convey, especially her difficult feelings
about both Peeta and Gale and the fact that Rue reminds
her of her sister, Prim. Some felt the character of Haymitch
had been cleaned up too much, diluting his relationship
with Katniss and the history of the Games – many missed
his pratfall from the stage during the reaping, an event he
doesn't even attend in the movie. The Avoxes are nowhere
to be seen, also removing the later subplot concerning
Darius from District 12. Katniss's dehydration and hear-
ing loss in the arena are both left out, as is Peeta's more
ruthless attitude in the arena, and the hybrid mutations
that contain elements of the failed Tributes don't appear
(the 'mutts' seen in the movie are little more than fierce
dog-like predators).

In other areas, the movie improved upon the source
novel. By cutting away from Katniss's point of view, the
movie gives a greater overview of life in Panem (something

Katniss can tell the reader about in the first-person book, but can't on screen). The emphasis in film is to show, rather than tell. Cutaways to Gale in District 12 watching Katniss and Peeta, with him unsure of how much their apparent love affair is real or not, helped to keep his character involved. Seneca Crane, in his running of the Games and his discussions with President Snow (another enlarged role that works well), is a more heavily featured character, and is given a wonderfully ironic send-off not sourced from the book. The replacement of District 11's supply of bread to Katniss – in return for her looking after Rue – by a full-scale rebellion helps make the point that unrest in the Districts is growing, empowered by the example of Katniss. This is an important element to seed for the sequels that, again, was missing from the original novel.

The film of *The Hunger Games* had several strengths that made it an improvement on some elements of the book. As a visual medium, the worlds of District 12 (very *Winter's Bone* poor and grey), the Capitol (eighties pop video meets Regency flounce, with a dash of John Waters) and the arena are brought to life in a definitive way, replacing individual readers' visualizations of Panem with those of the film-makers. Well-known character actors fill out smaller parts, making them more showy and providing added fun. The backstory of Panem is filled through propaganda films (an element that becomes more important in *Mockingjay*), while Peeta's habit of disarming threats through personable humour is heightened. It's a faithful retelling of the story of the book, but far more expansive in its visualization of the locations, characters and events.

With *Catching Fire* confirmed as a result of the box-office bonanza of *The Hunger Games*, many fans believed it was only a matter of time before Gary Ross was named again as the second movie's director. He'd helmed the tricky first film, delivering a movie that not only pleased most die-hard fans but also reached out to a wider mainstream audience (as evidenced by its massive box-office success worldwide). Ross had some definite idea about how he'd handle the sequel. 'I think that there may be some aesthetic departures,' said Ross. 'The arena in the second book is tropical and the arena in [the first] book is forests, so that in and of itself will make for a different wardrobe. I shot this in a very specific way that's very different than most franchises are shot. That had a lot to do with the urgency of what's going on and Katniss's point of view. I have some ideas about how to do *Catching Fire* slightly differently. It will look and feel slightly different from the first.'

Ross was already a successful filmmaker who rarely repeated himself: he'd never made a sequel or been involved in a 'franchise'. For him, the challenge of making *The Hunger Games* was to deliver a successful film adaptation of a very popular book. He'd done that to his own satisfaction. For Ross, there seemed to be little challenge in simply repeating himself with *Catching Fire* – the director felt he'd be better off channelling his creative energies into a completely new project.

Despite the cast members' enthusiastic support for Ross's continued involvement, Lionsgate eventually decided it was *The Hunger Games* itself that sold the movie, not the director. The same maxim had applied to other successful franchises, including *Harry Potter*, *Twilight* and James Bond, which had regularly shuffled the directors while maintaining a consistency of approach. Ross had only directed three movies since 1998, and he was very particular about the material he committed to. He also liked a decent amount of time to work on development of scripts and to relish the challenge of working on something new, and *Catching Fire* was rushing into production to meet a pre-set release date in November 2013. Ross finally announced his regretful departure from the franchise in a detailed statement to the media.

'Despite recent speculation, and after difficult but sincere consideration, I have decided not to direct *Catching Fire*,' stated Ross. 'As a writer and a director, I simply don't have the time I need to write and prep the movie I would have wanted to make because of the fixed and tight production schedule. I loved making *The Hunger Games* – it was the happiest experience of my professional life. Lionsgate was supportive of me in a manner that few directors ever experience in a franchise: they empowered me to make the film I wanted to make and backed the movie in a way that requires no explanation beyond the remarkable results. And contrary to what has been reported, negotiations with Lionsgate have not been problematic. They have also been very understanding of me through this difficult decision. I also cannot say enough about the people I worked with: producer Nina Jacobson, a great collaborator and a true friend; the brilliant Suzanne Collins, who entrusted us with her most amazing and important story; the gifted and remarkable Jennifer Lawrence whose performance exceeded my wildest expectations, and the rest of the incredible cast, whom I am proud to call my friends. To the fans I want to say thank you for your support your faith, your enthusiasm and your trust. Hard as this may be to understand, I am trying to keep that trust with you. Thank you all. It's been a wonderful experience.'

Lionsgate responded with a statement of its own: 'We're very sorry that Gary Ross has chosen not to direct *Catching Fire*. We were really looking forward to making the movie with him. He did an incredible job on the first film and we are grateful for his work. This will not be the end of our relationship, as we consider Ross to be part of the Lionsgate family and look forward to working with him in the future.'

Although it didn't seem likely, both Ross and the studio had been smart enough to leave the door open if either

wanted him to return to helm *Mockingjay*, the third part
of *The Hunger Games*. In the meantime, Ross would go on
to make movies of Steinbeck's *East of Eden* (with Jennifer
Lawrence) and *Burial Rites*, based on a novel by Hannah
Kent. Now Lionsgate had very little time to find a suitable
director to handle *Catching Fire*.

PART TWO: THE FLAME

9
TEAM JENNIFER, TEAM JOSH, TEAM LIAM

Jennifer Lawrence found herself an instant star in the weeks following the release of *The Hunger Games*. She had gone from being a critically acclaimed indie movie darling in the likes of *The Poker House* and *Winter's Bone* to becoming a heroine for teenage girls and boys alike. She'd been working hard on the publicity circuit since the beginning of the year, culminating in a worldwide tour in support of the movie (often accompanied by co-stars Josh Hutcherson and Liam Hemsworth) during the first few weeks of its release.

Jennifer had been paid $500,000 for her role in the first film and was contracted to appear in any sequels. That was a low figure for the lead in a potential franchise, but given Jennifer had never been in this position before and given Lionsgate's strict budget control, that's what she was offered. Although now an Oscar-nominated actress, there was no proof yet that she could 'open' a big blockbuster movie. After her Oscar win and several weeks of record-breaking box office for *The Hunger Games*, the story had changed.

The first benefit to Jennifer and her main co-stars was the activation of 'escalators' written into their contracts. This meant that as the box-office take climbed above certain pre-set targets, the main players would receive bonus payments. It was estimated that these 'escalators' could bring Jennifer an additional $1 million by the end of the movie's theatrical run. This was a dramatic step up from the days when she was paid 'scale' rates (the basic wage agreed by the actors' union) of $3,000 each week on *Winter's Bone*. The initial salaries paid to Josh and Liam were not specified, but it was expected that they too would receive a boost from similar contracted escalators. Given the way the fees for the stars of the *Twilight* saga had ballooned across the four films, it was expected the same would be true of *The Hunger Games*'s central trio. Kristen Stewart had been paid $2 million for the first *Twilight* movie in 2008, but that had hugely increased to $12.5 million for each of the final two movies, plus 7.5 per cent of the gross box office. Her co-stars Taylor Lautner and Robert Pattinson had been paid $1 million for the first film, but they were on a similar rate to Stewart by the final movies.

Lionsgate, taking a leaf from the *Twilight* and *Harry Potter* playbooks, decided to split the final novel in *The Hunger Games* trilogy into two films, announcing in July 2012 that *Mockingjay, Part 1* would be released on 21 November 2014, with *Mockingjay, Part 2* following a year later on 20 November 2015. With *Catching Fire* announced for release on 22 November 2013 that meant there would now be a *Hunger Games* movie every Thanksgiving holiday for the next three years.

Jennifer's increasingly visible quirky side, as displayed in many interviews and on late-night chatshow appearances, continued to make her new fans. She came across as a plain, down-to-earth girl who called it like she saw it and was not afraid of being candid. These traits quickly made her an internet favourite, with many websites compiling lists of her crazy, off-the-cuff quotes, like the time she told Jimmy Kimmel: 'I just went to the doctor today. I got a chest X-ray of my lungs and discovered that my breasts are uneven.' It was just another way that Jennifer stood out among her contemporary Hollywood peers, who tended to be much more coached and careful in their public pronouncements. For many, Hollywood veterans and fans alike, Jennifer's unaffected public persona came across as a dramatic breath of fresh air.

Jennifer quickly got tired of answering questions about the comparisons between *Twilight* and *The Hunger Games*. She said: 'They are both beloved series of books adapted into movies, with a young cast and a female lead . . . [The comparison] totally makes sense, and it doesn't bother me if people compare them. I don't think the *Twilight* films are terrible movies. Really, though, ours is very different and ultimately they are not all that comparable.'

Unlike the stars of some teen franchises, Jennifer had made sure to read all the books in Suzanne Collins's series. 'It was important to read the books, because I imagined myself at a Q & A with people that loved the books,' she said. 'I love the *Twilight* books. I'm not even ashamed to say it, they are like methamphetamine to me. So when I heard Kristen Stewart say, "I only read the first one," I was like, "Oh man," because she wasn't a huge fan of the books. I was like, for the book lovers I should probably read the books.'

She was also quizzed about the violence implied, if not actually shown explicitly, in a movie about child-on-child deadly conflict. 'We weren't going to make a watered-down version,' she said. 'If you take the violence and brutality out of the movie, you take the entire heart out of it. You're protecting the audience from something that these poor innocent children aren't protected against. But by having the boundaries of the [MPPA] rating, it made the violence better and more realistic. Violence in real life is over so fast, and fights last a matter of seconds. We didn't do the long overdone death.'

There was some concern over the announced release date for *Catching Fire* as Jennifer was already locked to play Mystique in the sequel to *X-Men: First Class*. If Fox decided to exercise their option on her, shooting on the superhero movie could delay her availability for *Catching Fire*, thus potentially putting the production and release of *The Hunger Games* sequel in jeopardy. While it may have been briefly exciting (and no doubt a boost to her ego) to have two studios fighting over her immediate services, Jennifer knew it was in everyone's interests for a deal to be done. Fox conceded they'd need to delay shooting on the *X-Men* follow-up until January of the following year, allowing Jennifer to start on *Catching Fire* as planned in the fall of 2012. The deal included a caveat that if there was a similar conflict between the two franchises next time, then Fox would have priority on the young actress.

Beyond Panem, Jennifer had been hard at work and had a backlog of unreleased films that surfaced after *The Hunger Games* hit it big. Her lead role in thriller *House at the End of the Street* had been filmed in Ontario, Canada, a whole two years before it was eventually released. The first trailers for the movie hit cinemas just as *The Hunger Games* opened, promoting the film due for release in September 2012 (delayed from an original April release). During summer 2010 Jennifer had been based in Metcalfe, Ontario, where the production was filmed.

Directed by Mark Tonderai (a one-time radio DJ from Britain whose directorial debut was *Hush*, 2009), *House at the End of the Street* was based upon a short story by Jonathan Mostow, himself a director whose titles include *Breakdown* (1997), *Terminator 3* (2003) and *Surrogates*

(2009). The screenplay was by David Loucka, whose previous work included the Daniel Craig-starring *Dream House* (2011). The movie centred on a teenager, Elissa, played by Jennifer, who moves with her newly divorced mother to a new town, only to discover they are living next door to an infamous 'murder house' where two people perished. Oscar-nominated Elisabeth Shue (*Leaving Las Vegas*, 1995) was cast as Elissa's mother and Max Thieriot took the role of Ryan, sole survivor of the incident, whom Elissa befriends. However, Ryan may not be all that he seems.

The production team behind *House at the End of the Street* struck lucky in the timing of their casting of Jennifer, catching her on the cusp of her major breakthrough in *The Hunger Games* and her Oscar nomination for *Winter's Bone*. 'The minute you meet Jennifer, you realize this girl has a very long career ahead of her,' said producer Aaron Ryder. 'She's incredibly talented. Her work in *Winter's Bone* was one of the best performances I'd seen in a long time. She walked into my office for a general meeting before we even read the script and I couldn't figure out if she was thirty years old or eighteen. She has a maturity and wisdom about her that is rare. Some people are just naturally confident, and that's certainly the case with Jen. We were lucky to have her.'

The filmmakers had cast Jennifer just after the release of *Winter's Bone*, before she was nominated for an Oscar. 'With *The Hunger Games*, she became huge,' said director Mark Tonderai, 'but at the time, it was a risk. It obviously paid off. Jen seized the part and made a difficult, complicated role her own.'

For her part, Jennifer regarded the new movie as yet another challenge, a learning experience and a chance to make the kind of movie she'd not tackled before. 'This was something completely different for me,' she said. 'I had never worked in this genre [horror thriller] and it was an amazing experience to do something so completely out of my comfort zone. I really liked that it wasn't about scaring people with blood or what I think of as "boo" elements. The characters are very well developed and you find yourself getting scared for them in a personal way. You are both invested in the love story and afraid for Elissa. It is a very sophisticated way to frighten an audience.'

Jennifer found she shared much in common with Elisabeth Shue, who became an actress at the age of nineteen with *The Karate Kid* (1984), more or less mirroring Jennifer's current situation. The pair were able to compare notes as they bonded as mother and daughter, with Elisabeth offering Jennifer a few useful pointers in how to handle sudden fame. 'I had seen *Winter's Bone*, so I knew what an extraordinary actress Jen was,' said Elisabeth. 'There's a real stillness to her performance that is electrifying, especially in the moments of fear and panic. She's like a colt, feeling her legs for the first time, but she also has a maturity that is surprising for somebody her age.'

The film was completed in a twenty-eight-day shooting period, with Ottawa doubling for the story's setting of Pennsylvania. Although one scene required Jennifer's character to sing, the actress didn't actually provide the vocals, lip-synching instead to pre-recorded vocals by Sarah Rayne. Jennifer herself made the request for the substitution fearing that her singing voice was simply not good enough for the movie. Although she knew that the film would be seen by many people who'd become her fans in the wake of *The Hunger Games*, Jennifer regarded her role in *House at the End of the Street* as an opportunity to escape the image of Katniss Everdeen and remind audiences that she was capable of much more than simply being the 'girl on fire'.

Jennifer was top billed and featured heavily on the movie poster; there was no doubt that the film was being sold on the back of her new *Hunger Games* fame. The movie opened at number one at the US box office on the Friday and Saturday nights of its opening weekend, but didn't do the exceptional business of *The Hunger Games*. Released on 21 September 2012, *House at the End of the Street* finished the overall weekend at number two, taking $12.3 million, just behind cop thriller *End of Watch* so $13.1, with just under $1 million between them. The movie went on to gross a total of $42.7 million in the US against a production cost of just $6.9 million.

Critics noted that the best thing about the movie was Jennifer, who gave a good performance in an otherwise underwhelming film. 'Lawrence's natural, disarming screen presence is ill-suited to something as mannered and laboured as *House at the End of the Street*,' said the *Los Angeles Times*, while *Entertainment Weekly* commented 'the only mystery at work is how Lawrence's agent ever let her sign on'. *Variety* noted that Jennifer wasn't the Oscar-nominated star of *The Hunger Games* when this film was made, explaining the 'cognitive dissonance in watching the rising star of *Winter's Bone* and *The Hunger Games* trying to deliver a serious performance at the centre of such a schlocky spin on the girl-in-jeopardy genre'. The *Hollywood Reporter* said that only 'Jennifer Lawrence keeps it watchable'.

Jennifer's other major film before *Catching Fire* entered production was romantic comedy-drama *Silver Linings Playbook*, written and directed by David O. Russell. The film would see Jennifer score her second Oscar nomination for Best Actress, and this time she would go on to win, even if she spectacularly tripped on the steps, falling flat on her face on the way to the podium to collect her trophy. The way she dealt with that and her candid nature in many of the post-Oscar media interviews further endeared her to many movie watchers, plenty of whom had not yet caught her performance in the first instalment of *The Hunger Games* series.

In *Silver Linings Playbook* Jennifer played the recently widowed Tiffany Maxwell, a woman struggling with mental health issues, who encounters Patrick Solitano (Bradley Cooper), a man suffering bipolar disorder who has recently returned home from a spell in an institution to live with his parents (Robert De Niro and Jacki Weaver). The pair unexpectedly bond and find a new happiness when they prepare for and enter a dance competition together.

Silver Linings Playbook seemed like unlikely Oscar material on the surface, but the combination of the central performances and Russell's sensitive direction propelled the film into contention. In all it was nominated for a total of eight Academy Awards, including for Best Picture, Best Director, Best Adapted Screenplay and the four central acting awards, as well as for Best Film Editing. The only winner out of the eight, however, would be Jennifer for Best Actress.

It was an amazing outcome for what had been a rather troubled production and a leap of faith for Jennifer Lawrence in committing to the central part. Originally Matthew Quick's novel had been optioned by Sydney Pollack and Anthony Minghella (who died within months of each other in 2008). Writer-director David O. Russell, whose films included *Three Kings* (1999), *I Heart Huckabees* (2004) and *The Fighter* (2010), was drawn to the project because of resonances in his own life. His then teenage son had been diagnosed with autism as a toddler, but in later years the diagnosis was revised to a bipolar obsessive compulsive hybrid disorder. The parallels were clear, although Russell softened some of the edges of the novel in preparing it as a film. The project was put aside while the director made *The Fighter*, but the stars were originally going to be very different: Mark Wahlberg and Angelina Jolie. Even with those names lined up, Russell had not got his first choices of Vince Vaughn and Zooey Deschanel.

When the film was back in development Jolie's interest

had waned, and Russell set his sights on Jennifer Lawrence instead. Jennifer had a new experience auditioning for *Silver Linings Playbook* over video-conferencing facility Skype while on location in North Carolina shooting *The Hunger Games*. She was nervous about the audition, but not for the usual reasons. 'Well, as I am the least techno-logically inclined person ever, I was definitely anxious about doing the audition over Skype,' she said. 'I had never done anything like it before. Luckily, David started by having me jog in place alone in my apartment, which some-how helped ease some of the initial awkwardness, and we were able to jump right into the audition.'

A thirty-three-day shoot was arranged for Philadelphia with the production planning to wrap up before Thanksgiving 2011. That proved problematic for Jennifer's original co-star Mark Wahlberg. The $22 million movie looked to be in danger when Wahlberg opted to make the thriller *Contraband* instead, but Russell quickly lined up the much more suitable Bradley Cooper to keep the pro-duction on track. 'You're never their first choice,' said Cooper, whose star was riding high following 2009's comedy *The Hangover.* Neither leading actor had much time to prepare for their roles, with Jennifer particularly worried about the dance scenes. 'I'm such a bad dancer,' she said. '[Bradley's] very good. He moves very smoothly. I felt bad for him, because he's such a good dancer and I'm so bad. We rehearsed two hours a day and he didn't have to do much, but I was in need of the extra sessions so I could look less like a malfunctioning robot. The only thing I can do well is shoot bow and arrow.'

Working with Russell, however, proved to be right up Jennifer's street, and the making of *Silver Linings Playbook* met her usual requirement of pushing her in new direc-tions. 'It's a different way of working, keeping you on your feet,' she said of Russell's improvisational approach. 'He has a way of bringing out different sides that you wouldn't know you had because he takes you so outside your comfort zone. I can't work in an environment where they're constantly talking about how everything I'm doing is right. We would be in the middle of a take, and I'd hear David going, "It's so bad." And Bradley would be giving me this look, like, "Are you okay?" I'd just start cracking up. Sometimes you're going to suck, and it's great if somebody could just tell you when you're sucking.'

The critical reaction to Jennifer's performance was near unanimous and it was the opposite of 'sucking'. The film was widely critically acclaimed, with the *Hollywood Reporter* noting that 'the chemistry between Cooper and Lawrence makes them a delight to watch, their spiky rapport failing to conceal a mutual attraction'. *Time* magazine focused on Jennifer: 'The performances of these actors are reason enough to go. The reason to stay is Lawrence. Just twenty-one when the movie was shot, Lawrence is that rare young actress who plays, who is, grown-up.' *Entertainment Weekly* wrote 'Jennifer Lawrence, the girl on fire, is incandescent as Tiffany', while *Rolling Stone* said of Jennifer as Tiffany that she was 'rude, dirty, funny, foulmouthed, sloppy, sexy, vibrant and vulnerable, sometimes all in the same scene, even in the same breath. No list of Best Actress Oscar contenders would be complete without the electrifying Lawrence in the lead. She lights up the screen.'

The film had a quiet opening weekend as it only played in sixteen locations, taking less than $500,000, with overwhelming competition from the new James Bond movie, *Skyfall*, and the Steven Spielberg heritage drama, *Lincoln*. However, when the film opened wider in later weeks it quickly rose to blockbuster status itself, boosted further by the Oscar nominations. By the end of its run in theatres, *Silver Linings Playbook* had taken over $132 million in the US, and an additional $104 million worldwide, for a final gross of $236 million. Not bad for a limited budget romantic comedy, lacking in special effects and superheroes.

Jennifer's performance certainly appealed to the voters for the Academy Awards, who nominated her as Best Actress (for the second time in three years) alongside Jessica Chastain, veteran eighty-five-year-old French actress Emmanuelle Riva, nine-year-old Quvenzhané Wallis (making them together the oldest and youngest ever nominees) and Naomi Watts. Jennifer said of the process: 'It's an honour and an overwhelming compliment, but it's also a bizarre thing. All of a sudden you're at these parties and everybody's famous, and you feel like a loser. By the time of the actual Oscars, I was so sick of fittings and trains and corsets and people asking "What are you going to wear?" I had to go on a diet, because at all the parties there's champagne and hors d'oeuvres. I ate so much!'

Her fall on her way to the podium to collect her award made international headlines, but her reaction to tripping up in her voluminous Dior haute couture gown endeared her to many. 'Thank you so much,' she said to the Oscar audience, who were giving her a standing ovation. 'This is nuts. You guys are only standing up because I fell and you feel bad. That was embarrassing.' She then went on to wish Emmanuelle Riva a happy eighty-sixth birthday amid the usual Hollywood namechecks delivered at the Oscars. Afterwards, in between admitting to the Hollywood press corps that she was 'starving' and wanted a McDonald's burger and that she'd 'had a [vodka] shot' before coming to see them, a television interview with her was interrupted by Jack Nicholson attempting to chat her up, which caused Jennifer to cover her face in embarrassment. All in all, it was a memorable night for the rising young star.

Although an off-the-cuff hit on the interview circuit, Jennifer's attempt at hosting *Saturday Night Live* at the beginning of 2013 didn't come off as well. Deliberately written sketch material didn't seem to be her forte, compared with her own natural freewheeling moments of unexpected candour when promoting movies or being interviewed by the press or on television. Nonetheless, Jennifer gave the show her best shot alongside a cast of well-practised professional comedians. Among the sketches there was the inevitable spoof of her role in *The Hunger Games* at a post-game press conference and a pretend mocking of her fellow Oscar nominees. The nervousness that she displayed during the opening monologue dissipated as the show went on, but Jennifer never really seemed comfortable. *Entertainment Weekly* wrote of her *Saturday Night Live* debut: 'It's possible that being such a good actress actually worked to the host's disadvantage here; maybe the audience didn't laugh at Lawrence's lines because she delivered them a little too convincingly.' Her real wit was much more natural and much more endearing to her growing legion of fans, many of whom couldn't wait to see her return to the Games arena in *Catching Fire*.

Also propelled to a new level of stardom by *The Hunger Games* were Josh Hutcherson and Liam Hemsworth, who played the two men in Katniss's life, Peeta and Gale. Josh was finally seen in the poorly received remake of *Red Dawn* after *The Hunger Games* (although it was made before) had been released. There's no doubt that *Red Dawn* was rush-released in an attempt to cash in on his new-found visibility. Josh had two other movies out in 2012: *7 Days in Havana* and *The Forger*. A Spanish language anthology-film featuring seven segments named after the days of the week, each directed by a different person (including Benicio del Toro, Gaspar Noé and Laurent Cantet), *7 Days in Havana* chronicled a week in the Cuban capital. Josh appeared in del Toro's opening Monday segment, 'El Yuma' (slang for 'American'), as young American actor Teddy Atkins enjoying a particularly revealing night on the town. The *Hollywood Reporter* suggested Josh's participation might draw a curious audience to a film it otherwise dismissed as a production with 'a few veritable sweet spots, but winds up leaving a rather sour aftertaste'.

The Forger was a more straightforward Hollywood movie about art forgery that saw Josh co-starring with movie veteran Lauren Bacall and *Nashville* star Hayden Panettiere. The straight-to-DVD movie was released in the wake of *The Hunger Games* with Josh in the lead role of troubled fifteen-year-old Joshua who gets involved in the world of art forgery in Carmel, California. A voice role in the animated film *Epic* (2013) followed, before Josh was back on Peeta duty for *Catching Fire*.

Similarly, Liam found his new *Hunger Games* fame working for him. The character he was expecting to play in *The Expendables* but which was dropped at the last minute was reinstated for the sequel (and killed off, as the catalyst for the plot), so he briefly featured alongside ageing action stars Sylvester Stallone, Jason Statham, Jet Li, Dolph Lungren, Chuck Norris, Jean-Claude Van Damme, Arnold Schwarzenegger and Bruce Willis in *The Expendables 2*. Liam played 'Billy the kid', an ex-military sniper who saw action in Afghanistan, described by Stallone (the driving force behind the movies) as one of the 'next generation' of Expendables.

During 2013 Liam featured in a trio of new movies: *Love and Honor*, *Paranoia* and *Empire State*. Romantic drama *Love and Honor* was the feature film debut of director Danny Mooney and featured Liam as a Michigan soldier returning home from Vietnam at the end of the sixties to reconnect with his girlfriend. Thriller *Paranoia* was drawn from a novel by Joseph Finder (who worked on the screenplay) and starred Liam as an inventor fired for insubordination who becomes a corporate spy. Although it co-starred Harrison Ford and Richard Dreyfuss, the movie was a commercial and critical flop, with Liam coming in for particular criticism. Costing $35 million to make, the movie only grossed $7 million at the US box office.

Liam's third film of 2013, *Empire State*, fared better, even though it was released direct to DVD. Based on a true story, the film followed two childhood friends (Liam and Michael Angarano) who rob an armoured car depository and are pursued by a dogged cop (Dwayne Johnson). DVD Verdict noted that 'Hemsworth is fine as Chris, giving his character a subdued note that works well with the material'. The actor would get a chance to flex his muscles once more in his return to *The Hunger Games*, alongside Josh and Jennifer in *Catching Fire*.

10

CATCHING FIRE: INFLUENCES AND INSPIRATIONS

Catching Fire, Suzanne Collins's second novel in her *The Hunger Games* sequence, explores many of the themes and issues raised first time round, as well as introducing several brand new ones. The story expands the world of Panem and introduces a handful of new key characters who help Katniss Everdeen realize her ultimate destiny. The Quarter Quell – which sees Katniss forced to return to the Games arena – is initially a shock to her and she despairs at the news. However, by the end of the novel she has grasped the opportunity to turn the event to her own advantage and that of her friends and allies, who turn out to be far more numerous and better organized than she could ever have imagined.

Returning to District 12 from their victory in the 74th Hunger Games, Katniss Everdeen and Peeta Mellark take up residency in the Victors' Village, beside their neighbour

and successful mentor Haymitch Abernathy. Despite the
fact that her family has been saved from worry and want,
all is not right with Katniss. Her experiences in the arena
have left her suffering trauma, expressed through her nightmares. Her relationships with both Peeta and Gale (who is
now working in the mines, as both his and Katniss's fathers
did) are troubled and difficult, while the arrival of new
Head Peacekeeper Romulus Thread makes life in District
12 even tougher. Rumours of rebellions inspired by her
actions reach Katniss, further unsettling her – she doesn't
want to be the figurehead of a revolution, the spark that
ignites that fire. She just wants to live her simple life with
her family and friends, left alone by the Capitol. An unexpected visit from President Snow reveals to Katniss just
how angry the powers in the Capitol are with her. Snow
threatens Katniss and her family and friends if she does
not play up her relationship with Peeta and attempt to calm
the unrest in the various Districts during her forthcoming
Victory Tour.

During the Victory Tour, Katniss meets the families
of Rue and Thresh in District 11, and the crowd greet
her speech with Rue's four-note whistle and the District
12 three-fingered salute. As she is bundled off the stage,
Katniss witnesses the man who started the whistling shot
dead by Peacekeepers. When the tour reaches the Capitol,
Peeta stages a proposal of marriage to Katniss during a live
television interview with Caesar Flickerman. The couple
are congratulated by President Snow, who subtly confirms
to Katniss that she has not done enough to quell the rebellion or to satisfy him.

Katniss doesn't know whether to flee with her family
or remain in District 12. She intervenes when she sees
Gale being punished by Head Peacekeeper Thread, but
she is saved from punishment by Peeta and Haymitch.
Thread, meanwhile, continues his Capitol-sanctioned
crackdown on District 12. Katniss then finds out about

an attempted rebellion in District 8 and is visited by two runaways – Bonnie and Twill – who use the mockingjay symbol to communicate that they are part of the rebellion. They tell Katniss that they believe stories about the supposedly destroyed District 13 still surviving underground. Before she can investigate further, Katniss is distracted by preparations for a wedding-dress photo and video shoot, and then by the unexpected bombshell that as part of the once-every-twenty-five-years Quarter Quell she will have to return to the Games arena along with several other previous winners, including Peeta (who would inevitably take Haymitch's place if their mentor's name was drawn during the almost pointless reaping process). Forced to participate, the pair aim to protect each other above all else.

The 75th Hunger Games take place in a jungle arena with a saltwater lake. Katniss and Peeta ally themselves with District 4's previous Victors, twenty-four-year-old Finnick Odair and eighty-year-old Mags. They survive a poisonous fog that partially paralyses Peeta. He is saved by Mags, who dies allowing the others to flee. The surviving trio then join with Johanna Mason from District 7 and the older pair of Beetee and Wiress from District 3. Pooling their knowledge and resources, they discover much about how the arena is designed. In the end, Katniss is able to reuse a trick she learned Haymitch employed during the 50th Hunger Games and attacks the forcefield surrounding the arena. As a result, Katniss is paralysed and falls unconscious.

When she awakens, she is in District 13. She is informed that Peeta, Johanna and District 2 career Tribute Enobaria have been captured by the Capitol, while the other participants escaped the arena and brought her to District 13, the nerve centre of the growing rebellion. Gale visits Katniss and informs her that while her family are all safe, District 12 has been obliterated by Capitol bombing.

* * *

Catching Fire introduces new locations across Panem and further explores some familiar ones. In District 12, Katniss, her family, Peeta and Haymitch all live in the Victors' Village, a relatively up-market neighbourhood provided to each District for previous Games' Victors to live in as a reward for surviving the Games. The large homes offer plenty of space, but if a Victor dies, then their remaining family must vacate the property. The Victors' Village in District 12 is the only area not to be bombed by the Capitol, left as a monument to remind others of the consequences of rebellion.

During the Victory Tour, Katniss and Peeta visit each of the Districts, although only District 11, their first stop, is given any real attention in the text. This southern District focuses on agricultural production and is already under the control of especially vigilant and violent Peacekeepers (unlike District 12 in the first novel, where the Peacekeepers were rather lax). Many tracker-jacker nests were placed in the District, so the inhabitants have developed a special interest in medicinal remedies and herbs.

In the Capitol, Katniss attends a party at President Snow's mansion, located in the City Circle along which the chariots parade prior to the Games. It is during this party that Head Gamemaker Plutarch Heavensbee indicates to Katniss that he may be sympathetic to the rebellion by showing her the hidden mockingjay insignia on his watch (while also giving her a subtle hint as to the clock-like nature of the new arena).

Although thought to have been destroyed during the Dark Days, District 13 reappears at the climax of *Catching Fire*, with survivors revealed to be living underground and plotting against the Capitol. The leader of the District is President Alma Coin, who goes on to lead the revolt against the rulers of Panem.

* * *

There's a new twist to the Hunger Games introduced in *Catching Fire*: the Quarter Quell. Once every twenty-five years the Games feature the Quarter Quell, when the rules are revised to mark this special occasion. For the 25th Games, the Districts were forced to vote for who among their populations would become the Tributes sent to the Capitol, a way of reminding them that their previous rebellion was responsible for the Games that kill their children. For the next Quarter Quell, the 50th Games, four Tributes were required from each District, doubling the number of participants to forty-eight. Haymitch Abernathy from District 12 won those Games by using the arena's force-field as a weapon against other Tributes, annoying the Gamemakers and resulting in him paying a terrible price. The 75th Hunger Games sees the Tributes experiencing a new arena, based around a jungle environment and featuring a saltwater lake. This is only the surface appearance, however, as the arena is more complicated, resembling a clock face, with events running to a predetermined timetable.

For the 75th Hunger Games, President Snow announces that previous Victors will be reaped to return to the arena. For Katniss and Peeta, as the only District 12 winners besides Haymitch, it means a certain return to the battle. The details of the Quarter Quell rules are contained in envelopes locked in a special box said to date from the establishment of the Games seventy-five years before. There are many envelopes, supposedly dictating the rules for each Quarter Quell well into the future. However, Katniss suspects the rules of the 75th Games have been created especially to punish her for her act of rebellion, and whatever may or may not have been in the envelope, President Snow simply announced the rules he wanted to apply. It will turn out to be the final Hunger Games ever held in Panem.

* * *

Catching Fire adds new characters to the world of Panem. Bonnie and Twill are two female runaways from District 8 who are dressed as Peacekeepers when Katniss comes across them in the woods outside District 12. They prove their allegiance to the rebellion by showing Katniss a cracker with an image of a mockingjay on it, revealing to her that the bird on her pin has become a symbol of resistance. The pair had worked in a now destroyed factory making Peacekeeper uniforms (hence their disguises), and have escaped the Capitol's reprisals against the District 8 rebellion. They are heading to District 13, which they believe still exists underground. The characters were omitted from the film of *Catching Fire*, while in *Mockingjay* it is revealed that they never reached District 13 so are presumed to have perished en route after leaving Katniss.

Maysilee Donner does not properly appear in *Catching Fire* as a character, but we are told about her as part of the backstory of Haymitch Abernathy and the 50th Games. She was one of Haymitch's three fellow District 12 Tributes in the 50th Games and the original owner of the mockingjay pin now worn by Katniss. She secured a blowgun and darts from the Cornucopia, using them to quickly eliminate several other Tributes. She saved Haymitch, but after a temporary alliance she was killed by a flock of brightly coloured, genetically engineered birds of prey. Haymitch watched over her as she died, reminding Katniss of her own tribute to Rue. Unknown to Katniss, Maysilee was also best friends with her own mother.

Catching Fire reveals that the unnamed, inattentive Gamemaker who fell into a punch bowl during the training for the 74th Games – when Katniss fired an arrow at them to gain the Gamemakers' attention – had been Plutarch Heavensbee. He replaces the executed Seneca Crane as the new Head Gamemaker for the 75th Games, the Quarter Quell. He subtly indicates to Katniss that he may be involved with or at least sympathetic to the rebellion, although she cannot be sure of his true intentions. It is only when she awakens in District 13 that she discovers he is one of the leaders of the rebel movement and was the instigator of the plan to protect her and Peeta through staging a mass breakout of the Tributes from the Games arena.

The male Tribute from District 4 for the 75th Games, Finnick Odair, is a twenty-four-year-old well-trained, athletic career Tribute who takes a shine to Katniss during the Games preparations. He won his previous Games aged just fourteen, with a trident and net (District 4 is a fishing area). Initially wary, Katniss eventually allies herself with Finnick and his fellow District 4 Tribute, the eighty-year-old Mags. During the Games, Finnick resuscitates Peeta after he nearly drowns, further endearing himself to Katniss. Jabberjays sent into the arena to make sounds of the Tributes' friends and relatives being tortured in the Capitol harass Finnick with the sound of his 'poor, mad' District 4 girlfriend Annie Cresta, who won the 70th Games thanks to her swimming abilities, but witnessed her partner being beheaded, an act that drove her mad. She was reaped again for the 75th Games, but Mags volunteered to replace her.

Johanna Mason, the female Tribute from District 7, sees herself as a rival to Katniss and tries to outdo her in the rebelliousness stakes. Johanna won her Games by pretending to be weak and harmless, so luring the other Tributes into underestimating her and allowing her to triumph. In reality, she cares for nothing or no one but herself – she's a vicious, unstoppable killer. However, she is part of the rebellion team committed to keeping Katniss and Peeta alive in the arena, protecting them throughout the Games, and she removes the tracker in Katniss's arm with her knife. She is one of the group captured by the Capitol at the end of *Catching Fire*.

The Tributes from District 3 – Beetee and Wiress – are middle-aged experts in electronics and technology. Beetee is an inventor who uses his skills to help the rebels survive.

It is his plan to use wires and electricity to short-circuit the forcefield, partially carried out by Katniss. Wiress is mentally troubled, and though as smart as Beetee, she sometimes has difficulties communicating. She is the first to figure out the clock-like nature of the arena, but can only indicate it to the others through her repetition of the phrase 'tick tock'. They are nicknamed 'Nuts' and 'Volts' by Johanna Mason.

The other 75th Hunger Games Quarter Quell Tributes include Cashmere and Gloss, younger career Tribute siblings from District 1 (they kill Wiress, and in turn are killed by Johanna and Katniss); Brutus (who is killed by Peeta) and Enobaria (who boasts sharpened teeth with gold fang tips as weapons) from District 2, a pair of brutal career Tributes who make trouble for Katniss and her friends; an unnamed alcoholic District 5 male Tribute killed early in the Games by Finnick; a pair of drug-addicted 'morphlings' from District 6, one of whom saves Peeta from attacking 'muttations'; District 8's Cecelia and Woof, a young mother and a deaf old man who are eliminated on the first day of the Quarter Quell; and the District 11 Tributes for the 75th Games, Chaff, an old friend of Haymitch who lost his hand during a previous Games, and Seeder, both of whom are aware of the growing rebellion against the Capitol.

The majority of modern sequels – certainly in franchise movies – will try to do the same thing that was popular the first time round, only bigger and better. In that respect, the return to the arena in the *Catching Fire* novel is not unexpected, nor is the fact that Katniss is once again made to face the trials of the competition, as well as dealing with the effects on her from her previous participation. However, Suzanne Collins knew she had to do more than just re-stage *The Hunger Games*. In that respect, *Catching Fire* expands upon some of the thematic issues introduced in the first book.

The main lesson for Katniss through *Catching Fire* is one of mellowing her independence somewhat and the novel sees her become more comfortable cooperating with and relying on others. Since her father's death in a mining accident, she had found herself thrust into the role of holding her family together. Her mother withdrew, giving up her healing ways with herbs, and young Prim had to be looked after and provided for. Hunting in the woods – an illegal act punished by the Peacekeepers – was a way for Katniss to not only find food to feed her own family, but also as a way of gaining material to sell to others or to use as barter in The Hob. All alone, she filled several traditional roles: mother, father, provider and teacher (to Prim). When she first teams up with Gale to hunt, Katniss is wary and suspicious, her natural position in life. She prefers to work alone as it's safer, and she can't rely on anyone else. Gale is the first to break through her defences, and becomes a friend, beyond just being a useful ally in the hunt. He prepares her for the wider interdependence she will have to accept in order to survive.

During her first time in the arena, Katniss tried to survive – the basic theme of the books – alone, especially when she thought Peeta had joined the career Tributes. She found the adjustment to accepting him as a true ally difficult, and even by the end of the Games there is a question of whether her acceptance of Peeta is still simply play-acting for the cameras. Entering the arena for a second time, Katniss does not have that luxury. She knows going in that she and Peeta must work together, and she sets her goal as not her own survival but that of Peeta: she will protect him and ensure he survives. It's quite a change for her, and a sign of her growing maturity.

This extends beyond just Peeta. In various ways Katniss must work with Finnick Odair and Mags, Beetee, Wiress and even her rival Johanna Mason to survive the attacks of the other Tributes and finally to escape the arena. Unknown to her at that stage, the others are already working together to ensure her survival and that of Peeta. Katniss doesn't properly discover that she has become a symbol of the growing rebellion across the Districts until she is out of the arena and safely ensconced in District 13.

Katniss wants independence from any form of authority, symbolized most obviously by the Capitol and President Snow. Before winning the 74th Games, she effectively evaded the rules in District 12, aided by the lack of rigour in running the Peacekeepers displayed by Head Peacekeeper Cray. The black market that Katniss served and drew upon was quietly tolerated, as it was to the mutual benefit of many including Cray himself. However, with the arrival of Head Peacekeeper Thread, everything changes. Katniss is now a target, and Thread sets out to trap her by electrifying the fence surrounding the District (which Cray had rarely been bothered with previously). Returning to District 12, Katniss discovers that the authorities have her in their sights in a way they never had before.

This is symbolized right at the beginning of *Catching Fire* with the unprecedented visit of President Snow. Snow is a man who rarely leaves the Capitol, someone who has no interest in the Districts or their people except in the ways they can serve the economic and material needs of the Capitol. If he must, he'll visit a Victory Tour to make a speech, but that's it: he is certainly not a man who makes unannounced house calls, so his arrival at the Victors' Village in District 12 to see Katniss is a clear sign that she's now being paid special attention. Sure enough, he's there to make a not very subtle threat.

The Quarter Quell rules seem specifically designed – regardless of the pretence at using rules devised seventy-five years before – to exert control and authority over Katniss. She (specifically) and Peeta are forced back into the arena by the new all-Victors line-up with the clear intention that the problem she now represents will be eliminated. Both

Snow and his advisors miss the fact that their opposition is more organized than he (or Katniss, at this stage) ever suspects, and not only will aid be offered to Katniss in the arena, but a wider plan of dramatic resistance is under way, even within Snow's own ranks.

From their Romeo and Juliet moment when they threatened suicide at the end of the 74th Games, Katniss and Peeta became targets, as well as celebrity personalities much approved of by the watching masses in the Capitol (for their romance) and the Districts (for their rebellion). That makes a straightforward elimination of Katniss impossible for Snow (it would be easy to instruct Thread to simply have her killed), as in death she would become a martyr and an even greater symbol for the masses. Snow's plan involves Katniss dying very visibly in the arena as part of the system that made her famous in the first place. His own blindness to those around him (notably Plutarch Heavensbee) proves his personal Achilles heel.

Another theme expanded in *Catching Fire* (and present throughout *The Hunger Games* series, undoubtedly one of the things that makes them so popular with teen readers) is that of friendship and loyalty. Katniss has one significant friendship in District 12: Gale Hawthorne. As her emotions grow and change, she becomes confused about this – can it really be more than friendship and more like romance? She has other friends, such as the Mayor's daughter Madge Undersee (from whom she obtains the symbolic mockingjay pin, one of the elements altered in the movies), and even Greasy Sae, the old woman Katniss trades with in The Hob (and is presumably the old woman character who gives Katniss the mockingjay pin in the first movie). It is clear, though, that true friendship does not come easy to Katniss, due to her guarded personality, solitary ways and secretive nature. It takes a while for Peeta to break through her defences, even when they are sharing life-or-death situations in the arena.

Loyalty is clearly a strong force in the life of Katniss Everdeen, and it plays into her feelings about both Gale and Peeta. Gale has long been a supporter, helping her sharpen her hunting skills and to look after Prim. Without her knowing it, Peeta has also long been an admirer of Katniss, but she is slow to warm to him beyond the pretence of a 'star-crossed lovers' romance. Which one of those two she should choose over the other is one of the main emotionally troubling issues for Katniss. He's many miles away, but Gale is rarely far from her thoughts. The brief return home to District 12 has put both of them in different positions. Is Gale's disappearance into the mines an avoidance strategy? Is Peeta really willing to wait for her to choose at her own pace? Before anything can develop she is back in the Games, trying to protect herself and Peeta.

Family is another source of loyalty for Katniss: her mother has improved since her return from the arena and has taken up her herbalist interests and treatment of local ailments once again, and Prim is growing up to follow in Katniss's independent footsteps. Katniss still has to look after and provide for them, even with the advantages offered by life in the Victors' Village. Gale and Peeta also have their own familial loyalties, which sometimes conflict with their own emotional needs and wants. However, all three seem continually willing to put themselves out in order to support and aid others.

Suzanne Collins threads several consistent issues through all three novels, from the obvious ones – war, survival, trauma, love – to others that she intends to encourage readers to think about for themselves. Morality is a major question, especially as regards taking a life. The Games force the participants to kill their peers, and Katniss enters the arena on both occasions attempting to avoid having to take anyone's life. The times that she does kill, it is depicted as unavoidable, as it is often in self-defence or in the defence of others, such as Rue. As noted, Katniss has difficulties with authority, and as part of that she has trouble with obedience: she doesn't follow the rules at home in District 12, so it was always unlikely she would follow the rules in the Games arena either. She demonstrated this in the way she triumphed in the 74th Games, and she does so again in the Quarter Quell, using a strategy inspired by the actions of Haymitch Abernathy during the previous Quell, the 50th Games. Her actions in breaking the forcefield containing the arena echo those of Haymitch when he used a similar forcefield as a weapon, allowing him to win. Both are unconventional strategies, very much against the wishes of the Gamemakers, and both their actions offer some insight into their respective characters.

Sacrifice and redemption are embodied by various characters due to the very nature of the Games, but the trio of Katniss, Peeta and Gale make sacrifices for each other, and even for strangers (as Katniss does for Rue). It is in their natures, and they don't particularly expect to be rewarded for it – it is a mark of difference between them as moral operators compared to those who wield power from the Capitol. They are forced to participate in the Games (or in the case of Gale, stand by helplessly and watch) against their wishes, but once there they refuse to play by the imposed rules. Katniss struggles with her trauma, hoping she can find redemption for the acts against her nature that she was forced to carry out to ensure her survival or that of her friends. Her move from independence to a more willing interdependence during the 75th Games is a big step, and sets her up to be part of a communal effort to overthrow the Capitol in the next novel, *Mockingjay*.

One other issue developed further in *Catching Fire* (and again in *Mockingjay*) is the role of media in the world of Panem. The control of the only television channel allows the Capitol to shape and control society by what it selects to include and to eliminate from its communications. The broadcasting of the Games is an exaggerated form of contemporary pop culture events like *The X Factor* or *America's Got Talent*; it's an overblown gameshow where death is ever present. The audience is manipulated, especially in *Catching Fire* over the Katniss Everdeen wedding (where the dress selection is turned into a mini event in itself, following examples of celebrity or royal coverage). Propaganda is used against the population as a form of control and punishment (making them view their own children battle for survival is continually held up as the result of the rebellion seventy-five years in the past, a constant warning not to dare to try anything again). During the first two books, the media is a weapon deployed against the Districts. In *Mockingjay*, it is something turned against the Capitol, when Plutarch Heavensbee uses their best weapon against them.

II

CASTING *CATCHING FIRE*

For *Catching Fire*, the second movie in *The Hunger Games* trilogy, the core cast remained the same, with Jennifer Lawrence leading the ensemble as Katniss Everdeen, now the figurehead of a growing rebellion against the Capitol. Both Josh Hutcherson and Liam Hemsworth were also back as Peeta Mellark and Gale Hawthorne, with the latter enjoying a slightly expanded role. Paula Malcomson and Willow Shields put in brief appearances as Katniss's mother and her sister, Prim. Woody Harrelson reprised his role as Katniss's mentor, Haymitch Abernathy.

The forces of the Capitol were represented by Donald Sutherland as President Coriolanus Snow, who instigates the Victory Tour of the Districts that Katniss and Peeta embark upon. Elizabeth Banks returned as Effie Trinket, and Lenny Kravitz reprised his part as Capitol Games stylist Cinna. The returning actors were rounded out by Stanley Tucci as the Games' public anchorman Caesar

Flickerman and Toby Jones as Claudius Templesmith, the Games announcer.

One of the biggest new names to join *Catching Fire* was Philip Seymour Hoffman as Plutarch Heavensbee, the new Head Gamemaker and secret rebellion ally against the Capitol and President Snow. A distinctive actor and director, Philip won a Best Actor Oscar for his role as Truman Capote in the 2005 biopic, *Capote*. He was also Oscar-nominated three times in the Best Supporting Actor category for his roles in *Charlie Wilson's War* (2007), *Doubt* (2008) and as cult guru Lancaster Dodd in *The Master* (2012).

Philip Seymour Hoffman was born in Fairport, New York, in 1967. His mother, Marilyn O'Connor, was a family court judge and civil rights activist while his father, Gordon Hoffman, was an executive for the Xerox corporation. He was raised without any religious conviction in a household where his father was Protestant and his mother Catholic – they divorced when Philip was nine years old. He had two sisters, Jill and Emily, and a brother known as Gordy who scripted the 2002 film *Love Liza* in which Philip featured.

After studying at the Theatre School of the New York State Summer School of the Arts and the Circle in the Square summer theatre programme, Philip took personal acting tuition from drama coach Alan Langdon. In 1989 Philip received a Bachelor in Fine Arts in Drama from New York University's Tisch School of the Arts. Professionally, he set out to balance a career in film and television with regular work on the stage, co-founding the Bullstoi Ensemble and making his first screen appearance in a 1991 episode of *Law & Order*.

The following year saw Philip appear in four films, with *Scent of a Woman* (1992), starring Al Pacino, bringing him to the notice of a variety of filmmakers who would become future collaborators. Among the many movies he appeared in were *Twister* (1996), *Boogie Nights* (1997), *Magnolia* (1999, both directed by Paul Thomas Anderson: Philip made six films with him), *The Talented Mr Ripley* (1999) and *Mission: Impossible III* (2006). After his Oscar win for *Capote*, Philip won roles and acclaim in a distinctive run of movies including (besides the three for which he was Oscar-nominated) *Synecdoche, New York* (2008), *Moneyball* (2011) and *A Late Quartet* (2012). In 2010 he directed the romantic comedy-drama *Jack Goes Boating* and played the main role of Jack, a shy limo driver who tentatively begins a relationship with the equally shy Connie (Amy Ryan).

In July 2012 came the news that Philip was to join *The Hunger Games* sequel. Although he'd appeared in a movie franchise before (as the villain in *Mission: Impossible III*), it was an unusual film choice for the much-lauded actor. As the Head Gamemaker of the 75th Annual Hunger Games, his character would have an influential role in the staging of the Quarter Quell. Philip was the first of the new cast members to be announced, alongside the returning regulars.

Philip had a simple reason for joining the franchise. 'I liked the people involved,' he said. 'It's a great group of actors. The character was something I was attracted to. He's somebody who's part of the revolution, but you don't know it. The idea that somebody would be risking themselves in such an extreme way to join something that's dangerous because he thinks it's the future . . . that's interesting stuff, you know?'

Politics had never been far from Philip's movie roles or his personal life, where he followed his mother's lead in becoming involved in causes he supported. He had a lot of catching up to do before shooting *Catching Fire*, though, as he hadn't read any of Suzanne Collins's novels. 'I've read the script, which is true to the book,' he said. 'I'm reading it, because I really want to find out everything I need to know about this guy.' He was also happy to be joining the cast of an established franchise, something he'd rarely done before. 'Things always pass over, you know? I don't know what it will be like. But, you know, I'm not playing Katniss. I'm not in high-profile movies in that way too often.'

New director Francis Lawrence, who replaced Gary Ross (see Chapter 12), had his sights set on Philip. 'We came up with the idea for Phil pretty early on,' he said. 'He was the biggest role to cast and the most important role for the entire series, if you think in terms of new additions. He was the first one we went after, but he was in the middle of [a stage run of] *Death of a Salesman* and wasn't really interested in entertaining anything until he was done with that.'

As the role of Plutarch Heavensbee would be continuing into the next two movies, and would be expanded from the novels (as with President Snow), Lawrence wanted to be sure he secured the right man for the job – there was much the character had to accomplish. 'We did a fair amount of invention with him [Heavensbee] and Snow, so these are scenes that could possibly have happened in the background,' said Lawrence. 'They're not deviations, they're additions to the book. Because it's an antagonist-driven story, it was really important to see the scenes between Snow and Plutarch and to see the two of them plotting and manoeuvring.'

Lawrence added of his newest cast member: 'Plutarch is such an important character and Philip is one of the very best actors working right now, so we started talking to him and fortunately, he just loved the books, and he loved this story.' Once he was cast, Philip plunged into the world of Panem, reading the books and discovering what the fuss was all about. 'I was just sucked into them. I was blown away by what Suzanne had done. So the idea of being part of bringing this whole story to the screen in a worthy fashion interested me. It's challenging to take a character like this from the page into cinematic storytelling. I had to look into Plutarch a bit more, outside of what the book showed me. He has all the qualities that he had in the book, but I think he has even more now, so that was exciting.'

The Hunger Games series' star, Jennifer Lawrence, was awed to have Philip join the cast. 'It's a pinch me moment as an actor if you get to do a scene with Philip Seymour Hoffman,' she said. 'I think he's arguably one of the greatest actors of our time. He's such a smart, nice man and he embodies Plutarch in the most incredible way.'

Shockingly, Philip's contribution to *The Hunger Games* movies was tragically cut short due to his untimely death in February 2014 at the age of forty-six, as shooting of the *Mockingjay* movies was underway. Philip had been frank about his struggles with drugs over the years, but it seemed he couldn't conquer his demons as the cause of death was a suspected drug overdose. His untimely death left the producers of the final two movies of *The Hunger Games* series with a major problem due to the role Plutarch Heavensbee has in the story.

The next significant new character in *Catching Fire* was Finnick Odair, the twenty-four-year-old Tribute from District 4 who triumphed in the Games when he was only fourteen. It was a tough role to fill, with Canadian Taylor Kitsch (whose first leading role was in the ill-fated Disney sci-fi movie *John Carter*, 2012), *Twilight*'s Robert Pattinson, *The Lone Ranger*'s Armie Hammer, and *Tron: Legacy*'s Garrett Hedlund said to be up for the coveted role. Director Francis Lawrence was clear about what he was looking for – and he found it in British actor Sam Claflin. 'We saw tons of people for Finnick, but I always kept going back to Sam. He's a handsome, sexy, funny, athletic guy but he also can tap into real emotional power – that's what sold me most.'

Sam was born in 1986 in Ipswich, Suffolk, the third of four children. His father, Mark, worked for a charity radio station, while his mother Sue was a classroom assistant. His younger brother Joseph followed Sam into acting. Sam studied Performing Arts at Norwich City College in 2003, and then attended the London Academy of Music and Dramatic Art. His first major role was in the television miniseries *The Pillars of the Earth* in 2010, but he graduated to the big screen as Philip Swift in the fourth instalment of the *Pirates of the Caribbean* series, *On Stranger Tides* (2011). Three months before securing his role in *Catching Fire*, Sam was cast in the lead role in Hammer Films' thriller *The Quiet Ones*, although that wouldn't begin production until after he'd completed his role in *The Hunger Games* sequel.

'Finnick is a very complicated person,' said Claflin. 'He is not someone able to easily share his feelings and emotions because he feels that eyes are always on him. But he also is ready to fight for what he believes is right for the future of the world that he lives in. Ultimately, he becomes allies with Katniss, and he goes on a great journey.'

Jennifer Lawrence welcomed her new co-star to the world of Panem. 'Sam has this sweet, wonderful charm to him,' she said. 'When you put Finnick's sarcastic words in Sam's mouth they still come out dripping with charm and that's a really hard thing to pull off, yet Sam does [it]. I couldn't see anybody else playing Finnick because he was so amazing.'

For his part, Sam was happy that the majority of his screen time would put him opposite Jennifer. He said of Finnick's role in relation to Katniss: 'He tries to charm the pants off of her, basically, and that doesn't work out as planned. Every other girl falls over him, but Katniss doesn't. I think there's an element of that which intrigues him.'

Supporting Finnick was his very own Haymitch

Abernathy, in the form of eighty-year-old Mags, a former Victor turned mentor. Cast in the role was veteran actress Lynn Cohen, best known as Miranda's nanny Magda on the hit television series *Sex and the City*. A character actress for many years, Lynn was born in 1933 in Kansas City, Missouri, and came late to acting, starting to rack up credits from the early nineties. She appeared in *I Shot Andy Warhol* (1996), *The Station Agent* (2003) and *Synecdoche, New York* (2008, alongside Philip Seymour Hoffman). She played Israeli Prime Minister Golda Meir in Steven Spielberg's *Munich* (2005). Her television roles have included regular parts on *Law & Order* (as a judge), *Nurse Jackie* and *Damages*. She was ideal for the elderly, small, yet powerful Mags, whose time alongside Katniss in the arena is dramatically cut short. Although the younger Best Supporting Actress Oscar winner Melissa Leo (*The Fighter*, 2010) was rumoured for the role, age won out for Lynn, who came to audition thanks to her granddaughter and a friend who both independently suggested she should play the part of the older mentor. 'Mags is a female to the very end, and strong and funny and crafty,' said Lynn. 'How can you resist that? How can you resist playing such a strong woman in a film about strong women?'

Katniss finds she has some unexpected allies in the arena among the other previous winners, including Johanna Mason, an unpredictable, axe-wielding Tribute from District 7; Beetee, a previous Victor who triumphed by using his brains over his opponents' brawn; and Wiress, the wily partner to Beetee from District 3. Three relatively well-known cinema names filled these pivotal roles.

Regarding Johanna Mason as an uninhibited character, the producers were looking for an equally uninhibited actress, and they found her in Jena Malone. Born in Sparks, Nevada, in 1984, Jena had a peripatetic childhood moving frequently with her mother and her mother's female partner; she had lived in twenty-seven different places by the age of nine, including Lake Tahoe in California. Her father was of Norwegian descent. Her interest in acting was ignited by seeing her mother participate in community theatre. Home schooled, she achieved her General Educational Development certificate only after she was legally emancipated from her mother in 2000, at the age of sixteen. She'd made her professional movie debut four years earlier in *Bastard Out of Carolina* (1996), in which she played an abused young girl. The movie was directed by actress Anjelica Huston. The role won Jena an Independent Spirit Award for Best Debut Performance and a Screen Actors Guild Award for Outstanding Performance. Roles in episodic television dramas followed, including a Golden Globe-nominated turn in *Hope* in 1997. She appeared in several high-profile movies, such as *Contact* (1997, playing the younger version of Jodie Foster's character), *Stepmom* (1998) and *For Love of the Game* (1999). Her first lead role came in *Donnie Darko* (2001) as Gretchen Ross, the girlfriend of Jake Gyllenhaal. She co-produced *American Girl* (2002), in which she also starred, and played the lead character in *Saved!* (2004). Her other films included *Cold Mountain* (2003), *Pride & Prejudice* (2005, as Lydia Bennett), horror thriller *The Ruins* (2008) and steampunk fantasy *Sucker Punch* (2011).

'Her audition was so intense, so raw and so dangerous,' said producer Nina Jacobson. 'There was nobody else we could even really think about casting once we'd seen her. She felt tough in a way that came from being damaged, not tough because she was just trying to intimidate.'

The actress was really keen to get to grips with the unpredictable Johanna Mason, whom she'd also be playing in *Mockingjay*. 'I think Johanna's biggest strength, and the one that I was most interested in exploring, is her unpredictability,' said Jena. 'She's not consistently angry, she's not consistently nice. I just feel there's this thing where you never really know what you're going to get from her.' There was one scene that gave the actress pause for thought: a near-nude scene beside Katniss, Peeta and Haymitch in an elevator. 'We're very faithful to the adaptation,' she said, 'so in the elevator I did have to pretty much almost take everything off.'

Like Philip Seymour Hoffman, Jeffrey Wright was another distinguished actor who'd not read *The Hunger Games* when he was up for a key role in *Catching Fire*. He rapidly rectified that. 'As soon as I discovered how rich this material was, how complicated and relevant it was, I got really excited,' the actor said. *Catching Fire* producer Jon Kilik felt Jeffrey was ideal for the role of the smart electronics specialist who finds himself back in the arena. 'Beetee required a very unique individual – somebody who's smart and methodical, and also dangerous. Jeffrey has that versatility and talent.'

Born in 1965 in Washington, DC, Jeffrey was studying political science and intended to go to law school when the allure of an acting career took hold of him. He quit New York University after just two months to pursue life as a full-time actor. He first trod the boards in Off Broadway productions, before appearing in his first film, *Presumed Innocent* (1990) with Harrison Ford. He continued to mix acclaimed and award-winning theatre roles with work in film and television, including movies like Woody Allen's *Celebrity* (1998), *The Manchurian Candidate* (2004), two James Bond movies, *Casino Royale* (2006) and *Quantum of Solace* (2008), and television shows such as *Angels in America* (2003, repeating his acclaimed stage performance), *House* (2011) and period gangster drama *Boardwalk Empire* (2013).

Of Beetee, Jeffrey said: 'What's driving him is his sense of mistrust against the very idea of the Games and against the idea of a society of exclusion. He must use his best ideas and technological know-how to try to escape. What's interesting about the way that Suzanne Collins has drawn these characters and the way we're attempting to portray them is that they're all, to some extent, damaged warriors. It starts to become a real examination of the price that warriors pay for what they do . . . Issues around war and the consequences of war, the consequences on warriors and people – the human elements of that – I don't think [society] can address [that] enough.'

Beetee was paired with the District 3 Tribute Wiress, played by Amanda Plummer, best-known for *The Fisher King* (1991) and *Pulp Fiction* (1994). 'Wiress and Beetee make for a curious and eccentric pair and working with Amanda was fantastic,' said Wright. 'She's such an open actor, so generous and so fragile and their relationship becomes a very personal one.' Wiress allies herself with Katniss, and is the one to provide the key to figuring out how the arena works. Her repeated utterances of 'tick tock' lead Katniss to the conclusion that the arena functions as a clock. Suffering from a confused mental state, Wiress relies on Beetee, the only person able to clearly understand her. 'They have a really special relationship,' said Amanda of Wiress and Beetee, 'where Wiress has the feeling that he's got her back and she's got his back.'

The daughter of actor Christopher Plummer, Amanda Plummer was born in 1957 in New York City. She began her acting career in the eighties, with roles in *The World According to Garp* (1982), alongside Robin Williams, and Alan Rudolph's afterlife fantasy *Made in Heaven* (1987). A regular on stage (and a Tony Award winner), Amanda made a host of movies after *Pulp Fiction*, as well as appearing in various television shows such as *The Outer Limits*, *Law & Order: SVU* and *Hannibal*.

Opponents who trouble Katniss and her friends and allies in the arena during the Quarter Quell include the surviving career Tributes from District 2, Brutus and Enobaria.

Landing the two roles were actors Bruno Gunn and Meta Golding. Meta was struck by the secrecy surrounding her audition: 'I couldn't even tell anybody I had the audition,' she said. 'But I knew the casting director, and she said, "Just come in. We're going to improvise." I knew about the character – that she was this fierce warrior.'

For his part, Bruno set out to familiarize himself with the world of Panem and the people in it. 'I spent a lot of time building a backstory about who Brutus was – did he have brothers and sisters? What happened to his mom and dad?' he said. 'I put a chip on his shoulder, and made that part of the process. Something might have happened to one of my family members that made me eager to get back into the game. Or the fact that the District 2 tribute, Cato, was one of the last people to die in the 74th Games. It could be about justice, or revenge, or trying to bring some glory to District 2. We've been trained since birth; we've had the best of everything. It's our job to stay fit, to stay strong, to be the backbone of Panem, to bring warrior mentality to the Games.'

Meta saw the experienced survivors who have to return to the arena in *Catching Fire* as characters better built to cope with the privations visited upon them by the Capitol. 'Everybody who is a Victor has had to survive,' she said. 'I think of the Capitol as the villain. I think Enobaria is just the ultimate survivor. Just using her fierceness, her physicality and her competitiveness to win. Yes, it's vicious, but I think it's also a commentary on war and survival and the human spirit. It's in our DNA to survive. I think that's why [*The Hunger Games* book series] is so popular, because it's like high school, surviving high school – only in a much more violent way. Or even in the workplace – how do you survive in corporate America? This is just super-super-heightened and exaggerated.'

During the 74th Hunger Games, Katniss had defeated both Tributes from District 1, Marvel and Glimmer.

During her return to the arena for the Quarter Quell she encounters brother and sister Gloss and Cashmere, District 1's experienced previous winners – and they're looking for revenge. As siblings who'd won their respective Games, Gloss and Cashmere were figures of fascination for those in the Capitol who followed the Games. Katniss recalled that Gloss had been a winner of the Hunger Games when she was just a child.

Alan Ritchson won the role of Gloss, having originally auditioned for the larger part of Finnick Odair. He waited months for a call back to another audition, but when it came it was for a very different role. 'It doesn't happen that often that you get a call months later, but it was fun,' he said. Alan was born in 1984 in North Dakota and was best known, prior to *Catching Fire*, for his role as the underwater superhero Aquaman in *Smallville*, the long-running series that followed the teenage adventures of Clark Kent (Tom Welling) before he became Superman. Alan had begun his career as a model (for Abercrombie & Fitch, for whom Jennifer Lawrence had done some work early in her career). Having played a superhero, he wasn't too worried about being cast as one of the 'bad guys' in *Catching Fire*. 'Looking at this world, it is easy to say they are the villains, they are deadly, scary and mean,' he said of Gloss and his sister, Cashmere. 'You have to get inside their minds and hearts and understand who they are and the kind of position they are thrust into and their world.'

Stephanie Leigh Schlund described Cashmere as 'beautiful, but deadly'. Stephanie featured in *The Last Song* (2010), alongside Miley Cyrus and her *Catching Fire* co-star Liam Hemsworth, and had been a model on the television quiz show *The Price is Right* before becoming an actress. 'She's a master at manipulating crowds or one on one,' she said of Cashmere. 'She's confident, arrogant and fearless. [She and] her brother, Gloss, play off each other and find joy in winning their battles in the arena.'

*   *   *

Actors with a variety of experience played the other returning Tributes featured on screen in *Catching Fire*. Among
them was forty-one-year-old E. Roger Mitchell, playing
the District 11 Tribute Chaff. The Atlanta-based actor
had appeared in *Battle: Los Angeles* (2011), episodes of *The
Shield* and *One Tree Hill*, and had been seen in Tyler Perry
productions, including *Diary of a Mad Black Woman*
(2005) and *Daddy's Little Girls* (2007). In the novel Chaff is
a six-foot-tall warrior who lost his hand in the 45th Hunger
Games, thirty years before the current Quarter Quell.
Once friends with Katniss's mentor Haymitch, Chaff
had become a belligerent alcoholic. While trying to avoid
trouble, Chaff protected Katniss, but he came off worse in
an encounter with Brutus.

Chaff's fellow District 11 Tribute was Seeder, played
by actress and singer Maria Howell. Seen in episodes of
science-fiction television series *Revolution*, Maria had
appeared in the acclaimed movie *The Color Purple* back
in 1985. She'd learned to be less nervous in auditions. 'I
don't really get too nervous any more,' she said, 'because
being prepared alleviates most of that for me. Growing in
the craft and growing up in life gave me more confidence
going into things. So by the time *Revolution* and *Catching
Fire* happened, I was not as nervous. Auditioning is part of
the job, and I like to do my job to the best of my ability.'
Seeder, although much older, reminds Katniss of Rue, the
girl she'd tried to save during the previous Games. Katniss
admires her self-possession and willingness to stand up
to the Capitol, calling the Quarter Quell Games wrong
and arguing that President Snow could easily put a stop to
them, if he wanted to. There is also something motherly
about Seeder that Katniss recognizes, a caring ability she
misses in her own mother.

District 8 returning Victor Cecelia was played by
Elena Sanchez, a young actress and stuntwoman who had

performed in *21 Jump Street* (2012), *Looper* (2012) and *Olympus Has Fallen* (2013). She didn't have much to go on when building a character for Cecelia. 'Since Cecelia is only mentioned a few times in the book, the love she has for her children that are taken away from her as she is chosen for the Hunger Games becomes a defining characteristic,' said Elena. 'I have never had to make that kind of sacrifice. I tried to relate to her by thinking about what it would be like to give up some of the most important things in my life, but knowing that it was for a greater cause.' She's another mother figure (described as about thirty years old) whom Katniss allies with during the Games. Also an actor and stuntman, John Casino played the other Tribute from District 8, Woof. Said to be senile, despite his duties as a mentor to other Hunger Games competitors, Woof was the second oldest participant in the Quarter Quell, behind Mags.

Yet another stuntman and actor, Bobby Jordan, was cast as Blight, the male District 7 Tribute who joins Plutarch Heavensbee's rebellion. Blight was teamed with Johanna Mason and tasked with making sure that Wiress and Beetee survived the Games long enough to make contact with Katniss. Bobby had appeared in *Zombieland* (2009) and *The Watch* (2012), among other projects.

Two unknowns, Justin Hix and Megan Hayes, played the pair of Tributes from District 6, known as the 'morphlings' due to their post-Games addiction to the painkiller morphling. As a result their skin is discoloured pale yellow and their minds tend to wander. Although described as being in their sixties in the novel, the actors cast were significantly younger, with thirty-two-year-old Hayes having only taken up acting in 2007.

The remaining Tribute roles were filled by several young actors, many making their first on screen appearances. The District 5 Tributes were played by James Logan and Ivette Li-Sanchez, with Daniel Bernhardt and Marian Green as the District 9 Victors, and the returning champions from District 10 being played by Jackson Spidell and Tiffany Waxler.

Finally, Romulus Thread, the head Peacekeeper of District 12 who is tasked with enforcing the Capitol's will using any means necessary, was played by Patrick St. Esprit, from the television series *Sons of Anarchy*, who was born in 1955. He was familiar with playing military types, having taken such roles in movies such as *We Were Soldiers* (2002), *United 93* (2006) and *Green Zone* (2010). He'd previously played police officers on television and featured in the J. J. Abrams movie *Super 8* (2011). As a Capitol loyalist, Thread is described as being harsh and unforgiving, and the part gave Patrick his biggest movie role to date, completing the main cast of *Catching Fire*.

12
MAKING *CATCHING FIRE*

The Hunger Games confirmed Jennifer Lawrence's position as a major star, combining her Oscar nomination for *Winter's Bone* with the lead role in a major movie franchise. Working with Suzanne Collins, director Gary Ross had completed a screenplay that captured the novel and assembled a cast that brought the characters to life. The film opened to great reviews and superb box office, but Ross himself was moving on to pastures new. For many fans there was a moment of panic, as to their minds Ross had delivered the perfect film. Now someone new would be taking over on *Catching Fire* . . . but who?

With five months to go before shooting, *Catching Fire* was without a director. For Lionsgate, the film – the entire franchise – was bigger than any one director, so they were confident they could find someone suitable. While many directors may not have fitted, either because they were too individual or idiosyncratic to take on a sequel or a franchise movie, many others would be entirely sympathetic to the material and to the cast.

Names were touted in the media, some less serious contenders than others, but they made for an interesting snapshot of Hollywood's movers and shakers. Among the names were action specialist Michael Bay, deeply identified with the *Transformers* franchise; Oscar-winner Kathryn Bigelow, someone who would fit well with Jennifer Lawrence's preference for working with female directors; *Harry Potter* director David Yates; Doug Liman, helmer of teen sci-fi thriller *Jumper* (2008); John Chu, who later handled *G. I. Joe: Retaliation* (2013); Bill Condon, who tackled *Twilight: Breaking Dawn, Part 1* (2011); and another *Harry Potter* director, Alfonso Cuarón, who handled *Harry Potter and the Prisoner of Azkaban* (2004). All were good candidates, many with experience of big-budget fantasy movies aimed at the teen audience. Nowhere on any of the lists, though, was the name Francis Lawrence.

By mid-April 2012, the list of directors seriously considered by Lionsgate was down to just two: Francis Lawrence and Bennett Miller. Little-known, Miller was a childhood friend of Philip Seymour Hoffman who'd directed the actor in the biopic *Capote* (2005). He'd made three movies, and none of them featured extensive special effects or were part of ongoing blockbuster franchises. Along with *Capote*, his other two movies – *The Cruise* (1998) and *Moneyball* (2011) – were character pieces. Miller had been Oscar-nominated for *Capote* and had won widespread acclaim for *Moneyball*, and was seen as an up-and-coming talent. Lionsgate may have felt it would be in their interest to snag him on the way up. At the time he was sounded out for *Catching Fire*, however, he was already deep in pre-production on *Foxcatcher* (2014), a 'true life' story set to enter production by the end of the year. *Catching Fire* was already on a tight schedule, based around availability of the leading actress, and needed a director who could start right away. The fact that the shortlist had shrunk to two within a week of Gary Ross's departure emphasized the urgency. That left Francis Lawrence.

Lawrence was an interesting choice (and was not related to Jennifer). He had extensive experience helming effects-driven action movies having begun his filmmaking career (after dozens of music videos) with the fantasy action double-whammy of *Constantine* (2005) and *I Am Legend* (2007). He'd done some television work, including four episodes of Bible drama *Kings* (2009) and the pilot for the Kiefer Sutherland-led series *Touch* (2012). His most recent movie romance, *Water for Elephants* (2011), starred *Twilight*'s Robert Pattinson and Reese Witherspoon. The $38 million budget *Water for Elephants* had grossed $58 million in the US and the same sum internationally, while reviews had dubbed the beautiful-looking movie to be saccharine. The movie had been a critical and box-office failure, so Lawrence was on the lookout for a new project.

Just under a week after the exit of Gary Ross, Lionsgate confirmed it had completed negotiations with Lawrence. His experience of large-scale filmmaking and stylish approach to visual effects had won him the gig, as *Catching Fire* was spread over a much larger and more exotic canvas. The Victory Tour that opens *Catching Fire* was a chance for a skilled filmmaker to broaden the world of Panem and put their own stamp on *The Hunger Games*. 'I thought we could grow visually, because we were seeing more of the Districts, the Capitol, and a whole new arena,' said the new director. Lawrence was facing a daunting challenge, as *Catching Fire* would have to wrap its principal photography by the end of 2012 in order to free up star Jennifer Lawrence to go to London to shoot her *X-Men* sequel in January 2013.

Producer Nina Jacobson knew what the film needed. 'We were looking for somebody who had a real passion for the books, and for this book in particular. From our first conversation, Francis had so much insight into the characters and into the dynamics between them, we were won over.'

Lawrence had put a lot of effort into winning the job, and felt he was ready for the journey ahead. '*Catching Fire* opens the world of Panem up and you start to learn more about the characters, as the story pushes them forward,' he said. 'It is the most technically complex film I have ever done, and yet I think the coolest thing about it is simply the strength of the story itself. I'm really proud of how emotional it is. Fans will enjoy seeing many new facets to Panem, but it's also a story that stands on its own.'

Lawrence had the advantage of having seen Gary Ross's take on *The Hunger Games*. 'I definitely think it's the cast,' he said of the strengths of the previous film. 'Jen and Josh and Elizabeth and Stanley, Donald Sutherland, they were amazing. I also think there were some aesthetic choices made that were very nice. I really liked the way District 12 looks and feels, this thirties Appalachia feeling. Some of the choices in the Capitol were pretty great in terms of the fascist, brutalist architecture. There's a lot for me to grab on to and to run with in [the next] one.'

For his part, Lawrence was attracted to the rich world of *The Hunger Games* as revealed in Suzanne Collins's original novels. 'Suzanne started all of this with an idea of a theme, and she wanted to create a series of stories for young adults about the consequences of war,' he said. 'Suzanne approached it without pulling any punches, so she's not talking down to the teenagers, she's actually treating them as smart people and treating them as adults, which I think teenagers appreciated, but I also think it's why it helped crossover into the adult world. She created a really rich world, filled it with compelling characters, and told a great story with a really truly amazing character, Katniss, at the centre of it. You can relate to her because she's so real, she's not a superhero. She's flawed. It allows [readers] to put themselves in her shoes, imagine yourself in her situation, and buy into the decisions she's making.'

Rumours had surfaced shortly after the debut of *The Hunger Games* that Lionsgate might lift an idea from the *Harry Potter* and *Twilight* series and split the final novel into two movies. It was a gambit that had paid off hugely for other teen franchises, with more screen time available to tell the story, a bigger canvas for the director and cast to play on, and an increased box-office presence (and so profit) for the studio.

The split was confirmed in July 2012, when the release dates were announced for *Mockingjay, Part 1* and *Part 2* as 21 November 2014 and 20 November 2015 respectively. Along with the 22 November 2013 release date for *Catching Fire*, the next three films in *The Hunger Games* series were set to be Thanksgiving holiday blockbusters. Additionally, new director Francis Lawrence would be on board for the rest of the series. 'I signed on originally for one movie,' he confirmed. 'As I started I didn't think at all about who would have to take care of the subsequent films. When they made the announcement that the *Mockingjay* films were going to be coming out on the next two Thanksgivings, I realized they were going to have to be starting the first one while I was still finishing *Catching Fire*. I started thinking to myself, "Well, that will be interesting. There's going to be some other guy around, some other girl around, directing *Mockingjay* while I'm finishing this?" Within maybe eight or ten weeks of preparation on *Catching Fire*, though, it was obvious that the collaboration was working really well and I was approached to do *Mockingjay* too. To know that I'm seeing these stories out, that I'm going to get to do the book that I think, personally, gives the whole meaning to the series, is very exciting.'

* * *

By June 2012, casting was in full swing, with Philip Seymour Hoffman confirmed as Plutarch Heavensbee, Jena Malone pipping Mia Wasikowska to the part of Johanna Mason and Amanda Plummer confirmed in July in the role of Wiress. Finding actors for Finnick and Beetee took longer, but the production rapidly settled on Sam Claflin and Jeffrey Wright. Over the next few weeks the other, more minor, roles were filled (see Chapter 11).

Elizabeth Banks, back as the flamboyantly coutured Effie Trinket, was looking forward to welcoming the new cast. 'Sam Claflin gave me a tummy flutter in *Snow White and the Huntsman* so I couldn't be happier that he's taking on the role of Finnick Odair,' she posted on her personal blog. 'Jena Malone will play Katniss's sarcastic "frenemy" Johanna Mason. She's got grit and spunk in spades. Quote me on that. The amazing Jeffrey Wright will play fan fave Beetee. We worked together on Oliver Stone's *W* – he's never less than perfection. I'm excited to work with everyone in the cast, and you know I can't wait to transform into Effie again – crazy nail art, wigs, and all.'

Woody Harrelson spoke about the casting of Philip Seymour Hoffman, and declared he was looking forward to the scenes that Haymitch Abernathy and Plutarch Heavensbee would be sharing. 'There definitely will be some [scenes] that we have together. I think he is just one of the greats, so I am really looking forward to working with him. We've never worked together, but we've known each other for a while and we've hung out a few times.'

Francis Lawrence had big plans for developing Woody's role in the second film. 'One of the things I really like about this book is you start to see why Haymitch is the way he is,' said Lawrence, 'so [Woody] and I did a fair amount of work in terms of that, in terms of understanding Post-Traumatic Stress Disorder. Also, we started messing around a lot with some real humanity in Haymitch because he can be quite cynical and sarcastic at times, but I think there's a more human side to him in this one as well.'

Finnick Odair was also a role that Lawrence was very happy to have filled. '[Sam Claflin] is very athletic, which is great. He's in great shape. He's very charismatic,' Lawrence said. 'But I was also looking in the long term. There's a rogue-like quality to him in this book. And long term, he's actually an emotional character and a very loyal character who's in love; a character who experienced quite a lot of sadness. He was really able to tap into that, as well as being really charming and sexy and handsome as hell.'

Josh Hutcherson declared that Peeta would be in even better shape. 'I've been working out a lot, getting back in the right shape for the role – because this last year, I sort of split my time and enjoyed myself – so I've been paying for that for the last month-and-a-half or so, getting back into the gym and eating healthy.' As well as a physical workout, Josh knew that the second film would put Peeta through the emotional wringer. 'It's such a tough position that I know Peeta is put in where he is in absolute love with this girl and she acts like she's in love with him, but he knows that she isn't – and that is heartbreaking. As an actor, it's something that I'm really excited to play because it's such a conflicting emotion . . . It's really intense and exciting.'

He was looking forward to playing opposite Jennifer once more, especially as the pair had won the MTV Movie Award for Best Kiss! 'Jennifer and I are such good friends,' Josh said. 'One of the hardest parts for us is to pretend we're in love. It feels so cheesy, because we're in love with each other in real life as really good friends and just switching that dynamic over was like, "Can we actually do this? We're so goofy and silly together, can we actually pretend that we're seriously lovers?" It's good to know that people say "Yes, you can."'

* * *

Producer Nina Jacobson was in something of a panic when she considered the next film. 'We were five months from when we needed to start shooting and we had no script and no director,' she said. Once Francis Lawrence was on board, she had him sit down with Suzanne Collins to begin to map out the urgently needed script. None of the other departments could get to work without it, although the novel provided many clues to likely environments and the kind of costumes needed. The first third of the novel was the trickiest to tackle, as it was the densest part of the story detailing the journey of Katniss and Peeta around Panem on their Victory Tour, as well as Katniss's return home to District 12 where she struggles to come to terms with her experiences. One thing that was definitely going to be different from the novel was the way the movie would introduce District 13. According to Lawrence, 'It was fun figuring out new ways around things and new ways of doing things.'

Although the film would be 'very true to the book', producer Jacobson knew that cutting some elements, such as Bonnie and Twill, the District 8 runaways who first alert Katniss to her role in sparking an uprising, would inevitably upset some readers. 'It's as agonizing for us to lose things from the book as it is for a fan. I want every single thing in there. But you know what? If you have to give up something in order to give more time to Katniss and Gale, or to Effie as she starts to feel a conscience, you make the sacrifices in order to serve the characters and themes that are more essential.'

Jacobson's aim for the second film was clear: 'We're very excited to advance Katniss's evolution. We see her growing into somebody who is much more the master of her own destiny, as opposed to a pawn in the agendas of others. We see an ethical and social consciousness awakened in her, and yet at the same time, we also see the very human resistance that she feels to having to become a hero, when all she really wants to do is go home.'

In working out how the character of Katniss would develop and how the world of Panem might change, the director had the original novel as a road map, but the film required much more. In consultation with Suzanne Collins, Lawrence broke down the story of the second book and reworked the core elements so they would function better on screen. 'There will never be anybody that knows these characters and the world of Panem as well as Suzanne,' said Lawrence. 'I know people really love and trust what Suzanne has to say about them. She became a vital part of finding the best ways to tell this part of the story.'

Working on the final script were Simon Beaufoy and Michael deBruyn (a pseudonym for *Toy Story 3* screenwriter Michael Arndt). Beaufoy, writer of *Slumdog Millionaire*, was attracted to work on *Catching Fire* due to its central female hero. 'What I really love about the books is it isn't even up for discussion that she's a girl,' Beaufoy said of Katniss Everdeen. 'There's no discussion that she shouldn't be killing people because she's a girl. We've done gender politics. This is about life and death. It makes the gender politics seem finicky and not terribly interesting.'

By September 2012, Lawrence and his cast were on location in Atlanta, Georgia, to begin shooting on *Catching Fire*, under the production codename 'The Idiom'. 'One of the very first things we shot that I like quite a lot is a good-bye before [Katniss] goes into the arena, with Liam,' said Lawrence. 'We shot it because we needed summer foliage and summer flowers. We actually shot it while we were in prep. Very first thing we went out into the meadow, out in the mountains in North Georgia and shot this sequence over three or four hours or so, and I really like it. Jennifer and Liam are really good in it.'

Shooting would finish in December, following a trip to Hawaii to capture shots relating to Katniss's new experiences back in the Games arena. Only after shooting had been under way for a few weeks were the names of the final cast members (mainly the other Tributes taking part in the Quarter Quell) revealed. During shooting, in November 2012, Lionsgate confirmed that Francis Lawrence would be staying in Panem to helm the two-film adaptation of *Mockingjay*. It meant that by the time the series was completed Lawrence would have directed three out of the four of *The Hunger Games* movies.

That November the cast and crew were in Hawaii, with the island used as a location for the water-based sections of the arena. 'This arena is like no other,' the director said. 'Special care went into creating it by the Gamemaker and it plays a large role in our story. It's a very interactive arena, and its secrets make it far trickier.'

The biggest development in the story was that the characters in the arena had an opportunity to team up, something forbidden during the previous movie. As ex-perienced Tributes, they also all came to the new arena with the physical skills, intelligence and knowledge that allowed them individually to be winners. 'These Tributes have all won the Games before, and they are now smarter, more skilled and savvier about forming alliances,' said Lawrence. 'Alliances become a big theme in this story for Katniss and Peeta as they try to figure who they can and cannot trust.'

Lawrence was keen to continue the focus on Katniss, but this time she's very much a reluctant hero, someone who doesn't want to be the symbol of resistance. 'It's one of the things that I think we all relate to in Katniss – that she has these very personal needs to protect her own family, which are not selfish needs but that conflict with some of the new things being asked of her,' said Lawrence. 'She doesn't want people looking up to her, because she has enough to worry about, yet she is discovering that she can't escape that, either. It's really what makes her so believable as a character, that she never set out to be anyone's hero.'

Jennifer Lawrence said of working with her new

director: 'Francis is a brilliant choice . . . every actor that has ever worked for him is in love with him and adores him and that goes a long, long way. He's such a great director because he's so freeing, but you also feel like you're in good hands. You know that he knows the material, he knows your character, he knows why he's asking you to do something and he's not restricting in any way . . .'

Josh Hutcherson was pleased with the new direction he saw the characters moving in, from the Victory Tour through to Peeta volunteering to take the place of Tribute Haymitch Abernathy as the male representative from District 12, putting him in the arena once more by the side of Katniss Everdeen. 'It's really hard for us being paraded around against our will,' he said of Peeta and Katniss. 'We've both been trying to get back to our old routine, but now we're different, we have notoriety and it's also tough to go back home after such intense battles. They're both going through a big transition. Peeta has realized that Katniss only pretended to be in love with him during the Games in order to stay alive and get back to her family, but Peeta has always been in love with her, and will always be in love with her. That's what makes it such an interesting relationship. The whole thing is very different from the first time around because whereas they thought they were just going into the arena alone, now they are learning the importance of making strong alliances.'

Another whose life had changed since the events of the first film was Gale Hawthorne. Liam Hemsworth was determined to make the most of his smaller part as the other man on the mind of Katniss. 'Gale's now working in the mines and he's still trying to survive. But his anger is growing more and more every day because of all the things that the Capitol is doing to the Districts. Now I think he's starting to feel a responsibility to stand up to that.' As well as the Capitol's oppression, Liam was sure that Gale would have Katniss in his thoughts. 'Gale feels like he's a bit in the dark. He's unsure as to his place in her life now that so much has changed. When he sees his best friend having to return to the Games again, I think it lights a fire inside him. It's exciting for me because Gale's whole story is becoming more complex.'

As the environments of Panem expanded in *Catching Fire*, so too did the demands on the costume department, which had to create many more outfits reflecting the different Districts and the wider world of the Capitol. Trish Summerville, who'd previously worked on the English language version of *The Girl with the Dragon Tattoo* (2011), was new to *The Hunger Games* phenomenon and had to go beyond her predecessor's work. She'd previously worked with Lawrence when he was making music videos, and she saw *Catching Fire* as an opportunity to bring some of the more avant-garde fashion of the pop world to Panem. 'Francis and I started off discussing making the look a little darker and also a bit more chic,' she said, 'a bit more fashion-forward, while still keeping that sense of the weird and perverse that clearly marks the Capitol.'

The most prominent follower of Panem fashion is Effie Trinket, whose demeanour grows ever more frantic as the films progress, an emotional state that Summerville felt could be reflected in her outlandish clothing. She turned to the work of designer Alexander McQueen, as she felt his distinctive, often over-the-top designs were ideal for the Capitol. She had his fashion house 'construct' the dress Effie wears for the Victory Tour. 'I wanted to have a tribute to McQueen [who died in 2010], because I've been really inspired by his fashion and his structural pieces,' Summerville said. 'Elizabeth [Banks] really let us torture her for some of these pieces. Her shoes are insane, especially a couple of pairs of McQueen shoes that kept her on the ball of her foot at all times. But she endured it all for the beauty of it, so it goes right along with Effie's character.'

Other fashion houses were involved in the film, with suits from designer Juun.J being used to clothe Haymitch and Peeta, and Jean Paul Gaultier – whose work has appeared in films such as *The Cook, the Thief, His Wife & Her Lover* (1989), *The City of Lost Children* (1995), *The Fifth Element* (1997) and *Bad Education* (2004) – provided outfits for the guests attending President Snow's party in his mansion in the Capitol.

The most important costume, though, was the wedding dress designed in the film by Cinna for Katniss. Summerville looked beyond well-known fashion houses and movie costume designers, collaborating with twenty-eight-year-old Indonesian designer Tex Saverio. The brief was to capture the romance evident between Katniss and Peeta, but also to communicate through the outfit something of the darkness of the world in which Katniss now moves. 'The dress as seen in the film is definitely a work of art,' said Summerville. Saverio wanted to push his design skills in coming up with a suitably dazzling outfit for the film's lead character, reflecting many of her characteristics in its look. 'We wanted something even edgier and more avant-garde so we used the metallic upper frame that has qualities of a flame and then the skirt is full of ribbons and lace. The materials symbolize all the contradictions in Katniss,' he said.

Beyond the fashion-driven designs for denizens of the Capitol, Summerville paid close attention to the colour-coordinated wear for each of the main characters, using their clothes and various 'looks' to communicate something about each of them individually and about how they relate to each other. For example, she often put Peeta in shades of green, as that was said in the novel to be Katniss's favourite colour. It suggested that subconsciously he's trying to attract her. Gale, in his new job as a miner in District 12, would obviously be wearing a more subdued colour palette, but Summerville still felt she could help to define his character through colour. She made sure to make it appear as if he was trying to 'dress to impress' Katniss (as far as he could with District 12's limitations) every time he was near her. Even in the Capitol, clothes were used to connote character, as with Cinna, who despite being the designer of clothes worn by others is himself rather more restrained in what he wears. He contrasts nicely with the more superficial inhabitants of the Capitol through his use of darker tones against their more pastel colours. 'For Haymitch,' said Summerville, 'we used a lot of natural fibres and textural fabrics and I wanted to clean him up a bit, so that he's now a little more chic and streamlined, but still slightly off in that Haymitch fashion.'

Make-up designs were handled by Ve Neill, returning from the first movie. She needed to develop some rather unusual skin applications, such as the blisters caused by poison fog in the arena and the effects of the 'blood rain' on Johanna, Beetee and Wiress. She also had to depict the after-effects of such events as the whipping of Gale, as well as the outlandish and colourful make-up flaunted by those in the Capitol. 'This movie was a make-up artist's dream,' she said. 'We have blood, we have fantasy, and we have Effie, who is a whole other entity unto herself.'

Returning hair and wig designer Linda Flowers was equally thrilled by the possibilities that *The Hunger Games* series affords her that more ordinary movies cannot. 'This is one of the only movies I've done where the hair is such an important part of the storytelling. How often do you get to be a part of creating looks that people love copying and replicating?' The pair collaborated on the new looks for Effie Trinket throughout the movie. Said Neill: 'The first time we see Effie, she looks like a giant snowflake, which is pretty fabulous. Linda Flowers made this really amazing white snow encrusted wig. I followed suit and made her face almost white. She shows up like a beacon of winter.'

One key scene involved the dressing (or rather undress-ing) of Sam Claflin as Finnick Odair. The notorious scene in the book where Finnick teases Katniss with sugar cubes while wearing nothing but strategically placed netting was retained, to the delight of many fans – but with a few key changes. 'They did have to tone it down from what it is in the book because they can't make it too graphic, if you know what I'm saying,' admitted Claflin. 'Because it was just a knot covering his . . . I was definitely prepared to do anything, but the costumer said "Well we can't have you in nothing", so I'm kind of covered up. It was the scariest moment of my life.'

For the arena sequences, the cast would be encased in high-tech wetsuits for the new environment around which these Games take place. 'Honestly, I was expecting them to be horrible,' said Josh of the wetsuits, 'because the idea of being in a wetsuit for a whole movie sounds terrifying, but they actually were pretty comfortable once we found out you can actually pee through them – just go into the ocean and take care of your business.'

For director Francis Lawrence, the work of all his vari-ous department heads was vital in making it possible for him to dramatically and dynamically – not to mention col-ourfully – tell the story outlined by Suzanne Collins. 'We all worked together – Trish, Ve, Linda and their entire team – to create the look of the Capitol, so that every person you see has their own individual style,' said Lawrence. 'At the same time it's all tied into a unified new palette, with paler, almost ghostly make-up and geometrical looks. It was a tricky business and took an army of people to accomplish it.'

The aim with *Catching Fire* was to build upon what had been achieved with *The Hunger Games* and to open that world up, filling it with new characters and new environ-ments. The returning characters would go on new journeys, growing and changing as they went. 'I thought "I like these aesthetic choices that [Gary Ross] made and I like this cast, but now I can run with it,"' said Lawrence about his take during development. 'I can see more of District 12 and explore it in the winter to help sell emotion and theme. I can create the other Districts and I'll have a brand new arena. It's an anniversary year so I can create new things in the Capitol. I discovered there was loads for me to do and build and to work with that would be entirely different.'

The design challenges were even greater than those of the first movie. While *The Hunger Games* had to establish a look for both District 12 and the Capitol, *Catching Fire* would have to up the ante to include several more Districts seen during the Victory Tour, a lavish party hosted by President Snow in the heart of the Capitol, and an all-new arena incorporating a large body of water and an Amazon-style tropical jungle. 'We're excited to show the audience much more detail inside District 12, including the Victors' Village, to give our first glimpses on the Victors' Tour of Districts 11, 4 and 8, to expand the portrait of the sparkling Capitol, and bring them into a very impressive new arena,' said Lawrence.

Production designer Phil Messina returned, rising to the challenge of building on his original work. 'I knew coming in that everything was going to be upped from the last and that was the real hook for me,' he said. 'It's not simply that Francis wanted to make everything bigger for the sake of it. It was more about responding to the fact that the story is expanding, the stakes are growing. Everything we did was in service to that. Francis is extremely visual and he approaches things much like I do – we both like to talk in pictures.'

The second movie picked up the story a few months after the end of the first, with Katniss and Peeta ensconced in the Victors' Village, one of their rewards for surviving the Games. Even though this accommodation is a step up from the old home where Katniss previously lived, it's still not extravagant or luxurious, especially not when compared to the opulence Katniss witnessed in the Capitol. 'Their new world is elegant but still fairly simple,' noted Messina. 'I guess, in the context of District 12, if you have food and heat it's extravagant, but there's still a real contrast with President Snow's house. Katniss's house is sort of a mini version of Snow's palace, with a lot of the same aesthetic, so you also get the sense that she is not really as comfortable there as she was in her old, much smaller house.'

She doesn't have time to adjust to her new surroundings, however, as it is not long before Katniss and Peeta are launched upon their Victory Tour, presenting Messina with an all-new challenge. The concept behind the portrayal of the other Districts was to show Katniss that the lives of others, about whom each District knows little, are just as difficult as her own. In addition, the plan was to show in some subtle ways Katniss becoming aware of a growing resentment and even resistance to the Capitol. Messina was keen to incorporate these psychological story elements into the designs. 'We show in little bits and pieces what Katniss is gleaning – that there's a kind of grassroots rebellion that is just starting in different places. It's in things like the line of graffiti we painted [in the train tunnel]: "the odds are never in your favour".'

Back in the Capitol, preparing for the Quarter Quell Games, Katniss is once again exposed to an entirely different way of life. For President Snow's mansion the production located a twenties-built property in Atlanta called Swan House. This would be the base from which President Snow would devise his plans to quell the growing rebellion, and it would be here that Katniss and Peeta would attend a decadent party thrown by the President. 'It made real sense that Snow would live in this sort of elegant house with a park-like feeling right in the middle of the Capitol. The architecture feels very real, which allows the people of the Capitol to bring the outrageousness to it,' Messina said.

As the Quarter Quell was a kind of 'all-star' Hunger Games, Messina felt the training centre and the apartments in which the Tributes stay during their preparation time in the Capitol should be new, too. The atrium of the Atlanta Marriot Marquis hotel (originally designed by architect John Portman) was adapted to stand in as the venue where Katniss and co. would stay. The giant, space-age lobby-and-elevators area was ideal for the movie's requirements.

The biggest challenge was yet to come, with Messina scrutinizing the second novel to develop his visual take on the new Games arena. There was a whole new series of threats to the Tributes that would be incorporated into the arena, including violent monkeys who attack the humans, uncanny Jabberjays and 'natural' (actually contrived by the Gamemakers) deadly lightning strikes, poisonous fog banks and a Cornucopia surrounded by water. 'When we were scouting in Hawaii,' said Messina, 'we saw a lot of lava formations, and Francis and I came upon the idea that the Cornucopia should sit on a rock island that would feel harsh and foreboding.'

The island had to also convey the clock motif identified by Wiress as the key to unlocking the Games of the Quarter Quell. The scene in which the entire island was seen to spin, complete with the actors hanging on for dear life, was one of the more difficult for the production to realize. Majorly expanded from its depiction in the novel, it was a scene that director Lawrence felt was especially cinematic. 'The moment in the arena when the Gamemaker starts to spin the Cornucopia: I'm very proud of that. We designed a very cool sequence and created a spinning island. I've never seen anything like it.'

Messina noted: 'It was all about getting the right forces to act on the actors' bodies and to get the light spinning at the right speed, but it was also very important to find a design safe enough to put our cast on. We used a system that's similar to the Ferris wheel, just a friction drive wheel on the outside of a big ring.' The requirements saw the special effects team, led by coordinator Steve Cremin, design new ways of working with water and designing wave effects. 'It's extremely challenging to manage a million and a half gallons of water quickly, to be able to drain it, fill it and create waves in it. But we felt it could be done – and it was done,' he said.

Lawrence had even more challenges for his cast and crew when he decided to shoot some pivotal sequences of the movie in the all-encompassing IMAX giant screen format. The large-format immersive film technology was central to Lawrence's ideas of bringing audiences even further into the world of Panem and having them come even closer to the experiences of Katniss. 'I wanted the arena to be the most visceral experience possible, all as seen from Katniss's inner point of view,' the director explained. 'Seeing her world through IMAX opens up the screen up and takes you inside the imagery.'

Belgian cinematographer Jo Willems supervised the use of the IMAX equipment to achieve the ambitious scope and scale of Lawrence's vision. Aiming to intensify the experiences of each of the characters, but especially those of Katniss, and in an attempt to give the new arena a unique look, the IMAX cinematography offered *Hunger Games* fans a new immediacy in their second trip to Panem. For the scene where Katniss gets her first look at the new arena, Lawrence wanted the IMAX technology to offer a dramatic moment that would mark a change in environment visually. 'IMAX photography makes for the most incredible moment as we see through Katniss's eyes this gorgeous, threatening new world for the first time. We are all awestruck along with her,' said Lawrence. 'I had been warned that the cameras are bigger, bulkier, and more awkward to hand hold, but we figured out ways to do exactly what we wanted. After you've spent days sweating, getting bitten by mosquitoes, lugging heavy equipment through the jungle and waiting for the long turnaround time of the cameras, when you see the dailies and see how unbelievably stunning it is . . . that is pretty satisfying.'

Filming also took place at Clayton County's International Park, known locally as 'the Beach'. An artificial man-made sandbank and lagoon, the Beach was originally constructed for the 1996 Summer Olympics that took place in Atlanta, Georgia. Some of the Cornucopia scenes were filmed here under more controlled conditions than could be achieved in Hawaii.

Scenes were also shot in New Jersey, in the Ringwood State Park, for two days in January 2013, as New Jersey film commissioner Steven Gorelick confirmed. 'They filmed scenes for the beginning of the movie in Ramapo State Forest. The weather worked perfectly for them. The water froze and there was a little snow and they got some very good footage.' Shooting with Liam was uncomfortable for Jennifer in the chilly temperatures as the actress was suffering from flu, making the two-day shoot doubly challenging.

Despite all the safety precautions involved in modern filmmaking, it is still possible for the leading artists to suffer the odd knock or bump especially when making action movies – as Liam found out. 'I twisted my knee,' he said. 'I try to just fight through it. There's so many people standing around waiting for you to do your thing. You feel sort of obligated not to let everyone down.'

One scene Josh had been dreading filming was the proposal scene. He knew he'd have to get it right not only to please general moviegoers, but mainly because millions of fans would be scrutinizing his every move and gesture to ensure he was being faithful to the text. There was one major drawback Josh hadn't reckoned on. 'The very first time I did it I got down on one knee,' he said, 'and my pants ripped right underneath! That was a fun moment because we tried to keep the scene going, but all the while Stanley Tucci and Jennifer are sitting there. I'm just smiling, knowing it's ripped right in the middle . . . We were just laughing [so] we had to eventually stop. It was pretty funny, but a little embarrassing. It's not a good omen, the first time I try to propose to a girl I rip my pants!'

Filming in Hawaii wrapped in December 2012, just in time for cast and crew to enjoy a break over Christmas, but they'd be back in action in the New Year for scheduled pick-ups and additional shooting. Reshoots took place in January and February 2013, with Jennifer Lawrence having to dye her hair 'Katniss black' once more, while Josh Hutcherson had to revert to his 'Peeta blond' look. The reshoots came the week after the still-blonde Jennifer had picked up her *Silver Linings Playbook* Oscar in Los Angeles, with a quick visit to a Beverly Hills hair salon in between. The production returned to Hawaii for some brief pick-up shots, and the primary photography phase of the production concluded in April 2013, by which time Francis Lawrence was deep into editing footage and working on post-production. He had a tight schedule ahead of him to complete the movie for its November 2013 worldwide release and to prepare to begin shooting on *Mockingjay* that September.

Visual effects supervisor Janek Sirrs, whose immediate work before *Catching Fire* included the box-office blockbusters *The Avengers* and *Iron Man 3*, as well as Francis Lawrence's *I Am Legend*, was responsible for the teams who would produce the film's 1,000 visual effects shots. Having worked with the director before, Sirrs knew Lawrence would want the effects to serve the story and not stand out as empty spectacle. 'Francis tends toward a very naturalistic style so it was important that the effects didn't draw unwarranted attention,' said Sirrs. 'The goal was not to regard the effects-heavy sequences any differently from the "regular" sequences. Creating a totally believable, realistic world was paramount. If you're asking the audience to buy into an alternate reality then the last thing you want them to be paying attention to is the environment, rather than the performances. If the audience doesn't question how the visual effects work, then we know we've done our job properly.'

Lawrence was especially keen to use the post-production visual effects work to make clear distinctions between District 12 or the Capitol and the world inside the arena where the Games take place. Effects would be used to augment the hot, humid and oppressive feel of the jungle in which the Tributes struggle to survive. The team compiled a photographic database of various jungles worldwide (especially Costa Rica), then selected the kind of trees and foliage that would suit the planned environment. The effects would not work on their own, so extra steps had to be taken during shooting of the live action to help 'sell' the cinematic illusion.

'Between takes the actors were being constantly spritzed down with water, and smoke was pumped through the locations to create the illusion of moisture and mist hanging in the air to add to the realism,' said Sirrs. In addition, there was the challenge of realistically realizing the new Cornucopia, amid the photorealistic jungle elements. 'Every piece of foliage that you see there, all the palm trees, banyan trees, smaller bushes, and so on, are completely rendered 3D models, with all the individual leaves blowing in the wind adding a sense of lifelike movement.'

As often on large complex films, especially those with a limited production time and a set release date, some key visual effects work was farmed out to various independent companies. Among those working on *Catching Fire*, Oscar-winner Double Negative was particularly prominent. The British company had been in business since 1998, supplying effects work for such productions as *Sherlock Holmes* (2009), *Inception* (2010), the two-part *Harry Potter and the Deathly Hallows* (2010 and 2011) and James Bond adventure *Skyfall* (2012). Visual effects supervisor Adrian de Wet oversaw some 400 of *Catching Fire*'s key effects shots, including the Avenues of the Tributes sequence, and the fire effects of the outfits worn by Katniss and Peeta during President Snow's reception. For the Avenues of the Tributes, almost everything was digitally created including the roads, barriers, fountains, background buildings, the President's Circle and the layout of the Capitol visible behind the Tributes.

The company also contributed work to the arena environment, including additional poison fog effects, the tidal wave that strikes the Cornucopia and the deadly Jabberjays. The fog, in particular, was a tricky effect to achieve in a convincing manner. 'There was much discussion back and forth as to how the fog should behave,' said de Wet. 'The brief was that it should be like an unstoppable wave moving through the jungle. One of the challenges here was the sequence was shot without any fog, and then we had to add the fog while still keeping continuity of speed and direction, allowing the fog to interact with the jungle vegetation, all at IMAX resolution.'

Perhaps the most difficult of all the sequences in the book to bring to life on the screen was the monkey attack in which a horde of brightly coloured primates emerge from the jungle and strike at Katniss, Peeta and their allies. The sequence was the responsibility of Guy Williams of WETA Digital, the New Zealand company established by director Peter Jackson initially to provide effects work for his *The Lord of the Rings* movies. 'Francis wanted it to feel like a very real moment, as Katniss, Peeta and Finnick face an extreme threat to their survival,' said Williams. 'His idea was to build the scene so the audience starts out fascinated by the monkeys, only to get more and more anxious as it becomes clear how dangerous they are.'

Real-life primates were studied in depth to reveal how

they moved and how they behaved, with a close focus on two particular species: drills, an endangered species found in African forests that are powerfully built and have fearsome fangs, and mandrills, colourful monkeys that are the largest of their species. The combination of these two types fed into the creation of *Catching Fire*'s monkey creatures. 'We basically fused the more ferociously primal body of a drill with the garish colouring of the mandrill,' said Williams. 'Everything started from real monkeys, and our fantastic animation supervisor, Daniel Barrett, found tons of references from zoos, so we had a large reference library of movements from which to find just the right twitches and mannerisms.'

On set, to evoke the presence of the attacking monkeys for the cast, the effects crew rigged up cardboard cut-outs of the creatures and also used small stunt performers as stand-ins. 'I'm sure there are some out-takes that have me doing my best monkey impersonations as well!' said Sirrs. Along with water and waves, recreating the visual effect of animal fur in the digital realm is a huge challenge, especially when that fur is combined with water and has to appear realistic when wet. For Williams, all the hard work paid off in the final movie: 'When you are able to create something that feels so real to people, that is extremely fulfilling.'

For Jennifer Lawrence, shooting *Catching Fire* was a challenging experience that reunited her with old friends, introduced her to some new ones and left her nursing a few movie-related injuries. 'There were a lot of six-day weeks,' Jennifer said, 'and the schedule was exhausting. But it's just so much fun to get back with everybody. It's pretty much the same crew, and obviously Josh is the same. Francis is such an amazing visionary, I think he's doing an incredible job. I kicked myself. Only I didn't kick myself, I hit myself in the face with an eight-pound carbon fibre bow. My own arm betrayed me.'

13

RELEASING *CATCHING FIRE*

The hype was always going to be extraordinary for the second film in *The Hunger Games* series. The first movie had surprised many with its huge opening weekend at the box office and by the way the film appealed beyond those who were already fans of the novels. For many cinema-goers, *The Hunger Games* was the less-twee antidote to other teen screen fare like the *Harry Potter* series and the *Twilight* movies. All the indications were that *Catching Fire* could be an even bigger film with many movie pundits predicting the worldwide box office could even push the film over the $1 billion barrier.

The first teaser trailer hit cinemas cleverly attached to the final film in the *Twilight* series, *Breaking Dawn*, *Part 2*, on 16 November 2012 – almost a full year before the film would be released. Nothing more than a mockingjay pin – the logo for the film – aflame, the forty-second teaser ended with the legend 'Every revolution begins with a spark' and the release date of 22 November 2013. Continuing the efforts by Lionsgate to involve fans in promotion, the teaser was followed by the announcement of a sweepstakes competition allowing twelve fans to have their names listed in the end credits. Over the following months, into 2013, various key images, including distinctive solo character portraits, were strategically released to magazines such as *Entertainment Weekly* and on specific websites.

All this was mere prelude to the release of the full teaser trailer, first screened during the 2013 MTV Movie Awards on 14 April 2013, and presented by Liam Hemsworth in front of a giant, flaming mockingjay symbol. The two-minute trailer set up the underlying opposition between Katniss and President Snow – who describes Katniss as an unwelcome 'beacon of hope' for the downtrodden population – that would drive much of the movie. This was followed a month later by the reveal of the movie's newest poster, featuring Katniss – bow in hand – standing atop a rocky outcrop with the clouds in the sky behind her forming insubstantial angel wings. The heroic slogan read: 'The sun persists in rising, so I make myself stand.'

April also saw the film screening out of competition at the prestigious Cannes Film Festival in France, with most of the main cast, director Francis Lawrence and producers Jon Kilik and Nina Jacobson in attendance. The exposure gave the film a welcome boost of publicity and resulted in many video and print interviews to sustain fan interest until the November release. Another major part of the marketing strategy was the huge presence of *Catching Fire* at the San Diego Comic-Con in July. A major showcase for geek-friendly movies, games, television and comics, Comic-Con had grown hugely from a much more low-key event in the seventies to a platform, with over 130,000 attendees, that the Hollywood studios had been taking seriously for several years. As well as exclusive footage sneak-peeks, Lionsgate promised major cast members and a brand new trailer. A thirty-minute panel featured Jennifer, Liam and Josh alongside other cast members in the massive Hall H of the San Diego Convention Centre on the Saturday of the weekend event. The new two-and-a-half minute trailer kept the IMAX arena footage to a minimum, but did more work setting up wider events. When it hit the internet days later, the new trailer quickly reached 7.5 million views, making it one of the most viewed movie trailers of all time. The final trailer for the film debuted on television during the fourth game of the 2013 baseball World Series on Sunday, 27 October. Patient fans were finally rewarded with some in-arena footage, including images of Katniss running, screaming and shooting arrows. More action-oriented, with a voiceover by Donald Sutherland's President Snow, and more impactful at just over one minute long, the final trailer was the last chance to attract uncommitted moviegoers to check out the film on opening weekend.

Some of the more unusual promotional items of merchandise reflected the role of high fashion in life in the Capitol. The CoverGirl Capitol Collection *Catching Fire* make-up range and the Net-A-Porter ready-to-wear *Catching Fire* inspired fashion were seen by some to miss the entire point of the *Hunger Games* message. Heather Long, writing in the *Guardian*, took these items to task: 'There's just one massive problem with this "beauty campaign": the Capitol represents everything wrong with society in the *Hunger Games* trilogy. No one in their right mind should aspire to look like that. We're supposed to be horrified by it.' She went on to cite Suzanne Collins's original inspiration for the movies and highlighted that the point of the books (and the films) is that the superficial world of the Capitol should be rejected, not willingly embraced. 'The people who live there are so blinded by their lifestyle that they don't fully grasp that they're putting on "games" where children are killing each other,' wrote Long. 'In fact, they're cheering it on like most people do sports teams. They make bets on who will die and laugh about it. That's what CoverGirl is worshipping. It's as if no one read the books or even saw the first movie. These brands trying to capitalize on *The Hunger Games*'s popularity should have thrown their marketing ideas into the fire.'

Producer Nina Jacobson said they hadn't simply accepted such seemingly contradictory promotional ideas without giving them some serious thought. 'We talked about this a lot from the beginning,' said Jacobson. 'Suzanne and [Lionsgate's Chief Marketing Officer] Tim Palen have a very, very open relationship – communicative and candid. Tim has always said, "Above all, do no harm." I think that what we found was that there was a way to have this sort of meta campaign: a campaign for the Capitol. The way that I look at it is, we as filmmakers always try in our story-telling [to] identify with the Districts. Katniss represents the Districts, the poorest of the poor. As a nation, we have plenty of Capitol in us. That gap that exists between the Districts and the Capitol – between the 99 per cent and the one per cent – is so much a part of the way that we live. The Capitol Couture Campaign and the campaigns that play on all the excess of the Capitol are, in their own way, reminders not to let ourselves off the hook. These books are dystopian fiction, but we're talking about us. I feel that the campaign [sparks discussion about] Capitol values in the mainstream conversation. It's also very worthwhile for us all to be reminded that we're incriminated in that side of things too.'

Aside from seeming misfires on the make-up and fashion fronts (and the Subway 'fiery footlong collection' of sandwiches that didn't seem to reflect the *Hunger Games* ethos either), the marketing efforts by Lionsgate, their consultants and partners, were extremely effective. More in keeping with the books and films was the launch of the mobile game 'Panem Run' as the movie opened. An 'endless runner' game (in which the player keeps moving until they die), Panem Run took the player through various Districts, where they could collect supplies or hit archery targets. 'Being able to play as a citizen of Panem further expands the world-building experience we've created for fans,' said Danielle De Palma, Lionsgate Senior Vice President of Digital Marketing. 'The game provides an exciting new narrative for the core fans while offering a challenge for players of all skill levels.'

The international press junkets and premieres for the film in early- and mid-November were dubbed the '*Catching Fire* Victory Tour' by Lionsgate, and it took the main cast members and producers as well as director Francis Lawrence around the world to help launch the movie in each of the major territories. The director summed up what he felt he'd achieved with his first movie in the *Hunger Games* series. 'I really loved how the world opens up in the second book,' he said. 'The mythology opens up, the story's much more complex, you see more of the Districts and Capitol, and you really start to get a sense of the meaning of things. This one's very, very different. The arena's much more active. And the movie's about different things, thematically: it's about the beginning of rebellion, and Katniss becoming a symbol, and there's much more love story. I really connected with the overarching ideas of the entire series and the idea of the consequences of war: what it means to the world, how it changes people, the loss involved and the consequence of it all.' With the Victory Tour drawing to a close there was little cast, crew or marketeers could do except sit back and wait to see how many tickets sold over the opening weekend beginning on 22 November 2013.

As with the first film, the adaptation from book to screen saw many changes, some minor, some major, but all noticed by fans. It wasn't just Bonnie and Twill who went missing between the book and the film. While largely happy with the movie, some fans felt the heart of the story had gone missing somewhere between paper (or Kindle) and cinema screen.

The movie spends less time in District 12 than the book, compressing the time in which Katniss is dealing with her post-traumatic stress. She and Gale are also shown to have a much more relaxed relationship in the movie than depicted in the book (the film opens with them hunting together, rather than Katniss out alone). Both of them are trying to discover what they mean to each other and how Peeta figures in the picture. The slow build-up of the newly draconian repression of the Peacekeepers in District 12 is also not given the time or attention afforded it in the book.

The slowly dawning awareness by Katniss of the growing resistance across the Districts is downplayed by the movie, and the backstory surrounding Haymitch Abernathy is not focused on as much as in the book, removing one of the strongest echoes between the actions of Katniss and those of her mentor. In contrast, the role of Caesar Flickerman is enlarged in the film as he works far better on screen as a link between viewers and what's going on in the arena during the Games, as well as a window through which viewers get to see life in the Capitol. Similarly, the roles of President Snow and Plutarch Heavensbee are considerably enhanced, as the movie offers many more scenes away from Katniss (the first-person narration of the books eliminates this) that fill in the larger world, as well as the politics of Panem. The extrapolation of these important roles was one of the factors that attracted actors like Donald Sutherland and Philip Seymour Hoffman to the world of *The Hunger Games*.

The symbolic appearance of bread (as in the first book) is downplayed by the movie, as with the elimination of Bonnie and Twill, so also goes their mockingjay cracker. In the novel, bread is used in the arena as part of a code to trigger the moment of rebellion, but it is missing from the movie, making the timing of the group's actions appear rather more arbitrary. At the climax, rather than go after Enobaria, Finnick is put in the path of Katniss's arrow, giving him the chance (in a much more cinematic moment) to repeat the line from Haymitch about knowing who the enemy is, and so confirming his place as one of the rebels.

Even at 146 minutes (although matching many modern blockbuster movies), the *Catching Fire* movie simply couldn't find room for everything in the novel. Some things are compressed: as soon as new Head Peacekeeper Romulus Thread arrives he instigates a reign of terror, burning down The Hob black market. It is this, rather than being caught poaching, that causes Gale to run afoul of Thread and leads to his public whipping. The changes make the scenes much more cinematic and dynamic. Many more scenes are simply missing, such as Katniss discovering the fence around District 12 has now been electrified, her wedding-dress photoshoot, the bonding between Katniss and Peeta on the roof before the Quarter Quell, and the discovery that the Capitol always screens the same stock footage of the supposedly destroyed District 13. As the loss of Peeta's leg was never depicted in the first movie, he doesn't have a prosthetic – which slows him down during the escape from the poison fog in the novel – in the second, either. The scene in which Plutarch Heavensbee tips Katniss off about his affiliations and about the secret of the new arena by showing her a mockingjay watch is also missing. Although mentioned during the pre-Games television interview, Katniss's supposed pregnancy seems to be forgotten by the movie as soon as the characters enter the arena. The character of Effie Trinket is given a moment of humanity, pre-Games, that doesn't feature in the book, allowing Elisabeth Banks a key scene.

Each of the changes and omissions was thought through by the writers and cleared by the book's author. Even though the aim was for a faithful adaptation changes were inevitable. 'Whenever you're adapting something that's a twelve- or fourteen-hour read down to something that has to be around two hours, there's going to be some cuts,' said Lawrence. 'It's a real challenge to keep everything in. There are a few scenes that didn't make it.'

With a budget almost twice that of *The Hunger Games* at $130 million, *Catching Fire* was expected to look spectacular, but would the critics – who had largely welcomed the first movie – be as well-disposed second time round? The *San Francisco Chronicle* praised the strong performances, not often the high point of either action-dramas or franchise movies from Hollywood. 'Jennifer Lawrence does not act like someone in an action movie, but like someone in a life-and-death drama that happens to have lots of running and jumping. Director Francis Lawrence makes sure that not a single performance is below par. Every effort is made to portray this awful future world as something real and to have the actors react with the right sense of terror and entrapment. Philip Seymour Hoffman is a strong new addition as Plutarch Heavensbee, the new master of the games and the president's closest collaborator. Like [Donald] Sutherland, [Jennifer] Lawrence and the rest of the actors, he isn't slumming. He brings a magnetic and elusive calm to the role.'

The *New York Times* agreed, praising Jennifer. 'The actress is more expressive here than she was in the first movie [which goes] a long way to clarifying Katniss and turning a girl with a bow into the charismatic figure she was always meant to be.' *Rolling Stone* dubbed *Catching Fire* 'spectacular in every sense of the word . . . watch the sublime Jennifer Lawrence take the role of Katniss Everdeen to new levels of ferocity and feeling. Pop-culture escapism can be thrilling when dished out by experts. Katniss is a character worth a handful of sequels. And Lawrence lights up the screen. You'll follow her anywhere.'

More generally, the film won high praise, despite its position as just one entry in a multi-film story. 'An effective piece of melodramatic popular entertainment,' said the *Los Angeles Times*, while *Entertainment Weekly* said *Catching Fire* was 'smoothly exciting', and the *Hollywood Reporter* said the film was a 'carefully crafted action-drama in which the subversive seeds planted in the first story take welcome root', while *Variety* noted its 'revolutionary spirit . . . [Catching Fire] rewrites the rules, which not only makes for a more exciting death match, but also yields a rich socio-political critique in the process.'

There were some who didn't fall into line with the largely positive reviews, with the *New Yorker* highlighting a climax that came across as 'an incoherent, rapid blur that will send the audience scurrying back to the book to find out what's supposed to be going on'. The *Financial Times* took the view that *The Hunger Games* movies were 'truly the most cynically machine-tooled, ultimate fantasy yet penned and screened', while website Little White Lies said that while 'Jennifer Lawrence sparkles once again, this diluted sequel fails to ignite'.

None of the very few negative write-ups of *Catching Fire* did anything to damage its triumph at the domestic US and international box office, where it outshone the previous instalment. The film grabbed a November release record with a $158 million debut weekend in the US, beating the $152.5 March 2012 opening of the first movie. It beat the previous November release record holder, *The Twilight Saga: New Moon*, which had opened in November 2009 with $142.8 million. Only three films (irrespective of opening month) had taken more in their opening weekends than *Catching Fire*: *The Avengers* ($207.4 million), *Iron Man 3* ($174.1 million) and *Harry Potter and the Deathly Hallows, Part 2* ($169.2 million). It also closely matched *The Dark Knight Rises* as the highest 2D-only opening, just falling short of its $160.9 million in 2012. Although not released in 3D, *Catching Fire* did benefit from the decision to release the movie on IMAX screens, with the aspect ratio changing for the arena sequences. IMAX screenings alone over the opening weekend added $12.6 million to the domestic total.

Internationally, across sixty-three territories, the film took an additional $146.6 million making for an overall opening weekend total of $307.7 million, 45 per cent up on *The Hunger Games*'s $211.8 million worldwide opening the previous year. In Germany and Denmark the new film took three times as much at the box office as the first, while in the UK, Netherlands and Sweden *Catching Fire* took more than twice as much as *The Hunger Games*, revealing how the novels' popularity had spread further outside the US following the first movie.

The second and third weekends on release saw the movie take an additional $74.2 million and $26.2 million at the US box office before other releases took its place as the no. 1 movie, including Disney's *Frozen* and the second movie in Peter Jackson's series based on *The Hobbit*. By mid-December, outside the US the film had grossed $336.7 million, which when added to the US three-week total of $347.9 million gave an estimated worldwide box-office take of $684.6 million, almost matching the final overall figure for *The Hunger Games* of $691.2 million (which was after twenty-four weeks on release).

The fourth week saw the movie take $13.7 million at the US box office, followed by a dip to $8.8 million in the fifth, before the movie rallied once more (thanks to Christmas holiday attendance) to $10 million on the sixth week of release. The first three weeks of 2014 saw the movie take $7 million, $4.3 million and $2.9 million for an overall gross of $418 million in the US. *Catching Fire* was at the top of the list for the biggest grossing movie of 2013, beating out hot favourite *Iron Man 3* (on $409 million) and surprise hit *Despicable Me 2* (on $368 million). Internationally, *Catching Fire* scored an additional $433 million for a total take of $851 million after just two months on release, way ahead of *The Hunger Games*' final total of $691.2 million. It was anticipated that by the time it finished its theatrical run, *Catching Fire* would have crossed the $1 billion barrier worldwide. The prospects for the two *Mockingjay* movies over Thanksgiving of 2014 and 2015 were stratospheric.

PART THREE: THE REVOLUTION

14

HOLLYWOOD VICTORS

Jennifer Lawrence emerged from the arena after *Catching Fire* an even bigger Hollywood star than before. Not only was she heading up one of the most popular cinema franchises of recent years, she felt she brought something unique to the characterization of Katniss Everdeen. 'She's suffering from post-traumatic stress from the first Games,' said Jennifer of Katniss in *Catching Fire*. 'She's trying to get her life back. She is living in the Victors' Village now, she doesn't have to hunt any more – which makes her feel useless and bored – and there is part of her life that Gale will never understand. Peeta is the only one that truly knows what she went through. When she has to go back to the Capitol, it's not a foreign world to her any more. Not that she likes it, but she understands it now and how to work it.'

It could almost be a description of Jennifer's own adventures in filmmaking, rising from little-known indie actress to pampered Hollywood icon with her own Oscar over the course of a few years. Her Victors' Village was now Hollywood, and she'd find herself rebelling against the easy temptation to rest on her laurels following the amazing success of the first two movies in *The Hunger Games* saga. She knew she had two more to go, and could reasonably rely on them to be hits, but that didn't mean she wasn't going to challenge herself and attempt to fit in as many diverse parts as she sensibly could before *Mockingjay* hit cinemas.

Two other films that featured Jennifer would be released in the wake of *Catching Fire*. *Serena* was shot immediately after Jennifer wrapped on *Silver Linings Playbook* in early 2012, just as *The Hunger Games* was hitting theatres, and it reunited her with her *Silver Linings* co-star, Bradley Cooper. Jennifer had brought the screenplay to Cooper, asking him if he'd be interested in taking the male lead. Danish filmmaker Susanne Bier (*Things We Lost in the Fire*, 2007) directed from the 2008 Ron Rash historical novel. The film had once been mooted as a Darren Aronofsky project to star Angelina Jolie. Set in North Carolina in 1929, the story follows two newlyweds, George and Serena Pemberton, who strike out to make their fortune in the timber business. Serena proves herself to be not only a formidable businesswoman but also a pioneer who thrives in the wilderness. Things take a turn for the melodramatic when Serena discovers she cannot have children and in a manic fit of jealousy sets out to murder George's illegitimate son from a previous liaison. The married pair find themselves turning their cunning and guile upon each other. Jennifer's *Catching Fire* co-star Toby Jones also appeared.

This film – ideally suited to Jennifer's indie credibility – had been completed but sat on the shelf without a distributor. The long editing process embarked upon by perfectionist director Bier further added to delays. During editing, Bier said: 'It's coming along great, and they're wonderful.

It's set in a logging camp in 1929; it's very romantic and very dark. It isn't finished yet . . . but sometime during the spring [2014] it should be ready.' Like Jennifer, director Bier was also an Oscar winner, for *In a Better World* which won for Best Foreign Language Film in 2011. In late November 2013, just as *Catching Fire* was hitting big at the box office, producers began to shop *Serena* around potential distributors. It was expected that *Serena* would reach the film festival circuit from April 2014 before coming to cinemas, long after the late-2013 release of a third movie featuring Jennifer and Bradley Cooper, *American Hustle*. The other 'on the shelf' Jennifer Lawrence movie released in 2013 was the 2007-made *The Devil You Know*, that co-starred Lena Olin.

After November 2013's release of *Catching Fire*, Jennifer was set to dominate movie screens again during the Christmas holiday season thanks to the release of *American Hustle*. Set among con men (and women) in the seventies, David O. Russell's film was his follow-up to *Silver Linings Playbook* and it brought that film's two stars together again for a third time. With a screenplay written by Eric Warren Singer (and contributed to by the director), the film was based on an FBI operation of the late seventies/early eighties that led to the conviction of a United States senator, six members of the House of Representatives, a member of the New Jersey State Senate and members of the Philadelphia City Council, and an inspector for the Immigration and Naturalization Service. The FBI hired a convicted con artist to entrap several officials it believed were guilty of corruption in public office. Bribes were offered – and accepted – in return for political and business favours, resulting in the convictions.

Originally more provocatively titled 'American Bullshit', the screenplay had reached the upper echelons of the so-called 'black list' of highly rated yet unmade scripts. The film was eventually set up at Sony with *Argo* director Ben

Affleck originally to direct. When that didn't work out, David O. Russell picked up the project and cast Christian Bale in the starring role of con man Irving Rosenfeld and Amy Adams as Sydney Prosser, his partner-in-crime and mistress. Cooper was brought in to play wild card Federal Agent Richie DiMaso, with Jennifer cast as Irving Rosenfeld's big-mouthed wife, Rosalyn. It was shot in and around Boston, Massachusetts, between March and May 2013, immediately after Jennifer had wrapped on shooting the *X-Men* sequel. The making of the movie had been interrupted by the events surrounding the Boston Marathon bombings of April 2013.

The finished movie quickly started attracting Oscar buzz based on early clips and the first trailer. The period setting, immaculately realized through hair, make-up and fashions-that-time-forgot, as well as the little-remembered true-life story, struck a chord. Jennifer was immediately a Best Supporting Actress Oscar contender for 2014, thanks to her scene-stealing moments with a 'science oven' (her name for the then new-fangled microwave oven) and singing Paul McCartney's theme to the James Bond movie *Live and Let Die* while aggressively doing housework! Her win as Best Supporting Actress at the Golden Globes presaged her later Best Supporting Actress Oscar nomination, her third Oscar nod in just four years.

Director Russell was in a perfect position to determine if Jennifer's post-*Silver Linings Playbook* success and Oscar triumph had affected the young actress. '[She] didn't really change,' he said. Working with Jennifer was, according to the director, 'very dynamic and sweet and fun. She had an enormous amount of fun playing this role [with] all the insanity.' He described her role as that of an 'unhinged Long Island housewife. You ask a lot and she brings it. That was our talk on *Silver Linings Playbook*. That's what we both enjoy. Have a loose, trusting environment, and then she can bring it. That's what's fun to do.'

Russell had invented and written the role of Rosalyn especially for Jennifer, and she was happy to forgo a planned break from making movies in order to take the part. 'Rosalyn is 100 per cent a product of David's imagination,' she said. 'She's a manic, depressive alcoholic and I couldn't wait [to play it]. Plus, I got to make out with Christian Bale. I couldn't say no. Then when I was on set, I was like "This is much more important than a vacation." It's so much better for my brain to be creatively stimulated in this way, it reminded me: "This is what I love."' Just like Katniss in the Victors' Village, it appears that Jennifer too sometimes feels useless and bored if she isn't working on a new movie.

American Hustle proved to be a winner with critics, awards bodies and audiences alike. Released widely on 20 December 2013, the movie made the American Film Institute's list of the Top 10 Films of the Year, as well as scoring 10 Oscar nominations, including Best Film, Best Director, Best Actor (Christian Bale), Best Actress (Amy Adams), Best Supporting Actor (Bradley Cooper), Best Supporting Actress (Jennifer Lawrence), Best Original Screenplay, Best Costume Design, Best Production Design and Best Editing. In the event, the film won none of the categories it was nominated in. Although Katniss spends a lot of time kissing Peeta, in *American Hustle* Jennifer's character got her smooch on with Amy Adams's Sydney. 'She does a great job [kissing],' said Amy of Jennifer. 'She has very soft lips. She's a really awesome woman.'

Jennifer Lawrence would end 2013 as the star of the biggest grossing movie of the year with *Catching Fire*; the 'Entertainer of the Year' according to the Associated Press (AP), beating Miley Cyrus; and about to receive a third Oscar nomination. Jennifer was described in a statement from the AP as 'not only talented and beautiful, but . . . incredibly intelligent, genuine, funny and well-spoken in her public appearances and interviews. It's refreshing to see a young woman not squandering her talent and success by succumbing to the temptations many do in Hollywood and who actively speaks about the ridiculous behaviour of some of her peers.'

Jennifer returned to her childhood love of goofy movies for her cameo in 2014's comedy sequel *Dumb and Dumber To*. The original 1994 film was a favourite in the Lawrence household when Jennifer was growing up and wanted to join in with her brothers' raucous laughter at the antics of Lloyd (Jim Carey) and Harry (Jeff Daniels). In September 2013 it was confirmed that Jennifer would appear briefly in the film as a younger version of Kathleen Turner's character. Intended to be a secret cameo, news of Jennifer's participation in the long-time coming sequel leaked in the *Hollywood Reporter*. 'I have completely memorized *Dumb and Dumber*, *Anchorman*, and *Step Brothers*,' said Jennifer of her taste in movie comedy growing up. The sequel was shooting in Atlanta at the same time as *Mockingjay*, making it easy for Jennifer to appear. Many of the cast of *Mockingjay* made a day trip to the *Dumb and Dumber To* set, and the news of Jennifer's cameo made headlines worldwide.

Jennifer's other 2014 movie was her near-naked, all-blue reappearance as Mystique in the seventies-set *X-Men: Days of Future Past*. Functioning as both a sequel to the sixties-set *X-Men: First Class* (2011) and *The Wolverine* (2013), and a prequel to the earlier *X-Men* trilogy (whose final entry was 2006's *X-Men: The Last Stand*), the movie saw Wolverine travel back to the past from a dystopian future in order to save mankind's super-powered mutants from extermination. The movie brought together the separate teams of actors who played both the younger and older versions of many of the main characters, including James McAvoy and Patrick Stewart, both playing Professor

Xavier, and Michael Fassbender and Ian McKellen, both as Magneto.

For Jennifer, the superhero film offered her an opportunity to further develop her very unusual character. '[When] we find Raven, she's split off from Eric and Charles and she's her own agent,' she said. 'She has one mission of trying to assassinate somebody and it will be her first kill. Because we've seen her in the future and what she becomes, this is a turning point for her.' The actress was very happy that this time around her extensive make-up process had changed after she suffered severe skin irritation making the first movie. 'I'm so excited because I'm going to wear a body suit. It will be from the neck down so it will cut out time and the blisters. Some of the Mystique look is a little different, but we're still using the same paint,' she said. 'I'm naked. When I do get to wear clothes, I love the seventies outfits. She's different in this film, too. She was struggling – like a lot of normal humans – with the way she looked, and she was covered up a lot in the first movie, but this time she is mutant and proud.' The mutant movie was scheduled for release in May 2014.

Production on the back-to-back shoot for the two *Mockingjay* movies began in September 2013, before *Catching Fire* had opened at cinemas, so Jennifer was intensely busy between filming the final movies and worldwide promotional duties for the second *Hunger Games* film right through to the end of the year.

Jennifer's male co-stars had not been idle, planning future projects they hoped would capitalize on their *Hunger Games* fame. Josh Hutcherson was lined up to star in *Paradise Lost* (not based on John Milton's epic poem – Jennifer's frequent co-star Bradley Cooper had been working on a film version of that). This *Paradise Lost* was to be a biopic of drugs kingpin Pablo Escobar, with Benicio del Toro tipped to play the starring role. Josh would be playing surfer Nick, who falls in love with Escobar's daughter. The film was to be the directorial debut of Italian actor Andrea Di Stefano (Dario Argento's *Phantom of the Opera*, 1998), who'd also written the script. Di Stefano had featured opposite Johnny Depp in *Before Night Falls* (2000) and as the priest in Oscar-winner *The Life of Pi* (2012).

Josh was also expected to reprise his role of Sean Anderson in the latest entry in the *Journey* series of movies. *Journey 3: From the Earth to the Moon*, sequel to 2008's *Journey to the Centre of the Earth* and 2012's *Journey 2: The Mysterious Island*, was in development and would be based upon Jules Verne's 1865 French novel *From the Earth to the Moon*. Hutcherson had also established his own production company, JetLag Productions, through which he was planning to star in and produce a film entitled *Ape*. *Repo Men* (2010) director Miguel Sapochnik would direct the tale of a young man (Josh) struggling with the effect of mental illness on himself and those he loves, while also keeping a dark family secret. The script for the psychological thriller was by newcomer Jon Johnstone. Josh said '*Ape* is a passion project and to see it get made would truly be a dream come true.'

Liam Hemsworth was also plotting his future career with roles in action movie *Aurora Rising* and thriller *Cut Bank* (both due for release in 2014). In *Aurora Rising*, Liam was set to play a cocksure and reckless military pilot recruited to join an elite team who test fly the next generation of smart fighter planes, just as international hostilities break out. The screenplay was by rap video filmmaker Christian Gudegast, whose previous work included *A Man Apart* (2003). It was expected Gudegast would also direct *Aurora Rising*.

In *Cut Bank*, Liam joins co-stars John Malkovich, Bruce Dern and Billy Bob Thornton in a tale of a young man's attempt to escape the Montana small town of Cut Bank where he grew up, only to face a tough time when he arrives in the 'big city' with his girlfriend, Cassandra (Teresa Palmer). Liam (who replaced Armie Hammer) plays the young athlete turned auto-mechanic Dwayne McLaren, while Matt Shakman (*Psych*, *Revenge*) directed from a screenplay (highlighted on the 2009 'black list' of acclaimed screenplays) by Roberto Patino (*Sons of Anarchy*, *Prime Suspect*). The film began production in summer 2013 in Edmonton, Canada.

Finally, Sam Claflin, who'd been brought to new prominence with *Catching Fire* despite previous film hits *Snow White and the Huntsman* (2012) and *Pirates of the Caribbean: On Stranger Tides* (2011), would follow his first *Hunger Games* movie with some diverse roles. He executive produced (but did not star in) a short entitled *A Thousand Empty Glasses* directed by Andrew Nolan and written by Mark Finbow, suggesting – like Jennifer – he harboured ambitions to work behind the scenes in film production. The short focused on a drunken evening among a group of friends that results in one of them making a life-changing decision. It was nominated for Best UK Short at Raindance Film Festival 2012.

Either side of the two *Mockingjay* movies, Sam had a variety of projects lined up for release. He was set to lead the cast in *Posh*, which sees two first-year students at Oxford University join the infamous 'Riot Club' where a single evening's events can make or break someone's reputation for life. Written by Laura Wade (based upon her play) and directed by Lone Scherfig (*An Education*, 2009), the film would reunite Sam with his *Mockingjay* co-star Natalie Dormer. While in England, Sam was also lined up to feature in Hammer Films's newest horror movie *The Quiet Ones*, directed by John Pogue (*Quarantine 2: The Terminal*, 2011). He'd been shooting this movie when he'd got the call offering him the part of Finnick in *Catching Fire*, although *The Hunger Games* sequel would be released first. Inspired by true events, *The Quiet Ones* tells the story of a charismatic professor (Jared Harris) whose controversial methods lead his students down a dark path as part of a dangerous experiment to create a poltergeist from 'negative human energy'. The film was due for release in 2014, before *Mockingjay, Part 1*.

Also on Sam's slate were *Love, Rosie*, *The Laureate* and *Modern Life is Rubbish*. *Love, Rosie* was a romantic comedy Sam shot in Toronto in the summer of 2013 alongside *Mirror, Mirror* star Lily Collins. The pair played best friends since school who find their developing romantic feelings disrupting their lives. Christian Ditter directed from a screenplay by Juliette Towhidi (*Calendar Girls*, 2003). *The Laureate* would see Sam play the role of real-life poet Robert Graves in a stylish biopic written and directed by William Nunez. *Modern Life is Rubbish* was another romance in which Sam would play one half of a couple united in their love of music, but who are driven apart after a decade and have to face the tricky task of dividing up their extensive music collection. The film was written by Philip Gawthorne and directed by Daniel Gill.

All the main young actors leading *The Hunger Games* series were in a fortunate position: they had a pair of sure-fire hits in their future in the two *Mockingjay* movies, allowing them some latitude to choose the projects they wanted to tackle based on their own tastes, ambitions and future career plans.

15

MOCKINGJAY: INFLUENCES AND INSPIRATIONS

Mockingjay was the culmination of Suzanne Collins's work on *The Hunger Games* trilogy: this was the book that resolved many of the issues building through the two previous volumes, as well as increasing the stakes and the jeopardy faced by the main characters. New locations – primarily District 13 – were introduced, and old ones explored from a new angle. There were no Games this time, but the war that tears Panem apart functioned as a countrywide version of the Games, as Katniss and her allies penetrate the Capitol in an effort to overthrow President Snow. A new cast of characters presented Katniss Everdeen with a new set of moral dilemmas.

At the beginning of *Mockingjay* Katniss Everdeen has found a new life in District 13. Her home – District 12 – is gone, bombed into the dust by the Capitol. Her family and friends are safe, and Gale Hawthorne is with her in

District 13. Peeta Mellark, along with Johanna Mason, Enobaria and Annie Cresta have been captured by the Capitol. Peeta, who has been tortured, is seen interviewed by Caesar Flickerman, when he calls for a ceasefire between the rebels and the Capitol. District 13 is the base for the rebellion now breaking out across Panem, but Katniss is kept away from the fighting. Reluctantly she takes up another role: the 'mockingjay', a propaganda figurehead for the rebellion in posters and in propaganda films, called 'propos'. Former Head Gamemaker Plutarch Heavensbee is now a rebel filmmaker, producing these propaganda films.

Katniss has agreed to this role, but she sets her own terms: District 13 President Alma Coin must grant immunity for all the Hunger Games Tributes, including Katniss's friends, especially Peeta who some are now calling a traitor . . . and – most surprising of all to her friends (and the reader) – Katniss wants the opportunity to kill President Snow herself, an act of revenge for his assaults on her through the Games and on her friends in District 12.

A visit to District 8 to make a propaganda film puts Katniss amid the action for the first time when a hospital is destroyed. Electronics wizard Beetee hacks the Capitol's transmissions and broadcasts a rebellion 'propos' film over the airwaves. The Capitol attacks District 13, but the rebels survive in deep bunkers after a warning from Peeta. Katniss realizes the Capitol is making an example of Peeta, having him speak out against the rebels whenever she makes a broadcast: her words are literally hurting him. He is infused with tracker-jacker venom and conditioned to develop hatred for Katniss. A rebel rescue mission is mounted to retrieve Peeta and the other Tributes, but when they are reunited he attempts to kill Katniss as a result of his conditioning.

Gale devises a controversial but successful plan for an attack on District 2, and plans are prepared to assault the Capitol itself. Political games are being played among the rebels, however. Boggs, Coin's right-hand man and leader of Squad 451, explains to Katniss that the President fears the 'mockingjay' will replace her by popular acclaim after victory is won, so is using Peeta's condition to try to eliminate her, seeing Katniss as competition for the leadership. After Boggs is killed, Katniss takes over command of the squad (who were on a simple mission to produce 'propos'), telling them that they have a secret mission (which she has invented) to eliminate President Snow.

The urban warfare in the Capitol resembles Katniss's experiences in the Hunger Games, with mined pods, black waves of death and 'muttations' roaming the area. The Capitol declares Katniss and her rebel friends dead, while President Coin's broadcasts continue to use mockingjay imagery to fuel the fight. Battling to President Snow's mansion, Squad 451 lose several members including cameraman Castor, Mitchell (accidentally killed by Peeta) and Finnick, who is decapitated by lizard 'mutts' while in tunnels beneath the city.

Snow's mansion is surrounded by Capitol children as human shields to dissuade the rebels from attacking. As Katniss reaches the mansion, an air vehicle with Capitol markings drops supply packages that are really bombs, killing many. Rebel medics – including Prim, Katniss's sister – move in to help, but more bombs drop, severely burning Katniss and tragically killing Prim.

The war is won by the rebels but at great cost. During his trial Snow claims that the bombing of the children around his mansion that killed Prim was carried out by President Coin, not Capitol forces. Katniss realizes this is true, and may have been part of a plan originally devised by Gale. Poised to execute Snow using her signature bow, Katniss instead kills Coin, the true architect of the raid. Snow dies in the resulting riotous melee. After a suicide attempt, Katniss is eventually acquitted of murder due to insanity, and returns to District 12 with Haymitch. Months later a fully recovered Peeta arrives, and Katniss realizes he symbolized hope and strength for her throughout her ordeals. An epilogue set fifteen years later reveals that Katniss and Peeta have two children. The Hunger Games are a thing of the past, but Katniss fears what her children will think of their parents when they discover their true history.

The prime new location in *Mockingjay* is District 13, whose fate is remembered by the population of Panem as a warning of what happens when those who rule in the Capitol are angered. It was long believed that District 13, which specialized in nuclear technology and the mining of graphite, had been wiped off the map during the Dark Days that preceded the Hunger Games. In fact, the population survived underground, their leaders having agreed a mutual pact with the Capitol. District 13 controlled Panem's nuclear weapons, so the Capitol agreed to leave them alone, portraying the area as having been devastated to keep the rest of the remaining Districts in line.

District 13 became the base for the new rebellion against the Capitol. Life in the District is rather regimented, due to their limited resources, something that irritates Katniss. Food is carefully cultivated and equally carefully rationed to ensure everyone's survival. The rule of law is enforced, but the population are free citizens who also benefit from free education. Everyone over the age of fourteen is trained in military skills in preparation for the eventual assault on the Capitol. The rebellion has been many years in the planning, but the emergence of Katniss as a symbol of defiance during the 74th Games was the trigger for District 13's forces to spring into action.

District 8 and District 2 both feature in *Mockingjay* as the location of crucial battles in the war against the Capitol. As one of the first to openly rebel (in *Catching Fire*), District 8 was always going to be central to the rebellion's plans. It was from runaway District 8 residents Bonnie and Twill that Katniss first learned of the rumours of the survival of District 13, home of the rebellion. Katniss visits a hospital in District 8 as part of her propaganda duties; it is then deliberately targeted and bombed by Capitol forces. District 8 leader, Commander Paylor, commands greater loyalty from her followers than the rebellion's overall leader, President Coin.

As the home of weapon making, District 2 was also always a likely target for both sides in the war in Panem, more so for the rebels as the District was often seen as sympathetic and supportive of the rulers in the Capitol. Enobaria, the District 2 Tribute for the 75th Games, joined with the rebels after she was rescued from the clutches of the Capitol. District 2 is the last to fall to the rebels, with them particularly targeting 'the Nut' – the central mountain around which the District spreads, and in which the weapons cache was held – following an inspiring speech from Katniss to District 2's inhabitants.

Although there are no Games in *Mockingjay*, the dramatic urban warfare undertaken by Squad 451, including Katniss, in their attack on the Capitol serves the same purpose. The squad almost function as Tributes, sometimes working together and sometimes getting in each other's way, as they face off against a variety of obstacles, from the rampaging 'muttations', deadly light beams, traps in the form of pods or mines, to the Capitol's Peacekeeper troops. Their journey through the streets of the Capitol and in the tunnels underneath the city functions as a variation on a Hunger Games arena. Katniss discovers that her 'training' through two previous Hunger Games stands her in good stead in this real-world Quell.

Several new characters play key roles in the events of *Mockingjay*. Annie Cresta, from District 4, was reaped for the Quarter Quell Games, but was replaced by Mags who volunteered in her stead. She had been traumatized by her

previous experience in the arena when she won the 70th
Hunger Games and remained vulnerable. Her screaming is
simulated by Jabberjays and used by the Capitol to attack
Finnick, with whom she had a relationship. When they are
briefly reunited, Annie and Finnick are married and she
conceives a child with him, a son who is born after his death.
In the vote about whether to stage a final Hunger Games
to punish the Capitol by putting their children in a battle
to the death, Annie votes against – believing that would be
Finnick's wish. Annie is one of just seven winners of the
Hunger Games to survive the rebellion against the Capitol.

President Alma Coin is the leader of District 13 when
Katniss arrives there, but the Games veteran never really
trusts the older woman. Coin views Katniss as a threat to
her own political ambitions and future plans. She would
prefer if Katniss were a safely dead figurehead, rather than
a very much alive rabble-rouser who could usurp Coin's
ambitions to take over from Snow as President of Panem.
However, President Coin is clever enough to realize that
while Katniss is around, she can also be used in a manner
helpful to the rebellion, in the hope that she will be eliminated during the course of the war, either through Coin's
deliberate machinations or in battle. It is Coin who suggests holding a final Hunger Games to punish the Capitol
for their actions against the Districts. Coin briefly achieves
her aim and becomes President of Panem, before Katniss
executes summary justice in response to her war crimes
and for the killing of her sister, Prim.

Squad 451 is led by Boggs, Coin's aide-de-camp. He
wins the trust of Katniss despite his connections to the
President whom she does not trust, especially when he
reveals Coin's fear of her as a potential future rival for the
top political office. Boggs becomes bodyguard to Katniss
during their incursion into the Capitol. He loses both legs
after stepping on an undetected landmine, but before he
dies he warns Katniss about the forces aligned against her.

The rest of Squad 451 is made up of Homes (decapitated by the lizard 'muttations' that also claim the lives of Finnick and Castor), Jackson and Leeg 1 (both assumed killed when they stay behind to fight the 'muttations', letting the others flee), Leeg 2 (identical to her sister, so differentiated by number – she is killed by a poison dart), Mitchell (accidentally killed by Peeta during one of his tracker-jacker-induced rages) and Messalla (who is killed by a light ray from a pod that melts his skin).

Cressida is a film director from the Capitol, who joins the rebellion in District 13, bringing her experienced camera team with her. It is her job to make the rebellion 'propos', many of which feature Katniss Everdeen as the mockingjay. She and her team accompany Squad 451 on their mission into the Capitol, as media representatives embedded with the troops. When they are attacked, Cressida steps in to lead the survivors to temporary sanctuary in the store run by Tigris. After the war she tours the Districts making films revealing the damage done and the recovery efforts underway.

Castor and Pollux, just like the Greeks they are named after, are brothers. They are the camera crew for Cressida's 'propos' unit. Their equipment is built into body armour that makes them resemble an insect within a carapace. Pollux has lost his tongue, as he was once an Avox (a slave punished by the removal of their tongue) in the Capitol, and relies on Castor to interpret for him. When Castor is killed, along with Finnick and Homes, by lizard-like 'muttations' in the tunnels under the Capitol, Pollux is left to face life voiceless and alone.

Commander Paylor is the leader of rebel troops in District 8 whom Katniss meets when she is sent there to make a propaganda film. Paylor allows Katniss to visit the captured President Snow while he is awaiting execution, so giving him the opportunity to tell Katniss that he was not responsible for the bombing of the Capitol children used as human shields around his mansion. He convinces Katniss that such an action would not be to his benefit, but that instead it benefitted President Coin. Katniss recognizes the bombing as part of an old plan Gale was involved in developing. As a result, she executes Coin instead of Snow. Paylor then succeeds Coin as the new President of Panem.

Dr Aurelius is based in District 13 and takes care of Katniss during her recovery after the Quarter Quell. He also helped examine Peeta's 'hijacking' when the Capitol exposed him to high doses of tracker-jacker poison and showed him images of Katniss in order to generate a conditioned hatred for her within him. After Prim's death, Dr Aurelius is assigned as therapist to Katniss, although as she rarely feels like talking during their sessions he occasionally has a snooze instead. He acts for the defence during the trial of Katniss following her killing of President Coin, suggesting that as a result of her experiences in both Hunger Games and during the rebellion against the Capitol she has become mentally unstable.

Delly Cartwright was a friend of Peeta in District 12, and is one of the refugees who survive the bombing and make their way to District 13. When Peeta is in recovery after being rescued from captivity in the Capitol, Delly helps him by retelling memories of their childhoods growing up together. It is hoped that this memory 'therapy' might help him recover and escape the grip of the tracker-jacker venom pumped into his system by the Capitol.

Tigris is a one-time stylist for the Hunger Games who now works in an underwear shop located in the Capitol. She has subjected herself to many cosmetic surgical operations to give herself a feline appearance, with the results looking too strange even for the outlandish people of the Capitol. Shunned and resentful, Tigris retreated to her shop. She helps Katniss and the survivors of Squad 451, giving them refuge in her store and supplying them with the materials they need to disguise themselves as Capitol inhabitants.

Lyme is a Games Victor from District 2 who leads the rebels from her District against the Peacekeepers in an assault on 'the Nut', the mountain used as a command-and-control centre for Capitol forces. Although not directly addressed in the text, it is assumed that Lyme perished in the fighting as she is not among the surviving seven Games veterans gathered together by President Coin when the war is won.

Throughout the three novels in *The Hunger Games* series there is an increase in scale. The first novel is on the smallest level, concerned as it is primarily with Katniss Everdeen and her then limited view of Panem. She only knows about the world outside District 12 through what she's heard from her parents or older people in the District, or through the obviously slanted Capitol broadcasts. The prospect of being reaped to take part in the Games is such a large part of any young person's life that she's more than aware of the Games, their official history and the reasons for their continuation. She doesn't like any of this, but as revealed in her conversations with best friend Gale, there's little she thinks she can do about any of it except follow through on her small, personal 'rebellions' that involve her hunting and buying and selling in The Hob, District 12's Peacekeeper-tolerated black market.

Her direct involvement in the Games changes all that: through her battle for survival she becomes aware of the larger world of Panem. Her trip through the Capitol reveals the truth of the inequality that plagues the world in which she lives. Her ultimate act of rebellion is a personal expression of her dissent, her disapproval of the rules of the game (both in the Games and in the wider political and economic sense) that she and her people must live by. She has little thought that her actions and her defiant refusal to toe the line might have reverberations beyond her own survival (and that of Peeta). However, others were watching and paying attention, others who could see a way that the 'girl on fire' could be co-opted to their cause.

The scale increases in *Catching Fire*, as Katniss discovers she has become a symbol of hope, something people across the Districts of Panem can believe in. At first, she refuses this responsibility, being largely only interested in the welfare of her immediate family – her mother and Prim – and then that of her friends and colleagues, Peeta, Gale and Haymitch. Initially unaware of her manipulation by the rebel forces during her time in the arena for the Quarter Quell, she finds her priorities changing. She grows from someone essentially selfish, concerned with her own well-being and that of those closest to her, to someone involved in group effort and teamwork to ensure the survival of more than just herself or Peeta.

During the events of *Mockingjay* the scale increases still further. Katniss comes to an uncomfortable accommodation with her position as the figurehead of the rebellion. She has become someone able to put duty above personal desire. Her relationships with Gale and Peeta have become increasingly complicated and compromised, both by what she's had to do, and also by aspects of the war that both men get involved in. Katniss is no longer a teenager, sticking her tongue out at authority. She's now an adult whose wider concerns have moved from the personal to the national. She's involved in a real war, a fight for the future of Panem, and has a responsibility to thousands of people, rather than just her family, her mother and sister. The war has taken her from home, has – in fact – destroyed her home, and it has altered her view of the world from that of a teenager to that of an adult. Her experiences have been an extreme rite of passage, introducing her to a more adult world, with real responsibilities and real consequences of her actions. Katniss Everdeen is someone who can move the inhabitants of the Districts of Panem from despair to hope, a vast difference from the girl readers first meet casually hunting in the woods, thinking that alone is a big enough act of rebellion.

While the themes of the previous books continue and are developed through *Mockingjay* – such as survival, the effect of war on participants and civilians, authority, control and rebellion, friendship, loyalty and family (all tested to breaking point), trauma and love – there are some issues of morality that are especially amplified in the final book. Katniss finds her loyalty tested as she encounters what appears to be forms of betrayal by those closest to her. For a while, she is not entirely sure of Peeta's loyalties or the effect captivity in the Capitol has truly had on him. Similarly, she comes to look upon the actions Gale undertakes – justified, he claims, due to war – and wonders whether he is not in danger of committing war crimes. These are the people closest to her that she has put her faith in, but the events of the war seem to be changing both of them beyond her recognition.

A big issue in *Mockingjay* is how appearances can be deceptive and things may not be exactly how they appear or what someone claims they are. From the beginning of *The Hunger Games* this theme has been lurking: the Capitol controls the information available to the Districts, so they believe District 13 no longer exists and see in that a threat to their own continued tolerance by the Capitol. As Katniss discovers, this is not true. On the surface, Coin appears to be the 'good' President and Snow is clearly the 'evil' President. As the war against the Capitol draws to a close, though, Katniss discovers that there is a huge degree of moral ambiguity on both sides – neither is exactly what they seem. She is involved in the making of propaganda films, and witnesses how both the rebels and the Capitol distort the truth and manipulate information to suit their own ends. She sees Peeta apparently betraying the rebellion on a broadcast from the Capitol, but she knows him and knows that cannot be true. Yet, when he is rescued and returned to her side in District 13, he is certainly not himself. Part of his rehabilitation involves the creation of what is effectively a simulation in the game of 'Real or Not?' that attempts to provoke Peeta into sorting his fake memories from the real ones. Gale seems to be fighting for the same cause as Katniss, but his methods change and he goes down a moral path that she simply cannot follow. There is a disconnect between the image – how Katniss sees the world and the people in it – and the reality, the way things actually are.

In a review in the *Baltimore Sun*, *Mockingjay* was described as 'traversing morally ambiguous terrain' and this is clearly an aim of Suzanne Collins in concluding her trilogy. In war, things are never as simple as 'good' rebels and 'bad' oppressors. There is good and bad on both sides, there are heroes and villains on both sides, and there is right and wrong on both sides. Actions that after the fact could be construed as war crimes (such as Coin's deniable black-operation bombing of the Capitol children surrounding President Snow's mansion) are committed using the argument that the ends justify the means. Katniss takes a different view, that if the victory of the rebels is to be a moral one as well as simply a physical one, it has to be achieved with a clean conscience. If the Victors restage the Hunger Games, as suggested by Coin, but this time make the children of the Capitol fight, how are they any different from the oppressors they have fought and overthrown?

The *Christian Science Monitor* called *Mockingjay* the 'most brutal of the trilogy' because it is the book in which there is a reckoning for many of the characters. Many of them end up in very different places from where they were when readers first met them (morally, as well as geographically). Katniss fears her most solid relationships, those with Gale and Peeta, have been compromised due to the vicissitudes of war. She has lost some of her closest allies in the battle with the Capitol, among them Boggs and Finnick.

Most hurtful of all, her sister Prim is killed in the act of helping others, when she rushes to the aid of the bombed children at Snow's mansion.

Katniss took her first step to becoming the 'mockingjay' of the rebellion when she instinctively stepped forward and volunteered to take Prim's place in the 74th Hunger Games when her sister was reaped on her first entry. Her act was not a conscious decision; it was an unconscious primal response, a protective instinct. It might be easy to conclude that it was all for nothing, as Prim dies in the end anyway, but Katniss has to console herself with the knowledge that so much else has been achieved in the fight for freedom that resulted from that moment, that so many thousands of people will benefit with new, freer lives thanks to the sacrifices made by others, Prim included. Through the three novels, Katniss learns the true price of war and how to live with its consequences.

She has one tough moral lesson to wrestle with before she has completed her journey. Throughout the three novels, one question has continually exercised Katniss: when is it ever right to kill? Fighting, killing and death are what underpin the Hunger Games, and it is the enforcement of the Games by the Capitol that keeps the Districts in line: it is better that there is a little annual sacrifice than the full-scale devastation of an attack on the Districts, as the surviving Districts believe happened to District 13. During her time in the Games arena, Katniss has struggled not to kill, to avoid conflicts and to focus simply on her survival. That proves to be an impossible task, a tightrope she cannot walk, and in the end she has to act, if only to defend herself or others around her, such as Rue and Peeta. Even then, she tries to keep the deaths she is responsible for to a minimum. That changes with the war. There is a relativism applied: how many must be killed to ensure freedom for the majority? Is war always worth fighting to achieve a principle or an aim, whatever the cost? Katniss is intimately involved in the war as the poster girl for rebellion, but she can have little effect on the higher level decisions over strategy or direction.

This is an area, however, where Gale finds he is able to make a contribution, both in terms of ideas and in being morally free to act as he does. Katniss finally comes face to face with the decision to kill when she has her requested chance to execute President Snow. Now she must consider: when is killing justified and when is it simply an act of revenge? Her sister Prim is dead, but whose fault was that? Is Snow telling the truth in indicating that Coin may not be morally as 'clean' as she appears. Katniss is faced with an agonizing decision, and her ultimate choice is one that looks forward rather than back. The regressive step would have been to exact her revenge, to kill Snow and hope that it would bring her some level of satisfaction regarding Prim, however unlikely that may seem. That's not the choice she makes. Katniss takes the forward-looking option, and in killing Coin instead frees Panem from a possible future tyrant, a second Snow. This, too, can be seen as an act of revenge, but it is not only that. Her killing of Coin has a greater purpose, one in line with the freedom that she, her family and her friends have been fighting for all along.

Throughout the three books Katniss has wrestled with the agonies of growing up amid extraordinary events. While all the young readers of *The Hunger Games* trilogy will no doubt have their own trials to bear while growing up (from high school through to taking up adult life), they are unlikely to be as dramatic as those confronting Katniss Everdeen. There is one way, though, in which today's teenage readers do in some respects share a world with Katniss. Suzanne Collins has always been quick to attribute her interest in communicating the realities of war to the young through her work as a legacy from her father, the result of a long ago war in Vietnam that today's teenagers may know little about. However, they have grown up in a post 9/11 world. The attacks on the World Trade Center and the ensuing 'war on terror' are the backdrop to their world: the first decade or more of the twenty-first century has been one of constant warfare, with the United States and her allies and supporters involved in conflicts in the Middle East and around the world. The readers of *The Hunger Games* books might recognize something of their own reality in the morally compromised world of Panem, in the actions of both Coin and Snow, and hopefully in the moral fortitude of the girl on fire, Katniss Everdeen.

16

CASTING *MOCKINGJAY*

With two films in production from the final novel in *The Hunger Games* trilogy, there were new key roles to be filled, some requiring actors to commit to the lengthy 150-day production process of the back-to-back filming of the final entries in the hugely successful movie series.

One of the larger parts appearing in both instalments of *Mockingjay* is that of Alma Coin, President of District 13 (the technologically sophisticated District believed destroyed) and leader of the rebellion against the Capitol in Panem. In the novel *Catching Fire* the characters of Bonnie and Twill (excised from the movie) had shown Katniss that the television news footage of District 13 always showed the same mockingjay flying in the same pattern across the corner of the screen, indicating that the Capitol was recycling old footage and not showing the current state of the District at all. This was the seed that would lead to Katniss uncovering the true situation in District 13.

The role of President Coin was a pivotal one to the story of *Mockingjay* and required a certain type of star-name actress. As production on the pair of movies began in September 2013 (under the codenames 'C4' or 'Seashore', following 'Artemis' and 'The Idiom' for the first two movies), it was announced that acclaimed actress Julianne Moore had won the role of Coin. Described in the novel as in her fifties and with 'grey hair that falls in an unbroken sheet to her shoulders', Coin's hair proves interesting to Katniss, who notes: 'I'm somewhat fascinated by her hair, since it's so uniform, so without a fall, a wisp, even a split end. Her eyes are grey, but not like those of people from the Seam. They're very pale, as if almost all the colour has been sucked out of them. The colour of slush that you wish would melt away.' At fifty-two, Julianne was the right age, but her vibrant flaming-red hair would have to change.

Born in 1960, Julianne started her acting career with television roles in the mid-eighties, including a stint on the daytime soap opera *As the World Turns* for which she won a Daytime Emmy Award. She made her film debut in 1990 with *Tales from the Darkside: The Movie*, playing the screaming victim of a mummy. While continuing her stage career in such productions as *Uncle Vanya*, she came to prominence for movie audiences with a dramatic role in Robert Altman's *Short Cuts* (1993). Her monologue in the film – which she delivered naked from the waist down – was described by Hollywood trade paper *Variety* as 'no doubt the most discussed scene'. She starred in Todd Haynes's *Safe* (1995) as a woman allergic to the modern world, and in Steven Spielberg's *The Lost World: Jurassic Park* (1997), sequel to his *Jurassic Park*. Roles in diverse movies such as *The Big Lebowski* (1998), the remake of *Psycho* (1998) and Paul Thomas Anderson's quirky *Magnolia* (1999) solidified her screen image. She took the Jodie Foster role of Clarice Starling in *Hannibal* (2001), the sequel to *The Silence of the Lambs* (1991), and appeared in the science-fiction thriller

Children of Men (2006). *The Kids Are All Right* (2010) saw her co-star with Annette Bening as one half of a lesbian couple whose teenage children set out to get to know their sperm-donor father (Josh Hutcherson played one of her kids). The film brought Julianne her sixth Golden Globe nomination and a second BAFTA nomination. She starred as vice-presidential nominee Sarah Palin in the 2012 HBO television movie *Game Change* that chronicled the 2008 campaign (written by *Mockingjay*'s screenwriter Danny Strong), winning Best Actress Golden Globe, Primetime Emmy and Screen Actors Guild awards.

'There's never been a definite plan to any of it,' she said of the career trajectory that led her to *Mockingjay*. She was very familiar with the books, having readers in her own family. 'My son read them when they first came out . . . and then my daughter a few years ago started reading *The Hunger Games*. We were on vacation and I didn't bring a book to read. I picked up her book and read it that afternoon, and then downloaded the other two on my iPad and tore through them. They're books about war, but with adolescent overtones. It's about, what is totalitarianism, what is revolution? How do people compromise, how do we repeat our mistakes? It's heartbreaking. I was really impressed by the books, so I'm delighted to be doing it.'

She was determined that her screen President Coin should match readers' expectations, so her distinctive red hair went grey for the movie. 'I think everybody tries very hard to honour the book because there's so many people who have invested themselves in it,' she said. Producer Nina Jacobson noted: 'You'll see that Julianne Moore's role in *Mockingjay* is much bigger in the movie than it is in the book.'

Rush (2013) and *Game of Thrones* actress Natalie Dormer joined the cast of *Mockingjay* as Cressida, director of the television coverage of the Games who switches sides to join

Katniss in her battle against the Capitol. Natalie was born in Reading, England, in 1982, a straight-A student and vice-captain of the netball squad at school. She trained in dance at the Allenova School of Dancing and intended to go on to study history at Cambridge University, but failed to achieve the exam grades needed. Instead she auditioned for drama schools and trained at the Webber Douglas Academy of Dramatic Art in London.

Six months after graduating she scored her first movie role, a small part as Victoria in the Heath Ledger-starring version of *Casanova* (2005) – director Lasse Hallström was so impressed with her comic timing he enlarged her role. Out of work for nine months, she happily accepted a guest role in an episode of the television detective series *Rebus* (based on the novels of Ian Rankin). She said being out of work 'was the best lesson I could have had in the first twelve months of my career' and that it taught her about the precarious nature of acting as a vocation. Her career blossomed with a regular role as Anne Boleyn in the first two seasons of *The Tudors* in 2007–8, an episode of Agatha Christie's *Marple* television series and a variety of small film roles.

Her breakthrough came in fantasy series *Game of Thrones* when she was cast as the scheming Margaery Tyrell in 2011. In 2014 she would be seen starring opposite her *Mockingjay* co-star Sam Claflin in the movie *Posh*. In *Mockingjay*, Natalie would be sporting a rather dramatic half-shaved hairstyle. Joining Natalie on *Mockingjay* were Elden Henson (television mini-series *Eldorado*) and Wes Chatham (television series *The Unit*) as her cameramen brothers Pollux and Castor, and Evan Ross (television's *90210*) as her assistant, Messalla. Encouraged by Plutarch Heavensbee, the group flee the Capitol together and head for District 13 to join the growing rebellion.

Also best known for her television roles was actress Lily Rabe, cast in *Mockingjay Part 1* as Commander Lyme, a former Games champion turned rebel leader. Born in 1982 in New York City, Lily appeared as a variety of characters in supernatural anthology series *American Horror Story* and, like Jennifer Lawrence, she featured in two episodes of supernatural television series *Medium*. An experienced theatre actress, Lily appeared in a Broadway revival of *Steel Magnolias* in 2008, and in summer 2010 played Portia in *The Merchant of Venice* opposite Al Pacino as Shylock at Shakespeare in the Park in New York's Central Park. She was nominated for a Tony Award and continued to play the role in various productions. Lily also appeared in a variety of films including Hollywood satire *What Just Happened?* (2008), *All Good Things* (2010) and played early movie actress Mary Pickford in *The First* (2013).

As a past Victor of the Games, Lyme was from District 2 and one of the first from the area to join the rebellion. Although in the novel her character meets an undetermined grim fate, it was assumed that changes were made to the character for thirty-one-year-old slightly built Lily to play a 'middle-aged, muscular, six-feet tall veteran of the Games from over a generation ago'. An unforeseen scheduling conflict would see Rabe replaced in *Mockingjay Part 2* by twenty-seven-year-old, six-foot three-inch Gwendoline Christie, best known as Brienne of Tarth in hit fantasy show *Game of Thrones* – perhaps a better fit in the role.

A group of lesser known actors filled out the remaining main roles in the two *Mockingjay* movies. Mahershala Ali, best known for his roles in television science-fiction shows *The 4400* (2004–7) and *Alphas* (2011–12), was signed up to the role of Boggs, resident of District 13 and President Coin's right-hand man, until Katniss takes on the role of the 'mockingjay', when his function switches to being her bodyguard. During the bombing raid on District 8, Boggs steps in to protect Katniss, winning her trust.

Australian actress Stef Dawson was confirmed in

the role of Annie Cresta, love interest for Sam Claflin's Finnick Odair. She'd made a brief appearance in *Catching Fire* during the District 4 reaping, setting up her enlarged role in the final two movies. Born in Canberra, the young actress had appeared in several short films and some indie productions, but appearing in *The Hunger Games* movies would be her big break. She was also set to appear in horror film *13 Girls* in 2014. Annie Cresta won the 70th Games, during which she saw her District 4 partner beheaded. The only person seemingly able to calm her during moments of mental instability was Finnick, victor of the 65th Games. When she was reaped for the 75th Games, Mags stepped up and volunteered in her place. She later has a child with Finnick.

Broadway actress and singer (*Sister Act*) Patina Miller made her film debut in *Mockingjay*, playing the role of Commander Paylor from District 8. From 2007 she had appeared in thirty episodes of daytime soap opera *All My Children*. She went on to win a Tony Award in 2013 for her role in a revival of *Pippin*, a musical following the adventures of a young prince. Commander Paylor is one of the leaders of the rebellion from District 8 who later goes on to become the President of Panem. She becomes closely involved with Katniss when they team up to defend a hospital in District 8 from a Capitol bombing raid.

An addition to the cast of *Mockingjay* announced in December 2013 was veteran character actor Robert Knepper as Antonius (a character not in the book). Best known for playing T-Bag in the television series *Prison Break* (2005–9), and later appearing in *Heroes* (2009–10) and *Mob City* (2013), his career began in the mid-eighties with episodic television roles in series such as *Star Trek: The Next Generation* and the revival of *The Twilight Zone*. At the same time he was cast in *Mockingjay*, he took on the role of the 'Clock King' on superhero show *Arrow*.

There was some confusion among fans as to who Antonius might be, as there was no one in the *Mockingjay* novel of that name. Although it was expected that the two movies would expand upon the novel (see Chapter 17), this was the first time that a fairly well-known 'name' actor had been cast in a seemingly invented role. *Entertainment Weekly* (a champion of all things *Hunger Games*) speculated Antonius might be either a soldier fighting for the Capitol (as Knepper tended to play bad guys, and Capitol folks tended to have Roman names), or possibly a general advising President Snow (which seemed more likely). On the other hand, argued the magazine, he might be a character on the side of District 13, possibly a member of an expanded Squad 451. There were other possibilities. Antonius could be a member of the 'propos' film crew (who are rebels, but originally from the Capitol, explaining his Roman name) or he could be the man who tortures Peeta – something described second-hand in the book, but which will be seen on screen in the movies. The only clue was his pre-publicity designation as 'President Snow's Minister'. Whoever Antonius turned out to be, fans were quick to welcome Knepper to *The Hunger Games* family.

Filling out smaller roles in the final two films in *The Hunger Games* series were television regular Omid Abtahi as Homes, a soldier from District 13 and part of Squad 451, who is an ace at hitting targets at a long distance; Misty and Kim Ormiston as Leeg 1 and Leeg 2, twin rebellion soldiers from District 13 and also members of Squad 451; and television veteran Kimiko Gelman as Venia, alongside Nelson Ascencio as Flavius and Bruce Bundy as Octavia – all members of the prep team who regularly prepare Katniss for public appearances.

17

MAKING *MOCKINGJAY*

The process of turning *Mockingjay*, the final book of *The Hunger Games* trilogy, into two blockbuster movies was a long and fraught one that by necessity overlapped with the post-production and promotion of *Catching Fire*. Shooting followed close on the heels of the release of the second movie, with both *Mockingjay* movies set for release over the Thanksgiving holidays of 2014 and 2015. Everything, however, began with the script.

A year before the release of *Catching Fire*, Lionsgate were powering ahead on their two-film adaptation of *Mockingjay*. As with the second film, a new voice was brought in to tackle the first script. Emmy-winner Danny Strong (who wrote the 2012 Julianne Moore television film *Game Change*) started out as an actor, best known as misguided nerd Jonathan Levinson in *Buffy the Vampire Slayer* on television. His move into screenwriting came with *Recount* (2008), an HBO television movie about the disputed 2000 presidential election which brought him a Primetime Emmy for outstanding writing and a Writers' Guild award for Best Screenplay. *Game Change* followed, with Strong winning another Emmy for outstanding writing.

Strong's first movie screenplay was for the acclaimed film *The Butler* (2013), starring Forest Whitaker as Cecil Gaines, an African-American butler working in the White House who witnesses the major events of the twentieth century during his thirty-four-year residency (the character was loosely based on a real person). He was also the screenwriter for the film version of the Dan Brown novel *The Lost Symbol*, but the film was postponed so producers could first adapt Brown's then most recent novel about Robert Langdon, *Inferno*, starring Tom Hanks and due for release at the end of 2015. Strong had come far given he started writing simply to fill the time between acting auditions.

For the actor-turned-scribe, adapting *Mockingjay* was a very different gig from his previous movies, all based on real-life stories. The one similarity was that his work would be extrapolated from a pre-existing source, although this time it was a fictional tale with two previous movies to draw from. 'I was approached to pitch on it,' said Strong of his *Mockingjay* assignment, 'and I just literally holed myself up for a week and came up with a presentation for two movies. I pitched my little heart out, and got the job.'

Lionsgate wanted to see Strong's finished script for *Mockingjay, Part 1* before they would commit to having him complete the second film. 'They were looking for a writer for *Mockingjay* and they knew it was going to be a two-parter, so part of the pitch that I had to give was how I would write both parts,' said Strong. By February 2013 he'd turned in a draft of the first of the two films, which met with Lionsgate's full approval, so his option to begin work on the second movie was taken up.

Working on adapting novels like *The Lost Symbol* and *Mockingjay* wasn't all that different from working on his screenplays based on real-life events, according to Strong. 'It's all the same to me to a certain extent,' he said. 'I'm just trying to make the scenes work. It always has its own unique set of challenges. [With] the novels, you can change more, depending on the book. Some books you have more liberty for more creativity and some books you have less, because the books are great. You want to use as much of them as you can, and they're so wildly popular that it's not an open season for interpretation. I've done adaptations that haven't been made that weren't as high profile [as *Mockingjay*] in which I changed quite a bit.'

As so often in Hollywood, especially in franchise movies such as *The Hunger Games* series, Strong would not be the only writer involved. As well as input from the novels' author Suzanne Collins (as on the other films), the final movies would also have some script revisions by director Francis Lawrence and by another writer, Peter Craig, described by producer Nina Jacobson as 'a very gifted writer, he's done an amazing job for us in really bringing the third book to life as two movies that hold their own'. Craig, son of actress Sally Field, was a novelist who specialized in comic novels about father-child relationships, and whose screenplays included *The Town* (2010, co-written with the film's director and star Ben Affleck) and as-yet unmade sequels *Top Gun 2* and *Bad Boys III*.

The biggest decision facing the screenwriters and producers was how to split the book into two movies. It had been a successful move for the makers of the final *Harry Potter* and *Twilight* movies, so it was simply down to whether they could agree on where to divide Suzanne Collins's novel. 'I think they are two distinct stories,' said director Francis Lawrence of the division they finally decided upon. 'I think the objectives are very distinct. One is about getting Peeta back and one is about revenge, which is why I think they easily separate out. It allows us to explore what we need to within each of those stories.'

For producer Jon Kilik the split was an artistic rather than financial decision, and one he considered in depth. 'I thought about it very carefully for a really long time,' he said. 'We talked about a few different ways to do it and we finally came up with what we think is the right one. Suzanne was very involved [in] the third book, the whole revolution is so big. Even the first two [novels] were almost too big for one movie. The third book is even bigger, with the action of the revolution and the overthrow, so it just could not hold in one.'

Nina Jacobson agreed with the need to make *Mockingjay* two movies, released a year apart. 'We ultimately just felt that [for] every book we've had to shear a bit off in order to keep the momentum going, and every time we've been okay with what we've had to lose. [We have] more time to give to Prim and Katniss. There are characters who don't make the cut. Going into that [final] book, there's just too much rich-ness, too much complexity. We felt like we would lose too much to condense it into one film. We had to work closely with Suzanne to really think about where we split them.'

The involvement of Strong – known for his take on complex political situations in *Recount* and *Game Change* – seemed right for bringing *Mockingjay* to the screen. 'Suzanne wanted to write a series of books for teenagers about the consequence of war and what that means,' director Francis Lawrence said. 'When there's violence it damages people, there's loss, there's real consequence. To really get that and to give the series its meaning I think you need to get to *Mockingjay* and tell that story. The truth is that we're making the book – we're not reinventing the book. These people start out damaged in *Catching Fire*, they're much more damaged by the beginning of *Mockingjay*. The movie does go to dark places. Part of why I love those [books] is that Suzanne didn't pull any punches. I think [*Mockingjay* is] the book that gives the whole series its meaning.'

For some fans of *The Hunger Games*, *Mockingjay* contained many surprising and upsetting developments, and debate had raged among them as to which was the better book, *Catching Fire* or *Mockingjay*. Both had their passionate supporters. The problem for the filmmakers all the way through the process of filming *The Hunger Games* series had been the first-person nature of the books – that had to change significantly, especially on the third and fourth films in order to encompass the epic nature of the storytelling on the big screen.

'There are some new elements to it,' said Lawrence of the final story. 'I think one of the things is when you experience the movies vs. the book, the books are so inside Katniss's head; we're not in Katniss's head as much. We're not changing the book, and we're not messing with anything, [but] we are injecting some hope to it, and some warmth to it. And there will be some humour. So there's different layers that we're adding to it to make it richer.'

For some, *Mockingjay* told a much grimmer story as the novel focused on an account of war, while for others it was exactly the realistic take on the subject they expected. The filmmakers would find it difficult to reach both sets of *Hunger Games* fans, although the split into two films might help with the first focusing on rescuing Peeta from the Capitol and the second following Katniss in her insurgency against President Snow and her quest for vengeance. 'The fans of the book are going to get more of what they love by splitting the book into two movies,' said the director. 'I think for those that haven't read the book, what they're going to get are two distinct stories. I think it's only positive. The fun thing about *Mockingjay* is that we actually get to see the Capitol in a new way. We'll actually be down in the middle of the streets of the Capitol.'

There were several problems in the storytelling in *Mockingjay* that were fine in a book but simply would not work for the screen. Suffering Post-Traumatic Stress Disorder, Katniss was a passive character for much of the first section of the novel, an attribute that would not play well on screen – she would be transformed into a more active cinematic heroine. Peeta was absent for much of the book, but the film had to show what happens to him, even if much of it was unrelentingly grim. The movie also needed to show the fates of Johanna and Annie when they are held by the Capitol, as well as Effie Trinket (who is jailed, but not featured much in the novel), given that she's played by Elizabeth Banks and featured heavily in the previous two movies. The fate of Cinna would also be visualized on screen, unlike in the novel.

There are other story problems the filmmakers had to find ways of tackling, such as the drifting apart of Katniss and Gale, as well as the killing of Finnick Odair, as both men have been built up in the films as significant characters. Both roles would be expanded, with the death of Finnick playing a larger part in the actual course of the war. The same was expected for Squad 451, whose actions would be integrated into changing the tide of the war, rather than appearing inconsequential as in the novel. All of these changes were improvements to the story required by its transformation into cinema, rather than a written story that plays out in the reader's head. Films and novels have very different requirements, and having worked in television Suzanne Collins not only understood the changes needed, but would have a hand in devising the new approach to concluding her story for the screen.

Several key story points would have to remain – no matter how unsavoury – if Suzanne's main points in *Mockingjay* about the moral problems of warfare were to be maintained. The death of Prim (perhaps as a result of the actions of Gale) and the killing of Coin (and not the overall 'bad guy' Snow) by Katniss are so central to the novel that they'd be difficult to change. Here it was a case of the nuance of the on-screen presentation: as long as Suzanne's intentions were intact, the message would remain the same, however the films achieved it.

Filming began on the final two movies in mid-September 2013, with them being shot back-to-back – in essence, a five-hour movie that would be split in two during editing. 'There's something to be said for working with a gun to your head as opposed to working to develop something without a start date,' said Lawrence. 'It's a different set of muscles. You think about it harder.' The films returned to Atlanta, the base for all four movies, but would also shoot in Boston (as had *Catching Fire*), Los Angeles and Berlin, Germany, to capture the expanded wartime world of *Mockingjay*. Cast and crew had a break from the movie to take on their promotional duties for *Catching Fire* in late November, but were straight back to work afterwards. 'We start shooting again in Atlanta right after Thanksgiving until December 20,' said Lawrence during promotion on *Catching Fire*, 'then we break for Christmas and then we shoot for three more months in Atlanta and two months in Europe. We're mostly shooting in sequence.' The shoot would continue for 150 days, right through to May 2014.

While the initial focus would be on capturing the material for the first of the two movies, it made sense to also film scenes for the final movie if they took place in particular locations to which the production crew would not be returning. 'It's definitely one story, but there are two totally distinct and separate scripts,' noted Lawrence. 'We're front-loading shooting *Part 1* so that cut [edit] can be worked on while we're shooting *Part 2*. There's a little bit of overlap, and a little bit of peppering of scenes. We're going to shoot a scene before the first initial shoot day, a prep shoot day, where we'll shoot one of the final scenes of *Mockingjay, Part 2*, so that's actually the first thing that we're going to shoot. Then we'll pretty much start at the beginning of *Mockingjay, Part 1*, and do our best to stay in as linear order as possible. Certain characters have pretty extreme character arcs, so it'll help the [actors].'

During filming in Atlanta, a faulty fog machine caused Jennifer Lawrence a moment of discomfort and a moment of panic on the film's set. The machine malfunctioned, filling the set with dense smoke during the filming of a scene set in the underground tunnels of the Capitol. While exaggerated reports (such as that in the *National Enquirer*) had Jennifer in danger of 'choking to death', in actual fact large fans quickly cleared the smoke away, causing little more than mild discomfort. Jennifer took some time out from filming immediately after the accident, as she was suffering from nausea.

For Ve Neill, head of make-up on the movie, the third book presented new challenges: 'They go to war. We have a lot of distressed looking make-ups, as opposed to glamour. We have three make-up artists who are on all the time and we have one make-up artist who runs our tech unit, who works with us concurrently doing interior and pick-up shots. She sometimes has fifteen people working with her. Right now we're doing stuff in District 13, so we have twenty extra make-up artists, and there are even more people in the hair department. We have a lot of manpower because there are over 400 extras.'

The unexpected tragic death of Plutarch Heavensbee actor Philip Seymour Hoffman in February 2014 presented *Mockingjay*'s producers with a major challenge. The majority of Philip's work had been completed on the two-part *Mockingjay* adaptation, with just seven days shooting remaining on his schedule. Post-production work-arounds would need to be applied to complete the role Plutarch Heavensbee plays in the climax of *The Hunger Games* saga. Philip wasn't the first actor to die while shooting a movie. Marilyn Monroe (*Something's Got to Give*), Bruce Lee (*Game of Death*), his son Brandon Lee (*The Crow*), River Phoenix (*Dark Blood*) and Heath Ledger (*The Imaginarium of Doctor Parnassus*) all died while making movies. Some were abandoned altogether, while others recast, and yet others used doubles to complete scenes. In recent times, technology has allowed productions to cover for the loss of an actor, as in the use of a digital double for Oliver Reed in *Gladiator* (2000). It was expected that a combination of techniques, including CGI, would be used to complete Philip's final performance as Plutarch Heavensbee.

On the night of Philip's death, Lionsgate studio issued a statement: 'Philip Seymour Hoffman was a singular talent and one of the most gifted actors of our generation. We're very fortunate that he graced our *Hunger Games* family. Losing him in his prime is a tragedy, and we send our condolences to Philip's family.' It seems likely one of the two final films will be dedicated to Philip, in remembrance of an acclaimed actor who had enhanced *The Hunger Games* series with his undoubted talents.

Lawrence anticipated the final two movies would be an emotional experience for audiences and for the actors who had played their characters over a number of years. He saw these films as getting to the heart of the story that Suzanne had written. 'To me *Catching Fire* was the beginning of it,' Lawrence said, 'where you start to see that damage and it only gets worse. Obviously if you know *Mockingjay*, you know stuff is done to Peeta and so there's a lot more exploration of that. The ending of the book and the book itself is just really important to me. Because we are splitting it into two there's room for world growth. We're being very true to the book. When there's violence, it damages people, there's loss, there's real consequence. To really get that and to give the series its meaning I think you need to tell that story.'

Mockingjay would finally resolve the love story at the heart of *The Hunger Games* series: the triangle between Katniss, Peeta and Gale. It was one of director Francis Lawrence's aims to resolve that in a satisfactory manner, while also making great screen drama. 'I felt the love story in general was a bit buried in the first one, more than it was in the book,' he said of Gary Ross's film. 'I wanted to bring the love story up more to the surface. It's a very import-ant aspect of *Mockingjay*. It needed to get platformed and teed up in the appropriate way, so that all the right pay-offs happen later. There's a shared traumatic experience, the bonding there almost can't go away. But what happens when you go home? Suddenly you go home and you want your normal life again, and you might start disconnecting from that person, and you might start being into the other person again, right?'

The epic story of *The Hunger Games* would conclude with the two-part movie of *Mockingjay* released across two years, but it would also bring the conclusion of the more intimate personal story of Katniss Everdeen and her friends. Across the books, the question is asked: what is the price of war, and is it a price worth paying? In the end Panem is free and a brighter future awaits, but the cost of that victory hangs heavily upon Katniss Everdeen, and her future is blighted by her experiences in the Games arenas and in the battle to free her world. It's a story that began on the page, in the bestselling novels by Suzanne Collins, but one that was due to end in spectacular style in a pair of blockbuster movies on big screens around the planet.

18

THE HUNGER GAMES LEGACY

In many ways, it was the fans that made *The Hunger Games*. Suzanne Collins may have written the three novels, and a team of talented filmmakers and Hollywood stars may have turned those books into four blockbusting movies, but without the readers of the novels and the viewers of the films, *The Hunger Games* would not enjoy a lasting legacy.

The creativity of the fans who have drawn on Collins's work for their own takes on the world of *The Hunger Games* has given new life to the characters, situations, places and events from the original stories. Fan fiction, where fans write their own stories based in Panem, has run the gamut from extrapolating upon favourite characters, to following the untold adventures of minor characters from the trilogy, to crossover fiction bringing in characters from other franchises (often other teen fiction, such as *Harry Potter* or *Twilight*). Many websites post these fan stories for other fans to read, and those who own and control the

copyright for *The Hunger Games* usually turn a blind eye
to such activity, as long as it is not sold or otherwise prof-
ited from. Many sites often run competitions for costume
creators or for Halloween artwork.

Curating websites devoted to the books and films not
only showcased their own creativity, but also that of other
fans who uploaded their own art, fashion creations and
stories. Some websites ran 'fan of the month' profiles
featuring a diverse range of fans, chronicling their activi-
ties and providing a showroom for their unique creative
endeavours. Some sites, such as mockingjay.net, focused on
following every bit of news surrounding the making of each
of the movies. Every development was chronicled in great
detail, with photos of the areas in which filming was taking
place through to write-ups of the production in local news-
papers and interviews with those even peripherally involved.
Other sites scoured the web, collating in one place every
television interview clip, every red carpet appearance and
every magazine interview with the movies' stars.

Crafting, where fans created their own real-world items
inspired by *The Hunger Games* books and films, including making bows and arrows modelled after those wielded
by Katniss, necklaces and keychains, mockingjay pins,
charms and magnets, bookmarks, slogan T-shirts, party
favour parachutes based on those that bring sponsored
supplies to Games participants, and edible goods such as
cookies. Cosplay – in which fans recreate costumes worn
by the main characters, either based on descriptions in the
novels or directly upon the looks in the movies – is also
very popular.

Official *Hunger Games* merchandise exploded with the
arrival of the blockbuster movies. The questions of principle in merchandising based around a dystopia whose
author was attempting to send a message that included
anti-consumerism was not lost on many fans, who nonetheless snapped up many of the official products. Items

available included movie action figures of Katniss (and a Barbie doll based on her, as well as Peeta, Gale, Finnick and Effie); mockingjay pins, necklaces and keychains were inevitable; the movie soundtrack album; various Scholastic-published guidebook spin-offs; stationery sets (an odd choice for a generation who communicate via tweets and SMS!); and free-to-play video games, available across social media. Inevitably there were some bizarre items (beyond contentious CoverGirl and Subway promotions), such as pillowcases featuring Peeta's face, socks emblazoned with the name 'Katniss' up the calf, a mockingjay light bulb, a *Hunger Games*-themed votive candle holder and a magnetic poetry set. It's little wonder fans started to make their own items . . .

The Hunger Games made a huge impact culturally, initially through the books but perhaps more widely as a result of the films. One notable impact was an increase in the interest in archery among younger women, inspired by Katniss Everdeen's feats. Sales of bows and arrows reportedly tripled following the release of the first movie, along with an uptake in organized archery classes.

Reading continued to be popular among teens, with *The Hunger Games* trilogy building on the success of the *Twilight* and *Harry Potter* series: despite the naysayers, many young people love to read great stories (whether in print or on a Kindle or tablet). Veteran fantasy author Charles de Lint said: 'I can tell you what I hope the legacy of *The Hunger Games* will be . . . That it will be another step in the understanding that books are fun and entertaining, and that young readers will continue to choose them as part of the overall entertainment package they consume. It does my heart good to know for all the cries of the death of the book and reading that appear with regularity in the media, people, young and old, are nevertheless still choosing to read.'

Suzanne Collins's success with *The Hunger Games* was one more step in proving the legitimacy of 'young adult' fiction as a thriving subset of publishing. Other successful series found new audiences, such as *Beautiful Creatures* (2009, the first part of *The Caster Chronicles*), *Mortal Instruments* (which started in 2007) and the *City of Ember* (2003) series, which were all also made into movies. *The Hunger Games* books helped raise the profile of young adult literature and legitimized the form for many. Collins's stories, and the success of the films based upon them, also had a direct effect on the source material adapted to film. A host of young adult novels were rapidly set for cinema adaptation in 2014, including *Divergent*, *Vampire Academy*, *The Giver* and *The Maze Runner*, all after a slice of *The Hunger Games*'s cinematic success.

Television was getting in on the act, too, with undeniably *Hunger Games*-influenced series such as *Capture* (notably on 'teen' channel The CW). *Capture* – a reality show of the type that inspired Suzanne Collins in the first place – pitted two teams of twelve contestants against each other in a fight for survival in the 'hunting grounds' for one month without being captured. A 'Game Master' (sound familiar?) would control their environment and a 'Supply Station' (a Cornucopia?) would contain much-needed equipment, with the winners walking away with a $250,000 prize. Life imitating art, perhaps?

It was to be hoped, by Suzanne Collins in particular, that these examples weren't the only cultural impact of her trilogy. The messages in the books remain relevant to a young generation growing up in an age of total surveillance and seemingly constant (yet distant) warfare, a world where social interaction takes place through a screen, and the future is depicted as something to fear rather than something to hope for. Some kind of political engagement at any level is perhaps what the author most wanted her readers to achieve. 'What do you think about choices your government past or present, or other governments around the world make?' she once asked of her readers. 'What's your relationship to reality television versus your relationship to news? Was there anything that disturbed you because it reflected aspects of your own life, and what can you do about it?'

This call to, if not political action, at least a wider political understanding of the forces that shape the world these readers were growing up in was reinforced by the movies' President Snow, Donald Sutherland. 'I just hope that they see from this allegory that the future is unacceptable,' he said. 'If you look at the weather, if you look at fossil fuels, if you look at a political party that just says "no" only because they want to get elected – they have no concern for four years for the people . . .'

Asked if she'd contemplate a return to Panem, Suzanne Collins replied: 'Honestly, I feel like I never left it. The revisions of Book I overlapped with the writing of Book II, just as Book II overlapped with Book III. Since each book feeds into the next, I feel like part of my brain's been in Panem continuously.' With the amazing success of the trilogy and the additional boost of awareness of her story and her message provided by the movies, Suzanne must have faced the temptation to return to the world of *The Hunger Games* for new stories. However, her agent closed the door on that possibility. 'Another one?' said Jason Dravis, in response to the question asked so often by so many fans. 'No, the books are done.' He was emphatic that Suzanne had no plans to expand the trilogy beyond *Mockingjay*, no matter how much the fans might want it. There'd be no spin-offs featuring the adventures of Finnick, or books about Gale growing up in District 12. There was even less chance of a *Hunger Games: The Next Generation* following the children of Katniss and Peeta into the future. Nor would there be a prequel telling how the Hunger Games came to be (as suggested by one April Fool's internet prank in 2013). Perhaps a graphic novel comic book retelling the saga could help get girls into comics? Instead, the author has embarked on a similar, but brand new, trilogy, aimed at teen readers and no doubt containing some equally worthwhile messages and life lessons, but probably not about war.

While Suzanne has moved on to pastures new, particularly *Year of the Jungle*, her autobiographical picture book for children, and that brand new young adult science-fiction trilogy, there is a possibility that the world of *The Hunger Games* could be expanded in future movies. With *Mockingjay* already split across two films, the undoubted overall success, critically and financially, of the films might give filmmakers the idea that they should explore 'brand extensions'. *The Hobbit*, a much slimmer book than J. R. R. Tolkien's *The Lord of the Rings*, was turned into three very expansive movies by Peter Jackson, while Disney has purchased Lucasfilm and announced a new *Star Wars* trilogy, plus several 'standalone' movies further exploring characters, places and situations from the *Star Wars* universe. A new *Harry Potter* spin-off movie, *Fantastic Beasts and Where to Find Them*, is in development in 2014. Could something similar emerge for *The Hunger Games*? Perhaps a prequel, or further adventures for Jennifer Lawrence's Katniss Everdeen beyond the victory over the Capitol? Only time, and the machinations of Hollywood, will tell . . .

In the end, the biggest question was how *The Hunger Games* – in both its literary and cinematic incarnations – had proved to be such a runaway success. The books tapped into a well-recognized audience: teenage readers, largely (but not exclusively) female, going through the process of growing up. The exciting, first-person narrative, with a heroine at its centre, made for a page-turner blockbuster that spread through word of mouth and clever marketing.

The darkness evident in Panem appealed to teenagers, perhaps in their final years at school. The competitive world of American high school, where the pressure is on not only to succeed academically, but to be great at sports, to look beautiful and to have special skills, means there must be losers as well as a few winners. This sense of competition and the unfairness of the life of the average teenager, struggling to get out from under their parents' supervision, was reflected (albeit in exaggerated fictional form) in the books' Games arenas and the events that take place there. Just like Katniss, many teens feel torn between their parents (symbolizing a sense of familial duty) and their peers (incarnated in the books in the shapes of Peeta and Gale).

It didn't harm the books' chance of success that they also contained a series of political messages that hit home harder with young people in the wake of the Western economic collapse of 2008. That aspect hadn't escaped the woman who brought Katniss Everdeen to life on screen, Jennifer Lawrence. 'I was personally very excited when I first started reading these books, just that there was such a big series that young adults would be reading,' she said, 'and something that was actually very important. I think it's a wonderful message to show how powerful one voice can be. [Katniss is] one voice that speaks up and it started a rebellion. A movement [started] because one person said this isn't right, even when it's the scary thing to do.'

The Hunger Games movies made international stars of its young cast, while giving a few older character actors a wonderful platform. For her part, Jennifer Lawrence was looking beyond her star-making association with *The Hunger Games* and laying the foundation for her future screen appearances.

Several movie roles are planned, with some in pre-production as *Mockingjay* was shot. Jennifer is attached to *The Glass Castle*, a movie based on a bestselling 2005

memoir by Jeanette Walls that recounted her unconventional upbringing in a poor household with two deeply
dysfunctional parents. It certainly sounds like Jennifer's
kind of project – in line with *The Poker House* and *Winter's
Bone* – one that would play to her indie-movie sensibilities.
Paramount has the rights to film the book, and the movie
is being produced through Brad Pitt's Plan B company.
Anne Meredith (television movie *Secrets of Eden*, 2012)
had written the screenplay, and Jennifer's involvement was
confirmed in March 2013. Clare Danes and Mark Ruffalo
co-star as Rose Mary, Jeanette's mentally unbalanced
mother, and Rex Walls, her alcoholic, nomadic father.
Destin Daniel Cretton (*Short Term 12*, 2013) directs.

Several planned projects see Jennifer re-teamed with
Gary Ross, director of *The Hunger Games*. The first project
is *Burial Rites*, a film about a murder in an isolated community in nineteenth-century Iceland. Based on a novel by
Australian author Hannah Kent, the film will tell the story
of a woman (played by Jennifer) sent to a lonely farm in
1829 to await execution for killing her former employer.
However, the family who own the farm are reluctant to
share their home with an accused killer.

Jennifer is also set to feature in Gary Ross's new adapta-
tion of John Steinbeck's *East of Eden* – the original 1955
Elia Kazan movie made a star of James Dean. Jennifer took
the role of 'psychotic monster . . . with a malformed soul'
(as Steinbeck describes her) Cathy Ames, played by Jo Van
Fleet in the original. In the 1952 novel, which relocated the
Book of Genesis from the Bible to 1900s Salinas Valley,
California, Steinbeck depicted Cathy as an abused young
woman who becomes the madam of a brothel. Image
Entertainment will produce the movie, to be released by
Universal.

Also on Jennifer's ever busy schedule are several 'in
development' projects including *The Ends of the Earth*,
about the love affair between an oil baron and his adopted

daughter Lydie (to be played by Jennifer), and *The Rules of Inheritance*, in which a young woman struggles to deal with the loss of her parents. That film is to be directed by Susanne Bier, who'd directed Jennifer in *Serena*, and was scripted by Abi Morgan from Claire Bidwell Smith's true life memoir. As well as starring, Jennifer is a producer on the project.

The story of *The Hunger Games* may have concluded in book form for readers of *Mockingjay*, but the two-part film version meant that *The Hunger Games* would live on screen well into 2016, when *Mockingjay, Part 2* would be released on Blu-ray and DVD. The saga was a complicated story, meaningful and moving, yet simply told in straight-forward terms by an author whose principal aim was to make her young readers think about a whole variety of issues. Those readers responded to Suzanne Collins's tale in creative ways, expanding the world and characters of Panem in their own imaginations.

The Lionsgate-produced movies took *The Hunger Games* to another level, a mainstream, populist blockbuster series to compare with any other superhero or space-fantasy franchise. With *Catching Fire* the number one movie of 2013, there is every possibility that the two *Mockingjay* films will match or exceed its box-office success, even up against such popular cinematic franchise competition as the final movie in *The Hobbit* trilogy (in 2014) and the first movie in a new *Star Wars* trilogy (in 2015).

The Hunger Games saga works because Suzanne Collins looks at several negative trends in early-twenty-first-century Western society (primarily American, drawing upon her own culture) and exaggerates them for dramatic effect to produce a dystopian warning for us all. Katniss, while also being a great female role model and heroine, is a symbol of resistance. Alone, she cannot be the revolution against the Capitol, but she becomes a living metaphor for the act of rebellion. Suzanne's trilogy also looks at the ethics of war: when is it right to fight, and what is worth fighting for? What will be the consequences of taking a stand? All this is filtered through the character of Katniss Everdeen, who symbolizes both the individual fight (in the Games arena) and the collective struggle (in the mockingjay revolution). She takes a journey to discover the truth about her world: that appearances can be deceiving, and often the truth hurts. While all around her people project falseness, Katniss herself finds she cannot fake her emotions, even when her life depends upon it. Her actions – large and small – uncover the truth about the social and political control the Capitol has over the Districts. She stands against that dominant ideology and through her actions she sparks the will among the downtrodden and controlled populace to bring about change. At its heart, *The Hunger Games* trilogy is an entertainment, but it asks readers to consider the dark side of trends in current entertainment: how far will we go to amuse ourselves and others?

The ultimate success of *The Hunger Games* was down to two talented women: Suzanne Collins and Jennifer Lawrence. Suzanne created in Katniss Everdeen a heroine who captured the imagination of a generation of readers, and Jennifer then brought her to life on screen in a way that appealed equally to those who'd read the original novels and those who hadn't. Between them they brought *The Hunger Games* to a mass audience starving for inspiring fiction.

NOTE ON SOURCES

Many works were consulted in creating this *Brief Guide*, but primary among them were the three novels by Suzanne Collins – *The Hunger Games*, *Catching Fire* and *Mockingjay* – and the movies made from them. The cornucopia of coverage of *The Hunger Games* phenomenon consulted as research included:

Production Notes
For *The Hunger Games* and *Catching Fire* movies and Lionsgate press releases.

Fan websites
Mockingjay.net, thehob.org, welcometodistrict12.com, hungergamesmovie.org, hungergamestrilogy.net, hunger-games.net

Publications and websites
Entertainment Weekly, *New York Times*, *Schools Library Journal*, *Age*, *Empire*, *New Yorker*, *Hero Complex*, *Hollywood Life*, *Vanity Fair*, *ELLE*, *Interview*, *Hollywood*

Reporter, *Variety*, *Daily Telegraph*, *Guardian*, IGN, SFX,
MTV, IMDB, Scholastic.com, Movieline.com, Collider.
com, JenniferLawrence.org, boxofficemojo.com, digital-
spy.com, vulture.com, huffingtonpost.com, latimes.com,
wired.com, buzzfeed.com, cinemablend.com, theweek.
com, theatlantic.com, nationalpost.com, time.com,
foxnews.com, newsweek.com, i09.com, forbes.com, npr.
org, deadline.com, salon.com

Many thanks are due to Paul Simpson for repeatedly read-
ing the manuscript and hunting down howlers, and for
Brigid Cherry for her continued indulgence . . . Thanks
also to Duncan Proudfoot for commissioning the work,
Howard Watson for his meticulous copy editing, and all at
Constable & Robinson and Running Press.